Great Trials and the Law in the Historical Imagination

Great Trials and the Law in the Historical Imagination: A Law and Humanities Approach introduces readers to the history of law and issues in historical, legal, and artistic interpretation by examining six well-known historical trials through works of art that portray them.

Great Trials provides readers with an accessible, non-dogmatic introduction to the interdisciplinary 'law and humanities' approach to law, legal history, and legal interpretation. By examining how six famous/notorious trials in Western history have been portrayed in six major works of art, the book shows how issues of legal, historical, and artistic interpretation can become intertwined: the different ways we embed law in narrative, how we bring conscious and subconscious conceptions of history to our interpretation of law, and how aesthetic predilections and moral commitments to the law may influence our views of history. The book studies well-known depictions of the trials of Socrates, Cicero, Jesus, Thomas More, the Salem 'witches,' and John Scopes and provides innovative analyses of those works. The epilogue examines how historical methodology and historical imagination are crucial to both our understanding of the law and our aesthetic choices through various readings of Harper Lee's beloved character, Atticus Finch.

The first book to employ a 'law and humanities' approach to delve into the institution of the trial and what it means in different legal systems at different historical times, this book will appeal to academics, students, and others with interests in legal history, law and popular culture, and law and the humanities.

Russell L. Dees teaches law at the University of Copenhagen, Denmark. He holds a J.D. from the University of California at Berkeley and a Ph.D. from the Claremont Graduate University.

Great Trials and the Law in the Historical Imagination

A Law and Humanities Approach

Russell L. Dees

a GlassHouse Book

First published 2023
by Routledge
4 Park Square, Milton Park, Abingdon, Oxon OX14 4RN

and by Routledge
605 Third Avenue, New York, NY 10158

Routledge is an imprint of the Taylor & Francis Group, an informa business

© 2023 Russell L. Dees

The right of Russell L. Dees to be identified as author of this work has been asserted in accordance with sections 77 and 78 of the Copyright, Designs and Patents Act 1988.

All rights reserved. No part of this book may be reprinted or reproduced or utilised in any form or by any electronic, mechanical, or other means, now known or hereafter invented, including photocopying and recording, or in any information storage or retrieval system, without permission in writing from the publishers.

Trademark notice: Product or corporate names may be trademarks or registered trademarks, and are used only for identification and explanation without intent to infringe.

British Library Cataloguing-in-Publication Data
A catalogue record for this book is available from the British Library

Library of Congress Cataloging-in-Publication Data
Names: Dees, Russell L., author.
Title: Great trials and the law in the historical imagination: a law and humanities approach/Russell L. Dees.
Description: Abingdon, Oxon; New York: Routledge, 2023. |
Includes bibliographical references and index.
Identifiers: LCCN 2022005669 (print) | LCCN 2022005670 (ebook) |
ISBN 9781032299952 (hardback) | ISBN 9781032299969 (paperback) |
ISBN 9781003302971 (ebook)
Subjects: LCSH: Law in literature. | Law and literature. |
Literature–History and criticism.
Classification: LCC PN56.L33 D44 2023 (print) | LCC PN56.L33 (ebook) |
DDC 809/.933554–dc23/eng/20220518
LC record available at https://lccn.loc.gov/2022005669
LC ebook record available at https://lccn.loc.gov/2022005670

ISBN: 978-1-032-29995-2 (hbk)
ISBN: 978-1-032-29996-9 (pbk)
ISBN: 978-1-003-30297-1 (ebk)

DOI: 10.4324/9781003302971

Typeset in Bembo
by Deanta Global Publishing Services, Chennai, India

To my daughters

Contents

Acknowledgements ix

Introduction 1

PART I
Ancients 15

1 The Trial of Socrates (399 B.C.E.): Democracy and Truth in the *Apology* 17

2 Cicero and the Trial of Gaius Verres (70 B.C.E.): 'Civic Corruption,' the Rule of Law, and the Analogy of Republican Rome 33

3 The Trial of Jesus (30/33 C.E.): Law, Narrative, and *Nomos* in the *Gospel according to Mark* 56

PART II
Moderns 75

4 The Trial of Thomas More (1535): Authentic Selfhood and Procedural Law in *A Man for All Seasons* 77

5 The Salem Witch Trials (1692): The Tragedy of Law in Arthur Miller's *The Crucible* 96

6 The Great Monkey Trial (1925): Historical 'Memory' and the 'Politics of Eternity'	113
Epilogue: The Vicissitudes of a Fictional Character: Time, Atticus Finch, and Constitutional Evil	137
Appendix 1 Summary of Historical Background and New Testament Source Differences	155
Appendix 2 Procedural Issues in the Trial of Thomas More	162
Appendix 3 A Digression on Evolution and Religion	170
Index	175

Acknowledgements

I stand indebted to the many friends on whom I've inflicted earlier drafts of this book, all of whom have borne the burden good-naturedly. First and foremost, I must thank Ditlev Tamm, whose wit and erudition made teaching the course on which this book is based such a joy. I also want to thank our students, whose curiosity and enthusiasm was such an inspiration. For their patient and invaluable comments, I thank Richard Dees, Dan Hardt, Maria Beisheim, Karen-Margrethe Simonsen, and Helle Porsdam.

Introduction

This book is an exploration of how different societies in different historical eras engaged in the interpretation and implementation of law through trials. It is also an exploration of how works of drama and fiction portray trials in different historical ages and how they affect our perception of them. Every society and every age provide their own answers to the questions: What is law, and how is it to be applied in concrete circumstances? Yet, over time, the responses of Western jurists have tended to circle around two general theories: natural law theory and legal positivism.[1]

In *De re publica* III.22 (54–52 B.C.E.), the Roman statesman Cicero said: "True law is right reason in agreement with Nature." In other words, what "right reason" dictates *is* law. Thus, Christian apologist Augustine of Hippo could opine in the 5th century C.E. that an unjust law is no law at all. By contrast, Jeremy Bentham, building on premises established by Thomas Hobbes, proposed a command theory of law: "In whatever persons in any state the supreme power resides, it is the right of those persons to make Laws" (*A Fragment on Government* IV.7 (1776)). The law is whatever the sovereign dictates as law, whether for good or ill (and whether the sovereign is in the form of a king or a parliament or something else). Yet, no legal system fails to incorporate aspects of both natural law and legal positivism in one form or another.

For example, in the English common law system, the King in Parliament may pass positive laws that govern or supersede common-law (or judge-made) precedents. And common law judges may make law by applying "right reason" to the interpretation and construction of statutes or by applying customary usage or "right reason" to resolve disputes in the absence of statutes. But theories of legal interpretation find their most crucial test in the courtroom trial. It is here that human beings in the form of judges and juries have the most direct control over the interpretation and implementation of law that directly affects those individuals subject to its power. Thus, the trial as a legal institution holds a particular fascination and, perhaps, a key to the practice of law.

This book grew out of a course taught for many years by me and the distinguished legal historian Ditlev Tamm at the University of Copenhagen. Our idea was to build an approach to the history of law on a 'law and humanities'

DOI: 10.4324/9781003302971-1

basis. We and our students examined a variety of famous/notorious trials at different times in the history of Western civilization through literature and/ or films that dealt with them. This (we hoped) would allow us to teach legal history in a way that would be exciting and palatable to students. However, it would also allow us to study methodologies used in the so-called 'law and humanities' movement to explore how historical events – in this case, notorious trials – make up part of our mental landscape, so to speak, which in turn affects the way we interpret law generally. The course, then, had a dual purpose: to engage with historical trials in an attempt to discover what we can learn about them from the historian's perspective and to engage with our cultural perceptions of these trials as they are presented in art in order to gauge our judgments about the meaning of these trials (for us). This approach (it is hoped) helps to hone critical thinking skills and to unveil the various modes of reasoning we use – consciously and subconsciously – in our historical and legal analysis.

Almost everyone has heard of the trials discussed in this book, but few have studied them in detail except for specialists. Most people by far are familiar with them only through accounts rendered in works of fiction. The focus on trials has two methodological advantages for my purposes. Trials are by their nature 'dramatic.' There is no drama without conflict, and a trial is in its essence about conflict. Two sides claim to be right, and only one may win their dispute. This is why artists (playwrights especially) are often drawn to portray trials in works of fiction.

Moreover, the trials we remember best are those in which important conflicts in history are in one way or another aired in the courtroom. A trial can often provide insight into an historical era as the point at which the various conflicts of the time intersect. Consequently, we can use the proceedings of a particular trial to help us understand the broader currents of history that surrounded it. Indeed, the historical importance of a trial is usually what draws an artist to depict it. However, a literary depiction of a trial is not always interested in historical accuracy; and, even when it is, the artist is almost always more concerned with exploring other issues and themes. Thus, a literary representation of a trial *may* shed light on its historical setting, but it *certainly* reflects issues and attitudes of the time in which it was produced, which may provide insight into that historical era as well. Yet, even more importantly, the work of art may have influence on the way we think about a trial even today.

The Trial of the Chicago 7

To take a recent example: the popular writer and director Aaron Sorkin (responsible for the hit TV series *The West Wing* and the Academy Award-winning movie *The Social Network*) recently released a motion picture entitled *The Trial of the Chicago 7* (2020), depicting the 1969 trial of eight – then seven – representatives of radical movements opposed to the Vietnam

War whom the US government blamed for the riots outside the Chicago Democratic Party convention of 1968. The trial is not well-remembered today and was considered even at the time something of a farce – the government attempted to prove a conspiracy to riot among disparate groups that had engaged in little or no coordination together prior to the convention. An independent commission concluded in the Walker Report (which was released before the trial began) that the disturbance in Chicago had been a "police riot." President Lyndon Johnson's administration under which the event occurred determined not to prosecute anyone in connection with the disturbances.

However, President Richard Nixon disagreed. The idea of a Leftist 'conspiracy' resonated well with conservative elements in the deeply divided America of the 1960s. The American Right saw the Leftist 'counterculture' as a monolithic attack on conventional values, which (in fairness) it sometimes was – but not in the ways the Right conceived. In the actual trial, this clash of values played out in the courtroom. The prosecutors openly mocked defense witnesses. Defendants blatantly provoked and ridiculed the prosecution, the court, and the American system itself. Judge Julius Hoffmann made preposterous rulings and engaged in what, when it reversed the convictions of the defendants, the US Seventh Circuit Court of Appeals characterized as "a series of judicial remarks deprecating defense counsel and the defense case" (*United States v. Dellinger*, 472 F.2d 340, 386 (7th Cir. 1972)). In short, the trial provided an almost perfect cross-section of the social and political unrest of the 1960s.

Aaron Sorkin's depiction of the trial captures much of this clash of values, but the director also had another agenda. Sorkin's work has always had a moralistic tinge – a decided bias toward centrism. *The West Wing* was famous for providing Democrats with a fantasy president during the dark years of Republican George W. Bush. Sorkin's fictional president, Jed Bartlett, was fashioned to show that power did not have to give up compassion in order to be 'tough' but also that the exercise of power is often morally complex and rarely leaves one with 'a clean pair of hands.' Sorkin has a vision of the United States as a family whose members may have their issues with each other but still retain an abiding faith in their good will and common purpose. Thus, Republicans and Democrats may quarrel bitterly but ultimately come together for the good of the country.[2]

The Trial of the Chicago 7 is in the same vein. The film was released just prior to the US presidential election in 2020 when the US was more deeply divided than it had been since the 1960s. And this was not coincidental. The underlying message of the film was that, even in an America whose citizens are at loggerheads, we must appreciate and understand the positions and sincerity of those with whom we disagree. Sorkin goes out of his way to show that we are all flawed individuals with strengths and weaknesses, which are demonstrated by both government and defense representatives alike.

To make his point, Sorkin deliberately distorts the factual history of the Chicago 7 trial in major and minor ways to provide 'good' intentions to each side. For example, the prosecutor Richard Schultz is portrayed as accepting the job reluctantly, doubtful about its legal merits and what good a prosecution would do. When defendant Bobby Seale is ordered by the judge to be bound and gagged, Schultz appears to be shocked and revolted and moves for a mistrial as to Seale. He even stands up at the end of the movie in solemn respect as defendant Tom Hayden reads aloud in protest a list of the servicemen killed in Vietnam during the trial.[3] The real-life Schultz had no reservations about pursuing the prosecution and did not ask to sever Seale's case. Nor did he display any form of solidarity with any action of the defendants. Even the brutal treatment of Bobby Seale was toned down in the movie.

Similarly, in the movie, when the defendant and Yippie Abbie Hoffmann takes the stand as a witness, some of his testimony as depicted is accurate, but other statements were made up or taken from different contexts. Though ever the anarchist, Sorkin's Hoffmann comes off as quite a bit less radical and dangerous to the Establishment than he actually was. The pacifist David Dellinger did not lose control and strike a bailiff during the proceedings as he does in the film. Sorkin deliberately softens and roughens the edges of his characters in order to place them within a defined range of behavior that stresses both their human flaws and their basic decency. Ultimately, Sorkin wants to say that, however divided the United States seems at any particular time, there is a consensus underlying the rift that will unite Americans if it is allowed to.

The film is critically acclaimed (nominated for a Best Picture Oscar) and has been seen by millions of people. Since few have the living memory or expertise to question the filmic representation, Sorkin's interpretation of the Chicago conspiracy trial is likely to become 'orthodox' in the way Arthur Miller's *The Crucible* has overtaken our understanding of the Salem witch trials. In other words, even if people 'know' that *The Trial of the Chicago 7* is just a film and not intended to be utterly faithful to the historical record, they will undoubtedly resort by default to the film's portrayal when they think of the trial, thanks to the wide distribution of the movie. Thus, the film will have a cultural impact that may affect the way many people think about an historical event, which in turn may have an impact on the way they think about American society in general and the justice system in particular. This idea will be explored in subsequent chapters, but I wanted to hint at the mechanism of memory and culture through which we think about these things.

Law and humanities

The 'law and humanities' movement grew out of what was once known as the 'law and literature' movement, which began as a discipline in the early 1970s with James Boyd White's *The Legal Imagination* (1973). The movement started with the seemingly uncontroversial insight that law is a linguistic enterprise ("the activity of law is at heart a literary one").[4] Laws cannot be separated from the language in which they are formulated. Thus, law is a form of literature, and scholars began to see how the tools of literary criticism might aid in our understanding of how law works and what law means. This framing of 'law as literature' encouraged scholars to explore how rhetoric plays a role in the formation and interpretation of law, how narrative works as a way of couching legal ideas.

Scholars also began to see how works of literature provided insight into how law functions in a broader context. Works such as Sophocles' *Antigone* and Herman Melville's *Billy Budd* demonstrated what effects law has on individuals in society and how societal pressures affect the application of the law. In other words, literary works could be used as set-pieces to illustrate a kind of 'philosophy of law lite,' that is, provide a common basis for discussing issues in legal philosophy and practice. Gradually, a canon of literary works was developed into a discipline that we label as the 'law in literature' framing of the field. Once this notion was established, scholars also began to explore how concepts of law are inseparable from the context of society in general – how our understanding of history and culture affect our understanding of the law. As a result, it seemed more appropriate to label the movement as 'law and humanities' since the analysis was not strictly limited to literature but included history, culture, sociology, anthropology, etc.

'Law and humanities' is not a homogenous field, and different scholars have different approaches to it – in methodology and interpretation. By its nature, the field is interdisciplinary. Yet, the gravamen, so to speak, of the field is what was called in the Renaissance the *'studia humanitatis,'*[5] the study of that which makes us human. And foremost among what makes us 'human' is our interaction with other human beings. The human being is, as Aristotle put it, a *zoon politikon*, a being that is part of a community (specifically, a *polis*). To paraphrase Hannah Arendt, law creates the space in which a community develops. What lies outside this space is lawless and, properly speaking, not a community.[6]

Yet, the interdisciplinary nature of 'law and humanities' means that we need to take seriously the methodological concerns of traditionally separate fields.[7] We cannot be content just to 'think like lawyers.' We must also 'think like historians,' 'think like literary critics,' 'think like anthropologists' when the situation calls for it and be able to ascertain when the situation calls for it. This has become more and more apparent, for example, in the American legal profession with the dominance of the so-called 'originalist' school of legal interpretation. Put crudely, 'originalism' asserts that the binding legal interpretation of a statute or a constitutional provision is the 'intention' of its drafters or the 'general public meaning' to be attributed to it at the time it was adopted. This, of course, requires an historical interpretation of what was 'intended' at a particular point in history. Historians object that lawyers are insufficiently trained to understand how to evaluate the evidence as to what that 'intent' might be. Lawyers object that historians are insufficiently trained in legal reasoning to ascertain the juridical rationale behind a legal formulation. To which historians then argue that you must be an historian to understand how lawyers in a particular age used legal reasoning.[8] We wind up in an infinite regress. The well of history is deep, Thomas Mann tells us in *Joseph and His Brothers*, should we not say it is bottomless? The standard joke for those of us with both a law degree and a history degree has been that people should just listen to us! But, of course, that would beg a great many questions ... even assuming we all agreed with each other.

One of the tasks of this book is to explore and demonstrate how these issues arise and intertwine in legal and historical interpretation. I do not purport to square this hermeneutic circle by resolving any of them. I merely hope to point out by example what differences various approaches might uncover and suggest how to begin to traverse an interpretive pathway without stumbling into the most common pitfalls.

What is art?

One of the pitfalls, of course, is that we will be examining historical events through the prism of a work of art, which raises all the concerns I just indicated about *The Trial of the Chicago 7*. We accept without much thought that a work of art is not a work of history, but we sometimes fail to notice that a work of history may also be a work of art. But what do we mean when we say something is a 'work of art'? Is it art simply because the artist says it is (Marcel Duchamp's urinal)? Is it like Justice Potter Stewart's pronouncement on obscenity – 'I know it when I see it'? (*Jacobellis v. Ohio*, 378 U.S. 184, 197 (1964)). And if we detect 'art' in something, should we then jettison it from our quest for truth as Plato did the poets from *The Republic*? I cannot even pretend to have an answer here.

But I do have a paradigm with which I work when I evaluate a piece of art. Umberto Eco once said that a text "is a machine conceived in order to elicit interpretations."[9] To me, this helps to explain Archibald MacLeish's riddle in his poem "Ars Poetica" that a "poem should not mean but be." There is no single, definitive interpretation of a work of art – or if there is, it has failed as a work of art; it is mere kitsch or melodrama. A genuine work of art should be able to evoke and bear many interpretations, all of which shed light on itself. We need not end up in hermeneutic nihilism, however. Some interpretations may be better or worse than others. My personal criterion is that an interpretation of a work of art is 'better' when it can account for more of the elements of the work of art itself. In this way, as Eco also put it, a text can create its own model reader.[10] Yet, this still does not mean that there is (necessarily) a 'definitive' or 'authoritative' interpretation. Often, it is the point that, like life, a piece of art may be interpreted a number of different ways with no particular way being conclusive.

To illustrate by way of example: In Sophocles' play *Antigone*, two brothers have gone to war with each other (one against the city of Thebes, one defending the city), and both have been killed. The new ruler of Thebes, their uncle Kreon, decrees that one brother is to be buried with honors; the other (the traitor) is to be left unburied. Their sister Antigone defies the decree and 'buries' the dishonored brother anyway. This sets off a chain of events that destroys both Antigone and Kreon. The play has been read many different ways but always as a variation of four possibilities: 1) Kreon is right, Antigone is wrong, 2) Kreon is wrong, Antigone is right, 3) they are both right, or 4) they are both wrong. The play can easily bear all four interpretations (although, admittedly, the first is not an especially popular one). This possibility, I would argue, enhances the artistic power of the play because it forces the reader (or spectator) to grapple with the ambiguity of the playwright's language just as we grapple with moral ambiguities every day. There is no easy answer; what seems plausible changes, depending on the perspective we take. This, in turn, enhances our ability to appreciate the complexities we encounter in life. If we hold certain variables constant, we can observe certain things. If we hold other variables constant, we can discern other things – like Heisenberg's 'uncertainty principle' in which the exact position and momentum of an electron cannot be determined simultaneously.

To make the same point in a different way: William Shakespeare's *Merchant of Venice* is considered one of his 'problem' plays.[11] It is problematic for us in particular because of its implied (explicit?) antisemitism. The fact that we are reading the play from the other side of the Holocaust cannot help but affect our interpretation. Yet, although the Jew Shylock is clearly the 'villain' of this comedy, Shakespeare makes him a somewhat sympathetic figure. At least, we cannot help but be moved by the "Hath not a Jew eyes" speech in Act III. It is frequently quoted to illustrate a sentiment of tolerance and human fellowship. But we must not forget the end of the speech: "If you poison us do we not die? And if you wrong us shall we not revenge?" Shakespeare creates empathy but also undermines it. This same ambiguity may be seen in an overall interpretation of the plot. Shylock may be read as a villain through and through, seeking vengeance against the merchant Antonio for wrongs committed against him offstage before the play begins. The pound of flesh bargain, then, is a crafty snare from the very beginning. However, the play may also be read differently with Shylock as an almost forgiving figure in the first half of the play. He says the pound of flesh bargain is a "merry jest," and for all we know Shylock is sincere until his daughter Jessica robs him and runs off with a Christian. Only then does Shylock give vent to a lust for vengeance. The play may be read both ways with equal plausibility. What difference does it make? For one thing, it places the behavior of the so-called 'Christians' in the play in a different light. The hypocrisy of the Christians is there all along; but, if Shylock is sympathetic at the beginning, there is a supplemental irony and piquancy in the play. This, in turn, adds nuance and irony to the character of Portia, who may be read as a saint-like heroine or as a manipulative subverter of patriarchal values. The wealth of interpretive opportunity is what proves Shakespeare's genius in my opinion.[12]

The historical imagination

Professional historians will recognize in the title of this book a nod to the work of R.G. Collingwood and his groundbreaking treatise, *The Idea of History* (1946). I mean the reference only as a nod, but there *is* an affinity between Collingwood's approach to history and the 'law and humanities' approach to the law. For Collingwood, to know something about the past was to reconstruct what happened in the 'historical imagination,' that is, we must re-think or, as he calls it, 're-enact' the thoughts of the historical actors engaged in an historical event.[13] For Collingwood, the proper methodology for an historian was "a logic of question and answer"[14] –to understand an historical event (at least, as a preliminary matter), one must understand what the historical actors thought they were doing, which means understanding the intellectual framework in which they acted. In other words, in order to understand their 'answer' (action), we must understand the 'question' they were asking. There is a certain kinship here with the 'originalist' approach to legal interpretation discussed earlier and all the methodological issues that come with it. In his "Lectures on the Philosophy of History," Collingwood explicitly compares the historian's method of evaluating evidence to putting it into the witness box and interrogating it mercilessly.[15] And one of Collingwood's crucial insights is that people in different historical eras often asked different kinds of questions than we would.[16]

Collingwood's approach is often praised or condemned as 'historicist.' 'Historicism' has been understood in (at least) two different ways. In one sense, 'historicism' merely means taking seriously the historical context of an action: "understanding past agents requires understanding the thought context of their action and [Collingwood] was adamant that the historian should be sensitive to the differences between her own thought context and that of the agent."[17] Anachronism is a cardinal sin for the historian. We must never presume uniformity in the way past agents thought about things and the way we think about them. But this raises the question: if we believe the thinking of past agents is entwined in a particular (past) view of the world, might we not also be trapped in our own present-mindedness? Do we not constantly risk imposing (consciously or unconsciously) our thoughts/concepts/understandings on past agents? In this sense, 'historicism' implies not only a radical epistemic relativism but a radical epistemic nihilism. Every historian must struggle with the tension between these two senses, and this is where the 'historical imagination' becomes useful.

The historian engages in an antipodal process: to try to imagine the past 'as it was' from the perspective of the present 'as it is.' Quentin Skinner describes the role of the intellectual historian "as a kind of archaeologist, bringing buried intellectual treasure back to the surface, dusting it down and enabling us to reconsider what we think of it."[18] Yet, however far down archeologists dig, they themselves remain in the present.[19] They find the 'intellectual treasure' but must still interpret it by their own lights as best they can. The trick is to figure out how to separate what is 'original' from the accretions of later ages.

Collingwood makes clear the tentative nature of the historian's task. He speaks of history as a "web of imaginative construction" woven on fixed points of evidence. The web may change as new evidence is added or doubtful evidence removed or as the relationship between two points is reassessed. Evidence speaks to the question being asked. All history is "revisionist" history. All history is an *interpretation* of the evidence and an interpretation of what *is* evidence. And interpretations may differ as perspectives change just as in the interpretation of art. To conceive of history as a set of 'facts' carved into the stone of eternity is not just a mistake; it is a betrayal of intellect.

Each chapter of this book examines a text that attempts in one way or another to 're-imagine' an historical trial, albeit not necessarily as a trained historian or jurist would. Thus, each text provides an opportunity to examine a problem or set of problems that arises when we attempt to understand an historical event through the 'historical imagination.' Moreover, each text provides an opportunity to examine how the concept of 'law' or 'legal reasoning' may be historically conditioned, which raises implications for our own (current) legal understandings. Martha Nussbaum once observed that the legal imagination is comparable to the literary imagination.[20] It is my hope to indicate how it is comparable to the historical imagination as well.

This book is pitched for law students and undergraduates and legal professionals who may not be familiar with a 'law and humanities' approach to legal studies. It is also meant to introduce these issues to non-lawyers, to people who have a general interest in the topic but little or no training in law, history, or the humanities. It is also suitable to serve as a textbook for a 'law and humanities' approach to the history of law through the analysis of various trials in Western history. While much of the analysis will focus on legal issues and issues in historical interpretation, attention will also be paid to theories of literary criticism, where relevant, since they, too, contribute to a 'law and humanities' approach.

Most chapters will provide an historical overview of a specific trial and the legal system in which it took place, serving as an introduction to the significant factual and interpretive issues and controversies surrounding the historical trial itself. These provide the fixed points of evidence, so to speak, on which to weave our historical interpretation. Each chapter will also engage with a specific literary and/or filmic presentation of the historical trial in light of a particular issue or problem it illustrates from a 'law and humanities' perspective. Thus, there is no cookie-cutter approach to these chapters. They are intended to raise questions about historical interpretation and the works of art themselves and their reception in the culture. By focusing on one problem or set of issues, I do not mean to suggest that there are no other issues that may be raised. I merely mean to provide an example of how one might approach works of art that portray historical trials – whether it is peculiar to a particular artwork or applicable to works of art in general. Scattered throughout the text and among the notes will also be remarks on recent events that may prove illuminating to the points being made.

The book is organized in chronological order by trial. This has a certain obvious appeal, but it means that the discussion of some methodological and interpretive issues may not be optimally presented. That is, it might have made more logical sense to discuss certain philosophical problems in a different order than they appear in the book. I hope the reader may overlook this inelegance and synthesize the views presented into a general thesis.

The book is divided into two parts, 'Ancients' and 'Moderns.' The chapters on the 'ancients' are unified in their examination of problems that arise when we try to engage with and understand ancient history or ancient texts by trying to comprehend both the different mindsets of ancient actors and the (usually subconscious) assumptions we bring to our understanding of history. The chapters on the 'moderns' are unified in another way. While each work of art examined looks at a different historical trial, their authors were each in their own way responding to issues raised by the "Red Scare" (baited by Senator Joseph McCarthy and the House Un-American Activities Committee) in the late 1940s and early 1950s during which lives and reputations were ruined by innuendo and accusation alone. This is not to imply that the authors necessarily manifested any direct or literal reaction in their plays. Rather, I am working with the hypothesis that, with their different historical accounts, they were posing similar questions about law and evidence made pertinent by the controversies of their day, which provides a sort of 'common ground' for a comparison of these works and, in turn, allows for a more cogent basis for assessing how each author employed or was affected by the 'historical imagination.'

The notes to each chapter are not intended to provide an exhaustive overview but to give readers new to this approach a foothold to begin their own explorations of the subject. All translations are my own unless otherwise indicated.

Notes

1 Witness the debates over law between Hans Kelsen and Gustav Radbruch or the famous debate between Lon Fuller and H.L.A. Hart: H.L.A. Hart, "Positivism and the Separation of Law and Morals," 71 *Harv. L. Rev.* 593 (1958); Lon L. Fuller, "Positivism and Fidelity to Law – A Reply to Professor Hart," 71 *Harv. L. Rev.* 630 (1958). For an accessible overview of the general debate, see Frederick Schauer, "Law's Boundaries," 130 *Harv. L. Rev.* 2434 (2017). For a comparison of the Kelsen/Radbruch debate with the Hart/Fuller debate, see Frank Haldemann, "Gustav Radbruch vs. Hans Kelsen: A Debate on Nazi Law," 18(2) *Ratio Juris* (June 2005), pp.162–178.

2 This 'consensus' theme is not uncommon in American sensibilities. For example, the filmmaker Ken Burns became famous for his public television series *The Civil War* (1990), which was excellent in many ways. However, in his attempt to end the series on a positive note, Burns (perhaps, unconsciously) fell into a version of the "Lost Cause" interpretation of the war that became prominent after Reconstruction, which held that, because both sides were acting 'sincerely' on their beliefs, the war was a mere 'family squabble' that, once reconciled, strengthened the Union. Compare John Higham, "The Cult of the 'American Consensus': Homogenizing Our History," *Commentary* (February 1959).
3 Actually, it was David Dellinger who read the names, and it happened prior to the opening of court business on Vietnam Moratorium day in the midst of the trial.
4 James Boyd White, *Heracles' Bow: Essays on the Rhetoric and Poetics of the Law* (1985), p. xi.
5 On this idea, compare Benjamin G. Kohl, "The Changing Concept of the 'Studia Humanitatis' in the Early Renaissance," 6(2) *Renaissance Studies* (June 1992), pp. 185–120.
6 See Hannah Arendt, *Was ist Politik? Fragmente aus dem Nachlaß*, ed. by Ursula Ludz (2003 [1993]), p. 122.
7 On the general problems, see, for example, Jane B. Baron, "Law, Literature, and the Problems of Interdisciplinarity," 108(5) *Yale Law Journal* (March 1999), pp. 1059–1085.
8 For an excellent brief overview of the clash between historians and lawyers on 'originalism,' see Jonathan Gienapp, "Constitutional Originalism and History," *Process: a blog for american history* (20 March 2017).
9 Umberto Eco *et al.*, "Between Author and Text," *Interpretation and Overinterpretation*, ed. by Stefan Collini (1992), p. 85 (The Tannen Lectures on Human Values 1990).
10 Id., p. 64.
11 Even here, what counts as a 'problem' play is a problem for scholars. See F.S. Boas, *Shakespeare and His Predecessors* (1896) (a 'problem' play is one that deals with a particular moral or social 'problem' like an Ibsen play) and E.M.W. Tillyard, *Shakespeare's Problem Plays* (1950) (a 'problem' play is one that does not fit within traditional genres such as tragedy or comedy).
12 It is a technique frequently used by Shakespeare, particularly in the middle plays. In *Henry V*, for example, the über-patriot king Henry may be read as a hero or a war criminal. Hamlet may be read as faux-mad or genuinely mad or even both. See Norman Rabkin, "Rabbits, Ducks, and Henry V," 28(3) *Shakespeare Quarterly* (Summer, 1977), pp. 279–296; John Sutherland and Cedric Thomas Watts, *Henry V, War Criminal?: And Other Shakespeare Puzzles* (2000).
13 Collingwood explains:

> The historian's picture of his subject, whether that subject be a sequence of events or a past state of things, thus appears as a web of imaginative construction stretched between certain fixed points provided by the statements of his authorities.... We know that truth is to be had, not by swallowing what our authorities tell us, but by criticizing it; and thus the supposedly fixed points between which the historical imagination spins its web are not given to us ready made, they must be achieved by critical thinking.
>
> (*The Idea of History*, pp. 242–243)

Of course, Collingwood is not without his critics. *The Idea of History* was not completed before its author's death and was published posthumously. Therefore, some of his ideas seem not entirely thought through, not completely 'baked,' so to speak. I am merely suggesting a congeniality of spirit in approaches. For a sympathetic critique of Collingwood, see William H. Dray, *History as Re-enactment: R.G. Collingwood's Idea of History* (1995).

14 R.G. Collingwood, *An Autobiography* (1978 [1939]), p. 37.
15 Collingwood, "Lectures on the Philosophy of History," in *The Idea of History* (Revised ed. 2005), p. 378. Collingwood also compares the process to a detective trying to piece together a murder.
16 As he puts it, "the history of political theory is not the history of different answers given to one and the same question, but the history of a problem more or less constantly changing, whose solution was changing with it" (Collingwood, *Autobiography*, p. 62).
17 Karim Dharamsi, Giuseppina D'Oro, and Stephen Leach (eds.), *Collingwood on Philosophical Methodology* (2018), p. 5. The essays in this volume examine Collingwood's own attempt to avoid epistemic relativism in a theory of 'absolute presuppositions.' However, since I take a different approach, I shall not grapple with the issue of 'absolute presuppositions' here. I merely reiterate that all historical interpretation is an interpretation from the present – or from *some* present, which we should take into account as we assess the evidence it adduces.
18 Quentin Skinner, *Liberty before Liberalism* (1998), p. 112. Skinner acknowledges an affinity with Michel Foucault's 'archeology of knowledge.' He also accepts the Nietzschean/Foucauldian 'genealogy of ideas' as a suitable metaphor.
19 Bernard Williams makes an apt analogy:

> The ethnographer in the field can come to think as the people think with whom he is living, and he can enact their judgements and deliberations in his own person. But at the end of the line, these are not *his* thoughts. The difference from the historian is that the ethnographer may *lose* the end of the line: he may find it hard to come back to his regular life and may, as it used to be said, 'go native.' The historian cannot do that, unless he goes mad.
> (Dharamsi et al., *Collingwood on Philosophical Methodology*, p. 22)

20 Martha Nussbaum, *Poetic Justice: The Literary Imagination and Public Life* (1995) (likening it as well to Aristotle's *phronesis* or practical reasoning). Citing Wayne Booth, Nussbaum explains that

> the act of reading and assessing what one has read is ethically valuable precisely because it is constructed in a manner that demands both immersion and critical conversation, comparison of what one has read both with one's own unfolding experience and with the responses and arguments of other readers.
> (*Poetic Justice*, p. 9)

And, just as a good novel invites us to try to understand the actions of its characters in a particular social circumstance, so too must a good judge empathetically understand the context in which the parties to a case have acted. See also Ronald Dworkin, "Law as Interpretation," 9(1) *Critical Inquiry* (1982) (comparing common law reasoning to a chain novel).

References

Arendt, H. (2003 [1993]). *Was ist Politik? Fragmente aus dem Nachlaß*, U. Ludz (Ed.).
Baron, J. B. (March 1999). Law, literature, and the problems of interdisciplinarity. 108(5) *Yale Law Journal* 1059.
Boas, F. S. (1896). *Shakespeare and his predecessors*.
Collingwood, R. G. (revised ed. 2005 [1946]). *The idea of history*.
Collingwood, R. G. (1978 [1939]). *An autobiography*.
Dharamsi, K., D'Oro, G., & Leach, S. (Eds.) (2018). *Collingwood on philosophical methodology*.
Dray, W. H. (1995). *History as re-enactment: R. G. Collingwood's idea of history*.

Dworkin, R. (1982). Law as interpretation. 9(1) *Critical Inquiry* 179.
Eco, U. *et al.* (1992). Between author and text. In S. Collini (Ed.), *Interpretation and overinterpretation* (*The Tannen lectures on human values* 1990), 85.
Fuller, L. L. (1958). Positivism and fidelity to law — A reply to Professor Hart. 71 *Harvard Law Review* 630.
Gienapp, J. (20 March 2017). Constitutional originalism and history. *Process: A blog for American history*.
Haldemann, F. (June 2005). Radbruch vs. Kelsen: A debate on Nazi law. 18(2) *Ratio Juris* 162.
Hart, H. L. A. (1958). Positivism and the separation of law and morals. 71 *Harvard Law Review* 593.
Higham, J. (February 1959). The cult of the 'American consensus': Homogenizing our history. *Commentary*.
Kohl, B. G. (June 1992). The changing concept of 'studia humanitatis' in the early Renaissance. 6(2) *Renaissance Studies* 185.
Nussbaum, M. (1995). *Poetic justice: The literary imagination and public life*.
Rabkin, N. (Summer, 1977). Rabbits, Ducks, and Henry V. 28(3) *Shakespeare Quarterly* 279.
Schauer, F. (2017). Law's boundaries. 130 *Harvard Law Review* 2434.
Sutherland, J., & Watts, C. T. (2000). *Henry V, war criminal?: And other Shakespeare puzzles*.
Tillyard, E. M. W. (1950). *Shakespeare's problem plays*.
White, J. B. (1973). *The legal imagination*.
White, J. B. (1985). *Heracles' bow: Essays on the rhetoric and poetics of the law*.

Part I

Ancients

Chapter 1

The Trial of Socrates (399 B.C.E.)
Democracy and Truth in the *Apology*

Plato's *Apology of Socrates* is one of the foundational documents of Western civilization. And it is largely due to Plato's works, thanks to their artistry and philosophical depth, that the trial and death of Socrates of Athens has captured the imagination of so many writers, artists, and thinkers. For many, Socrates' trial conjures images of the imperturbable man of reason attempting to assuage the passions of the mob. His fate is the paradigm of unjust outcomes. It is the triumph of superstition over reason, the tyranny of the majority over the individual conscience. Socrates is Sophocles' *Antigone* come to life. He is Thomas More before Henry VIII – Atticus Finch before a lynching party in Maycomb, Alabama.

Of course, this vision of Socrates has always been disputed. Even today, students sometimes become so irritated with the pedantic and often exasperating Socrates to whom they are subjected in Plato's dialogues that hemlock seems more than just retribution for the old geezer. The extent to which the Athenians who judged Socrates may have shared this attitude raises questions about what a trial is for – particularly, in a democracy.

The problem of Socrates

Because Socrates left behind no writings of his own, we draw our picture of him from other sources, creating the so-called 'problem of Socrates.' The 'problem' is that we only know of Socrates as a character interpreted by a writer – specifically, Plato, Xenophon, and Aristophanes, who were contemporaries of Socrates and each of whom wrote works directly relevant to the trial: 1) Plato's *Apology of Socrates* (the Greek word *apologia*, usually transliterated as 'apology,' simply means 'defense') in which Plato claims to be an eyewitness to the trial,[1] 2) Xenophon's *Memorabilia* and *Apology of Socrates to the Jury* in which Xenophon (who was absent from Athens at the time) claims to report the trial based on accounts he heard from an eyewitness named Hermogenes,[2] and 3) Aristophanes' play *The Clouds* (originally performed in 423 B.C.E.) in which Socrates is satirically depicted as a Sophist, a corrupter of youth, and a blasphemer (the very charges laid against him at the trial).

DOI: 10.4324/9781003302971-3

Xenophon's reputation as a writer has waxed and waned over the centuries. Some find his works subtle and ironic; most find them plodding and superficial (at least, in comparison to Plato's). Whereas Plato's *Apology* is clearly acknowledged as a piece of superb writing, Xenophon's is not.[3] Moreover, Xenophon's account of Socrates differs in crucial ways from Plato's. In Xenophon's *Apology*, Socrates commits suicide by cop – or, in this instance, suicide by *dikastai* (jury/judges) (see discussion below). Socrates, from a desire to put an end to his own life, seems to be daring the jury/judges through *megalegoria* (lofty or arrogant speech) to condemn him. He does not so much defend himself against the charges as scoff at them. He deliberately alienates the jury/judges and even refuses to propose a counter-penalty (see below) once he has been found guilty.[4] The question is: does Xenophon's clumsier style make his account more or less credible than Plato's? That is, can we trust it more because he is not as great an artist as Plato and, hence, less likely (or able) to bend the facts in service to his overall artistic purpose?

For the opposite reasons, this question applies in spades to Aristophanes (to whom Plato alludes in the *Apology*). Aristophanes is indisputably a fine artist who can almost be counted on to twist 'facts' in the service of satire. In *The Clouds*, the character of Socrates runs a school called The Thinkery (*phronisterion*), where he teaches students the art of sophistry. Socrates gazes at the moon and stars through his legs, denies the existence of Zeus, and teaches Unjust Logic. The play's protagonist Strepsiades goes to Socrates in the hope of learning how to argue his way out of his debts. Unable to grasp Socrates' obscurantist doctrines, Strepsiades sends his son Pheidippides to the school, where the son (ostensibly) learns Socrates' arts – including how to justify sons beating their fathers.[5] Finally, Strepsiades takes his vengeance by burning down the school. The play is satirical, but we cannot help but notice that Aristophanes depicts Socrates as engaging in the very activities for which he will be charged and, ultimately, condemned 24 years later: impiety and corrupting the youth. Was Aristophanes merely mocking Socrates or was there a more serious purpose lurking beneath the satire? What are we to make of the fact that, in his *Symposium*, Plato draws a portrait of Aristophanes that reveals no explicit hostility to the playwright?[6] Moreover, what are we to make of the fact that, in the *Apology*, Socrates denies ever having taught about 'heavenly or underground things' as the Aristophanic Socrates does (*Apology* 19b–d)?[7]

Plato wrote at least 27 (almost certainly more) dialogues in which he develops his philosophical outlook; and, in every single one of them,[8] he uses Socrates as a major interlocutor. Not only does Plato depict Socrates' trial and execution in his dialogues, but scattered throughout the Platonic *oeuvre* are references to Socrates' accusers and to the charges against him. One, Anytus, appears as a character in Plato's *Meno*; Meletus is mentioned in the *Euthyphro*. This raises the question of whether Plato is depicting Socrates as he actually lived or merely using him as a mouthpiece for certain views (which may or may not be his own). The scholarly consensus[9] is that Plato's early dialogues (such as *Euthyphro*, *The Apology*, *Crito,* and *Phaedo*) are closer to the actual, historical Socrates than the later dialogues (such as *The Republic* and *Timaeus*) in which Socrates seems to defend positions contrary to those he took in earlier dialogues.

The *Apology* was written, of course, after the fact of Socrates' trial (assuming, as we reasonably do, the trial ever took place at all). How much longer afterwards it was written we can only speculate.[10] Yet, the *Apology* is clearly not a transcription of Plato's shorthand from the trial.[11] The sheer artistry of it would give that the lie. This literary excellence is often recognized to be the result of Plato's extraordinary talent rather than Socrates'. But the point can be pressed further. As Reginald Allen has shown, the *Apology* is not merely a masterful piece of writing. It is a quietly ironical parody of the standard defense speech of its day. Socrates' speech contains an exordium, prosthesis, statement of the case, refutation, digression, and peroration, the same formal parts which a student of rhetoric would have been taught to produce.[12]

The artistry may also be instructive to our understanding of it. So, we are left with the question: Is the Socrates we find in Plato purely fictional, mostly fictional, partly fictional or – accurate? How to interpret the sources is a fascinating, critical, and ultimately (perhaps) irresolvable task for historians. The answers one concocts will depend on the assumptions one makes and the approach one takes to the material, including how the historical events that preceded Socrates' trial may have led to it and affected its outcome.

The historical context

By 399 B.C.E., when Socrates' trial took place, Athens had already experienced more than 30 years of war with its rival Sparta – the Peloponnesian War so brilliantly and vividly presented in Thucydides' history. The war ended in 404 with the establishment of a pro-Sparta oligarchy in Athens, the Thirty Tyrants. The Thirty Tyrants restricted the rights and privileges of citizens and purged the city of democratic proponents. Socrates' relationship with the Thirty Tyrants is ambiguous. Two prominent figures linked to the Thirty, Critias and Charmides, were well-known associates of Socrates. Indeed, they appear in two Platonic dialogues named after them. Socrates was also associated with Alcibiades, a flamboyant aristocrat who proposed the disastrous Sicilian expedition during the Peloponnesian War and, when accused of sacrilege, fled to the enemy Sparta.[13] So, when democracy was restored to Athens in 403, there were reasons for Athenian democrats to be suspicious of Socrates. One of his accusers, Anytus, for example, went into exile rather than live under the Thirty.

Yet, Socrates also counted opponents of the Thirty among his acquaintances – for example, Lysias (who appears in Plato's dialogue *Phaedrus*) and his brother Polemarchus (who appears with his father in *The Republic*). As recounted in Plato's *Apology*, Socrates was asked by the Thirty to bring Leon of Salamis to them for execution. He did not. In Xenophon's *Memorabilia*, Socrates even publicly criticizes Critias. Nevertheless, at least as he is portrayed in the writings of Plato and Xenophon, Socrates expresses no more than a lukewarm approval of democracy as a form of government.[14] Indeed, many have read Plato (and, by implication, Socrates) as an enemy of democratic regimes.[15] This forms the core evidence for those who see Socrates' trial as essentially a political persecution: in effect, that the trial was an expedient for the newly-restored democracy to purge one of its enemies – much like the practice of ostracism, a process by which the citizens of Athens could expel a person (ostensibly, someone suspected of aspiring to illegitimate power) from the city for a period of ten years.[16]

What can Plato's *Apology* teach us about trials? Reading the text through a traditional historian's lens, we may make inferences about the nature of the ancient Greek legal system and attempt to place the information Plato gives us into the context of what we know from other sources. We may also learn something if we focus solely on the text and attempt to discern Plato's thoughts on the trial process and the assumptions underlying them. Whichever route or combination of routes we choose, however, much turns on *how* we approach and understand the text itself – which means grappling with the perennial methodological problem of historicism: is it possible to understand the past on its own terms or are we doomed forever to interpret it through present-day concepts?[17] This may ultimately be an irresolvable question, but let us try to articulate some of the problems with understanding the context of Plato's text and experiment with Collingwood's approach by re-imagining some of what Plato might have wanted to convey within the confines of that context.

The problem of historicism: liberalism and democracy

Our first challenge in interpreting the *Apology* and what it can teach us about trials is to think about what it means to read an ancient document. The past, they say, is a foreign country; they do things differently there.[18] Is it possible for us to comprehend ancient texts without becoming prey to our own modern (mis)understandings and prejudices? We may never be able to eliminate this potential for error, but we can test it by examining our assumptions.

As mentioned, many people view Socrates as a hero of free thinking, whose only 'fault' was listening to the beat of his own drum, and the Athenian democracy punished him for this lack of conformity. This is a very 'liberal' reading of the text. That is, it is the reading of someone steeped in the values of today's 'liberal democracy,' of someone who deeply believes in the value of what Isaiah Berlin called 'negative freedom,' the freedom not to be interfered with.[19] It is a powerful reading that has many resonances in the text. After all, Socrates' whole enterprise as articulated in the *Apology* is to seek true knowledge (which may also expose the 'ignorance' of those who only think they know something). This is the quest to which Socrates dedicated his life and vowed never to cease. The 'lesson' of the *Apology* is that the unexamined life is not worth living; and, like Socrates, we should all pursue 'truth' on our own, never accept anything on 'authority.' The logical inference is that the Athenian *nomos*[20] was flawed in that it did not protect the 'right' of individuals to pursue truth in their own way. We 'moderns' in our 'liberal democracies,' therefore, are superior to the Athenians in the safeguarding of such a 'right.'

But this is where the 'liberal' clashes with the 'democratic' reading of the text. The democracy of Athens was not 'liberal.' It was the purest form of democracy the West has yet experienced. At the center of Athenian democratic institutions was the concept of *isonomia* – equality before the law or, some say, equality maintained by law.[21] The *dikasterion* (the court) was one of the fundamental institutions for the preservation of *isonomia*,[22] the antonym of which was expressed by the *hubris* of tyranny – the assertion of power by one man instead of 'all,' the claim of being 'above the law.'[23]

The golden age of Athens had the most radically democratic government the world has yet seen. It was a 'direct' democracy – governmental decisions were made by 'all'[24] the citizens of the city. Decisions on public affairs were made by the *ekklesia* (the Assembly), which was a congregation (open to all male citizens over the age of 20) that met at regular intervals on the hill of Pnyx (from once a month to three or four times a month).[25] The agenda was set by the *boule* (Council of 500), which also proposed laws for the Assembly to vote on. Some 40,000 or so citizens were eligible, and there was a quorum requirement of 6,000. Athens was divided into geographical areas called 'demes,' which were assigned to one of ten tribes. The Council was made up of 500 members, 50 from each tribe. The Council of 500 met every day. Day-to-day administration was taken care of by *prytaneis* (executives). Each tribe in the Council served in rotation as *prytaneis*.[26] Most governmental offices and posts were selected by lot. Only a few crucial positions – such as military generals (*strategoi*) – were filled by election (where some 'expertise' was thought to be needed). But the fundamental assumption of Athenian democracy was that no one is 'entitled' – it is no one's 'business' – to rule over another citizen[27] (obviously, this principle excluded women, children, and slaves).

The Athenian jury trial

Reflecting this radical form of democracy, the Athenian legal system functioned in ways that were quite different from what we are used to. There were no lawyers, no public prosecutors. Litigants were expected to make their own arguments (though their speeches could be written for them) within a specified period (timed by water clocks) on a single day. This is why the art of rhetoric became so crucial in the litigious atmosphere of ancient Athens and why the so-called Sophists ('wise men'), who claimed to be able to teach the art of rhetoric, became so important. To win their case, the litigants had to persuade the *dikastai* to vote in their favor. This Greek term, *dikastai*, could be translated both as 'jurors' and as 'judges' – for, in fact, this body of citizens served both functions.[28] There were no professional judges and no system of appeal from a jury's verdict. There was a jury pool of 6,000 (600 from each tribe) designated each year.[29] Jurors presented themselves on the day of trial and were selected for a court randomly through an extremely complicated process by a device called a *kleroterion*.[30] Moreover, the juries were considerably larger than we are used to – some numbered as low as 201, but juries could be in the thousands. This procedure limited the opportunity for any of the parties to bribe the jurors.

However, the juries were so large not only because this discouraged bribery but also because it was assumed that the more people who engaged in the decision, the more likely the outcome would be correct – the same sort of logic we recognize in the concept of the 'wisdom of crowds.'[31] Faith is placed in the 'common sense' of the people as a whole. We have juries because people bring their knowledge and experience of life to their decisions as well as the values of the community. Collectively, they understand what sort of behavior is or is not acceptable within the confines of their society – this is the *nomos* by which they are to decide cases. The purpose of a trial for the litigants was to persuade the *dikastai*, the 'judges/jurors,' of the outcome that was best for Athens.

Private suits (*dikai*) could only be initiated by the party injured or a close relative on their behalf. Public suits (*graphai*) could be brought by 'public-minded' citizens – that is, by citizens who believed they were acting for the public good. Normally, they would claim to be acting on the basis of *nomos*. To prevent 'frivolous' lawsuits, a fine of 1,000 drachmas was imposed on anyone who initiated a *graphê* and did not garner at least 1/5 of the jurors' votes. Socrates makes an odd joke about this at 36b. Once each side had presented his case, the jury did not deliberate (about guilt or innocence, for example). They voted immediately. If the vote went against the defendant, the 'accuser' proposed a penalty and the defendant a counter-penalty. The jury would then choose one or the other – it could not devise its own creative remedy. As a rule, this tended to moderate proposed penalties.[32]

In this way, the Athenian jury system reflected a deep belief in democracy – the rule of the people. The people themselves could interpret law and decide legal issues – no other 'expertise' was needed (from judges or lawyers, for example). There was no separation of powers in government, no separation of religion from politics. Democracy meant direct, participatory democracy – literally, the will of the people expressed in real time, based upon their beliefs about what was best for their community's interests, which included religious beliefs. Religious rituals and festivals were part and parcel of the life of the *polis*, the city. Indeed, the thing many of us associate most closely with ancient Athens – the performance of the great tragedies of Aeschylus, Sophocles, and Euripides – was linked to festivals for the god Dionysus. Thus, any threat to the religious beliefs of the city would be deemed a threat to the values that upheld the city itself – at least, that is how ordinary Athenians would have viewed the matter.[33]

The trial in the *Apology*

At the age of 70, Socrates was formally charged through a *graphê asebeias*, a writ alleging impiety, by three Athenian citizens about whom we know little: Anytus, Lycon, and Meletus, who acted as chief prosecutor.[34] They alleged that Socrates 1) did not acknowledge the gods of the city, 2) introduced new divinities, and 3) corrupted the young. The proposed punishment was death. There were 500 or 501 members of the jury.[35] If 500, the vote to convict must have been 280 to 220, so that a change of 30 votes would have meant acquittal (see Plato, *Apology* 36a). Obviously, Socrates' defense of himself failed. The question is: why did he fail?[36]

A plausible and widespread interpretation of the *Apology* is that it was meant to be a devastating critique of democracy. Plato, it is argued, blamed the democracy of Athens for condemning his teacher and meant to stigmatize that form of regime forever as the rule of the poor and the ignorant. Lovers of truth should fear the demagoguery to which the mob is vulnerable. Some readers find in the *Apology* an archetype for the philosopher's encounter with society. Democracies (indeed, all regimes) are governed by opinion. A philosopher seeks truth, which is always a threat to opinion. Any philosopher who values his life will hide his wisdom lest he meet Socrates' fate. Thus does philosophy make cowards of us all.[37]

However, we should note that nowhere in the *Apology* does Socrates claim to know the 'truth' (or, at least, the 'truth' of anything significant). We (and Socrates and the jurors) remain in the cave, to borrow Plato's image from his great dialogue, *The Republic*. We may seek 'truth' but never get there. No one is privileged with exclusive or assured access to it. Socrates says at the beginning of his speech that the *arête* (virtue or excellence) of a juror is to determine whether the interlocutors speak justly or not. But how does one determine whether or not a speaker is speaking justly – given the difficulty of knowing *anything* for certain? As mentioned, the jurors were supposed to determine the dispute pursuant to *nomos*, their 'common sense' about what outcome would be best for Athens.

It is precisely this 'common opinion' that the jurors bring to their deliberations that Socrates must first address. He is charged with corrupting the youth and not believing in the gods of the city but in 'new divinities.' He knows that Athenians have preconceptions about him that might incline them toward a guilty verdict: preconceptions created, in part, by his 'old accusers' (including the comic poet Aristophanes) that he is a 'Sophist' who teaches about things heavenly and underground (read: about religious matters) and how to make the weaker argument appear the stronger. Since these 'old' charges are so similar to the 'later' accusations of Meletus, Anytus, and Lycon, Socrates must dissuade the jurors from prejudices they may bring with them, which he admits will be hard, like shadowboxing. Socrates resorts to two gambits to overcome the 'common opinion' of the jurors, both of which have some divine connection.

Access to truth: the oracle of Delphi and the *daimonion*

His first gambit is to provide an alternative explanation for his behavior. Socrates' accusers did not produce a single witness that he had ever been paid as a teacher or even taught anyone anything. His reputation comes from his persistent, public questioning of Athenians on the street and elsewhere, which he admits has irritated people. He does not deny he does this but, instead, provides a reason for it that contradicts the 'common opinion': He is obeying the oracle at Delphi, whose wisdom was solicited by his friend Chaerophon. This is the only place in the Platonic canon we have that mentions this oracle.

Socrates explains that, when the oracle proclaimed that no one was wiser than Socrates,[38] he was confused because he was not aware of being wise. Still, the oracle cannot lie, he asserts, for that is not the god's *themis*.[39] One explanation he offers is that the oracle is saying that the god is wise (*ho theos sophos*), but human wisdom is worth very little (23a5–7). Thus, while some might argue that Socrates' later behavior, which raises doubt about the oracle, is disobedient to the god,[40] another explanation might be that his subsequent investigation of the oracle was an attempt to understand it more fully. It was "necessary" to give his attention to the oracle of the god (*to tou theou*) (21e5) because the oracle (one is tempted to add, 'as usual') was ambiguous. Investigation was necessary because it was not clear what it meant. On this reading, it would be impious of Socrates *not* to inquire into it. Eventually, he comes to the conclusion that the oracle meant to say that the wisest man is probably the one like him who recognizes that he is not wise. Thus, his 'mission,' as it is sometimes called, of questioning citizens about their wisdom is "pursuant to the god" (*kata ton theon*) (23b5). But note that Socrates has no better insight into the truth of the oracle than others except through his investigation. He tells the story to refute the 'common opinion' that derives from Aristophanes and other 'old accusers.' Still, the evidence and reasoning he uses is available to all.

Socrates' second gambit is more daring if we reflect upon it: his admission that he trucks with a *daimonion*, the spirit that tells him when he is about to do wrong. The exact charge against Socrates "is specified at 24b: Socrates ἀδικεῖ (does wrong, s. c. to the city) by corrupting the youth and not believing in the gods (θεοί) which the city believes in but other new divinities (δαιμόνια καινά)."[41] Leaving aside the corruption of the youth for a moment, Socrates does not directly refute the charge of not believing in the *theoi* of the city. Rather, he achieves a rhetorical victory by suckering Meletus into asserting that Socrates is an atheist – to which Socrates replies, how can he be an atheist if he expressly believes in a *daimonion*, which is a sort of *theos*. Socrates also makes frequent reference in the speech to a *theos* whom he never names (though most Athenians would assume is Apollo). Is he trying to mitigate the charge of believing in new divinities by emphasizing his continued belief in the gods of the city? If so, why did he not make clear that he was referring to Apollo or any other god Athens accepted?[42] Is it simply a diversion?

After all, admitting to his *daimonion* is a virtual confession to the charge of believing in *daimonia kaina*, as Miles Burnyeat points out. It is literally a 'new divinity.' Moreover, knowledge he claims to derive from the *daimonion* has a different epistemological status from the oracle at Delphi, since his access to it is idiosyncratic. Plato has him admit as much in *Republic* 496c. Not everyone, it seems, has a *daimonion* to keep them on the correct path. No one else can see or hear his *daimonion*.[43] What use is it then for him to invoke this divine sign before the jury? What does this say about the modern conception of Socrates as a rationalist? Was he sincere in his belief? Or was it a pretense? If a pretense, did Plato present the information as a way of covering for his mentor? Or is Plato rationalizing Socrates' 'mistakes' as some form of divine inspiration?

Socrates' most passionate discourse comes at 29d when he explains why he will not give up his activity of questioning people: "As much as I cherish you, men of Athens, I shall obey the god (*to theo*) rather than you."[44] Socrates knows that speaking or acting against those in authority is dangerous. Yet, he is persuaded that he is not doing wrong. Otherwise, his *daimonion* would have warned him. Assuming he (or Plato) is telling the truth about all of this, how does Socrates know that his *daimonion* is not misleading him?[45] And why should the jury believe him? Socrates can only base it on a subjective feeling or go by past personal experience. He cannot justify his actions publicly except by anecdote, which is why he says he has kept away from politics and concentrated on private matters (31d–e). Yet, now he is on trial and *must* justify his actions.

Therefore, he provides some anecdotes. He cites, beginning at 32b, instances of his *daimonion* warning him away from actions that were wrong: for example, from trying the admirals from the battle of Arginusae together (this was when Athens was a democracy, and the city itself later condemned that trial as illegal (*paranomous*)) and from doing the murderous bidding of the Thirty Tyrants, who ordered the execution of Leon of Salamis (which Socrates labels 'unjust' and 'impious' but not necessarily 'illegal'). He offers this as proof to the jury with the added weight that he presents evidence of deeds, not words – presumably, to show that he really believes it or he would not have acted this way and put his life in jeopardy.[46] But how can other men assess the truth here?

The jurors cannot *know* whether the *daimonion*'s promptings are true or just – or even that they exist. They can only judge this on Socrates' say-so and the indices of truth he provides, such as the fact that he risked his life to follow them and that he risks his life now to remain obedient to it.[47] Such evidence may or may not persuade them. It is a thin basis of proof. Indeed, after they render their verdict, Socrates expresses surprise that so many voted to acquit. Socrates is in a unique position, thanks to what we today by analogy might (misleadingly) call 'revelation.' He has faith that he is acting justly because his *daimonion* does not interfere. No one else can have that form of 'certainty' – so, in a sense, in the context of the *Apology*, no one *is* wiser than Socrates. This is reflected in something else as well.

No man knowingly does wrong

Socrates consistently addresses the jurors as 'men of Athens' and never as *dikastai*[48] (even though Meletus does so) until after he has been condemned – and then only those who voted to acquit him (40a) – for the term, he says, is only used rightly with respect to them. What does he mean by this? Obviously, one reading is that the 'true' jurors (the ones actually doing justice) were those convinced by Socrates because they recognized that he spoke justly, which is the true excellence of a juror. However, his surprise (though it may be bravado) at how close the vote was indicates his awareness of the difficulty of the proofs he was providing. Still, had the law permitted the trial to go beyond one day, he says he would have persuaded them (37b).

Does this link up to Socrates' claim that no man knowingly does wrong? To reach the right result only required a bit more education of the jurors, Socrates seems to say. The tragedy is that there was insufficient time to bring the jury into the state of knowledge that Socrates possessed, thanks to his *daimonion*.[49]

The jury has no better access to the truth of the oracle than Socrates does and even less ability to assess the warnings of the *daimonion*, feeling no internal prodding themselves and having no evidence other than Socrates' anecdotes. Therefore, they cannot assess the truth of Socrates' claims except pursuant to their own judgment and experience. Plato presents us with all the evidence they had to go on. Perhaps, that is why there is no account of the prosecution's case: what matters is the kind of evidence Socrates could evince for his acquittal.

Ultimately, Socrates appeals to the jurors to remain true to their oaths and decide according to the laws and/or customs (*kata tous nomous*). Moreover, he says, they must eschew emotion in their decision-making, which is why he refuses to beg for his life or make appeals on behalf of his family. At the age of 70, he would not disgrace his good name to resort to such tactics. This, then, is the nature of the trial as explained by Socrates: it is to allow jurors to assess impartially the evidence and arguments of the interlocutors, but it is not (perhaps, never can be) a determination of the truth. We should pay careful attention to the equivalence Socrates places on 'truth' and 'justice.' In order to do justice, the court must know the truth. If truth cannot be demonstrated, justice cannot be done – except by accident. Our access to truth may be better or worse. We may, as Socrates demonstrates, be wiser by knowing we are not wise.[50]

As modern citizens in liberal democracies, we are disappointed by the outcome of the *Apology*, thanks to our partiality for the underdog. The text is a *defense* of Socrates. Therefore, narratologically, we root for him to win. Still, we accept we are reading a tragedy.[51] There is yet another irony to appreciate. As readers of the *Apology*, we place ourselves in the position of jurors. We cannot know the truth of Socrates' guilt or innocence – only whether or not we are persuaded of the existence of his *daimonion* – or, at least, the sincerity of Socrates' belief in it. If so, then we must believe that Socrates believed he was acting justly. Yet, if we are so persuaded, then we cannot but be persuaded that Socrates was guilty of at least one of the charges – believing in *daimonia kaina*.[52]

This brings us full circle: is Plato defending Socrates or subtly condemning him? The ambiguity indicates exquisite artistry. However, it changes the stakes in the question to be debated in the next chronological dialogue, the *Crito*. Traditionally, the *Apology* has been read as a defense of civil disobedience – because Socrates will follow the god rather than the (implied unjust) law of Athens. In the *Crito*, however, Socrates argues for deference to the laws (even if they are unjust?). Does it change our perception of this dynamic if Plato gives us reason to suppose Socrates was guilty?

Notes

1 Socrates mentions Plato in his speech at 34a and 38b. The number reference to the *Apology* here (known as the Stephanus number) is the traditional reference to the Greek edition of Plato's complete works by Henricus Stephanus in Geneva published in 1578. References to Aristotle's works have been given Bekker numbers based on an edition published by August Immaneul Bekker in the 19th century.

2 Xenophon's version was apparently written many years after the trial. Xenophon relates that Socrates predicted that the son of one of his accuser's, Anytus, would become a disgrace – which proved true, so that Anytus, though dead, enjoys a bad reputation (Xenophon, *Apology* 30–32).

3 Gregory Vlastos summarizes the differences between Plato's Socrates and Xenophon's Socrates in this way:

> 1) Xenophon's is a Socrates without irony and without paradox. Take these away from Plato's Socrates, and there is nothing left. 2) Xenophon's Socrates is so persuasive that, 'whenever he argued,' Xenophon declares, 'he gained a greater measure of assent from his hearers than any man I have ever known' (*Memorabilia* 4.6.16). Plato's Socrates is not persuasive at all. He wins every argument, but never manages to win over an opponent .... 3) Xenophon's Socrates discourses on theology and theodicy, argues for the existence of a divine mind .... Plato's refuses to argue over anything other than man and human affairs. 4) Plato's Socrates maintains that it is never right to repay evil with evil .... Xenophon's ... parrots the common opinion that the good man will 'excel in rendering benefits to his friends and injuries to his enemies' (*Memorabilia* 2.6.35).
>
> (Gregory Vlastos, "The Paradox of Socrates," in Gregory Vlastos (ed.), *The Philosophy of Socrates* (1971))

4 In another work, the *Symposium*, Xenophon hints that Socrates could easily have won his acquittal if he had so chosen. Socrates even extols his ability to act as a 'pimp,' Xenophon, *Symposium* 4.56–64.

5 It is interesting that, in the *Crito* – the dialogue that follows the *Apology* in the chronology of Socrates' life and deals with why Socrates refuses to flee Athens and accepts

death by hemlock – Plato has a personification of The Laws argue that Socrates has no more right to flout The Laws than a son does to strike back at a father. See *Crito* 50e–51b.

6 For an argument that Plato has a darker view of Aristophanes, see Arlene Saxonhouse, "The Net of Hephaestus: Aristophanes' Speech in Plato's *Symposium*," 13.1 *Interpretation* (1984), pp. 15–32; but see Anthony Hooper, "The Greatest Hope of All: Aristophanes on Human Nature in Plato's *Symposium*," 63(2) *Classical Quarterly* (December, 2013), pp. 567–579.

7 In the *Phaedo*, Plato has Socrates say he used to study the natural world (*phusis*) but gave it up (*Phaedo* 96a7–8).

8 With, perhaps, one exception – *The Laws* about which many scholars assume the Athenian Stranger is actually Socrates.

9 See Gregory Vlastos, *Socrates: Ironist and Moral Philosopher* (Cornell 1991). See also Charles H. Kahn, "Did Plato Write Socratic Dialogues?" 31(2) *The Classical Quarterly* (1981), pp. 305–320.

10 The speculation runs from shortly after the trial to as late as 386 B.C.E. See E. de Strycker and S.R. Slings, "Plato's Apology of Socrates," in Rachana Kamtekar (ed.), *Plato's* Euthyphro, Apology, *and* Crito: *Critical Essays* (2004).

11 Indeed, "there is, on the one hand, no single sentence in the Platonic *Apology* that Socrates could not actually have pronounced, and on the other, that the published work contains no passage so specifically un-Platonic that it cannot be Plato's work" (Donald Morrison, "On the Alleged Historical Reliability of Plato's *Apology*," 82 *Archiv f. Gesch. d. Philosophie* (2000), p. 244).

12 Id., pp. 243–244, citing Reginald Allen, *Socrates and Legal Obligation* (1980). This also reflects ironically on Socrates' claim at the beginning of the speech not to be a clever speaker. Is the sophisticated structure an indication that Socrates is lying or engaging in false modesty?

13 Alcibiades also appears in Plato's *Symposium*, and a dialogue attributed to Plato bears his name.

14 On Socrates' antidemocratic sentiments, see C.D.C. Reeve, *Socrates in the* Apology: *An Essay on Plato's* Apology of Socrates (1989), pp. 97–108 (concluding that Socrates was not antidemocratic). The Greek term *demokratia* was mostly used as a term of disparagement – and mostly by sympathizers of aristocracy. Aristotle uses the term to describe the 'corrupt' form of rule by the many, the positive form of which is the *politeia*, which is also the general word for what we would call a 'constitution.' See Chapter 2. However, as Thucydides recounts it, Pericles proudly proclaims Athens to be a *demokratia* in his funeral oration early in the Peloponnesian War (Thucydides, 2.37).

15 For an infamous version of this argument, see Karl Popper, *The Open Society and Its Enemies* (1945), Vol. 1 "The Spell of Plato," in which, interestingly, he accuses Plato of betraying Socrates' 'democratic' sentiments by placing totalitarian speeches in his mouth – especially in the *Republic*.

16 The term 'ostracism' derives from the Greek word *ostraka*, shards of pottery on which Athenians wrote the name of the person whom they wanted exiled when they voted. Plutarch tells the story that, when the vote to ostracize the Athenian general Aristides was underway, an illiterate voter (who did not know the general) asked him to write the name 'Aristides' on the shard for him. The general is supposed to have asked the voter what wrong Aristides had ever done him. "None," was the reply, "I'm just tired of always hearing him called 'the Just.'" Aristides then wrote down his own name. See Plutarch, "The Life of Aristides" 7, *Parallel Lives of the Noble Grecians and Romans,* Loeb Classical Library (1914). Lest the point be lost: Plutarch's purpose in telling the story is to emphasize what a silly form of government democracy is.

17 For example, Collingwood indicates some of the problems here:

> in ethics, a Greek word like δεῖ cannot be legitimately translated by using the word 'ought,' if that word carries with it the notion of what is sometimes called 'moral obligation.' Was there any Greek word or phrase to express that notion? The 'realists' said there was; but they stultified themselves by adding that the 'theories of moral obligation' expounded by Greek writers differed from modern theories such as Kant's about the same thing. How did they know that the Greek and Kantian theories were about the same thing? Oh, because δεῖ (or whatever word it was) is the Greek for 'ought'.
> (R.G. Collingwood, *An Autobiography* (1978 [1939]), p. 63)

18 See David Lowenthal, *The Past is a Foreign Country* (1985), the title of which derives from the first line of L.P. Hartley's novel *The Go-Between* (1953).
19 See Isaiah Berlin, "Two Concepts of Liberty," *Four Essays on Liberty* (1969). On the genealogy of the modern concept of freedom, see Quentin Skinner, *Liberty before Liberalism* (1998).
20 *Nomos* is a tricky word in ancient Greek with a fluid meaning that can be translated as 'law' but may encompass legal decrees, customs, mores, etc. See Chapter 3 below.
21 See Gregory Vlastos, "Isonomia," 74 *Am. J. Philology* 337, 356–361 (1953).
22 On this, see Mogens Hansen, "The Concepts of *Demos*, *Ekklesia*, and *Dikasterion* in Classical Athens," 50 *Greek, Roman, and Byzantine Studies* (2010).
23 Compare Kreon's claim in Sophocles' *Antigone* in his colloquy with his son Haimon (*Antigone* 734–39). Haimon argues that no city belongs to one man, but Kreon claims the city belongs by *nomos* to him who rules. It is important to note that nowhere in the text does Socrates question the legitimacy of the trial. He laments that he did not have enough time to persuade the 'men of Athens' to acquit him (37a). This may be a veiled critique of the Athenian law limiting such suits to a single day. Sparta, for example, did not. See John Burnet (ed.), *Plato's Apology*, p. 237. Still, he accepts the responsibility to persuade them of his innocence. "The law must be obeyed," he says, "and a defense speech must be made" (19a6–7).
24 There is dispute about whether women were also considered citizens of Athens even though they were excluded from political and judicial offices.
25 Laws proposed in this body could be challenged by a *graphe paranomon* (lawsuit that a proposed bill was unconstitutional or, literally, against the law) and quashed by the courts (*dikasteria*) if a majority of the 'jurors' voted for the prosecution. They could also be quashed by the next such assembly. See Hansen, "The Concepts of *Demos*, *Ekklesia*, and *Dikasterion* in Classical Athens."
26 It was presiding in this position as a member of his tribe that Socrates acted in the case of the admirals at Arginusae. See *Apology* 32b.
27 Contrast this, for example, with the arguments Socrates makes (at least, on the surface) in the *Republic*.
28 Although the court was presided over by the *archon basileus* ('king magistrate'), the official responsible for the enforcement of religious law. Once a party commences a case, this official presides over a preliminary hearing to determine whether the accusation is in accordance with the law and should be allowed to proceed. Plato depicts Socrates on his way to this hearing in the *Euthyphro*.
29 While decisions of 'juries' were not subject to control or appeal, the 'jury' pool took an oath at the beginning of the year to judge according to the laws and decrees of Athens. Unwritten laws could also be cited – e.g., 'everybody knows that.' See Douglas MacDowell, *The Law in Classical Athens* (1978) and, generally, Paul Gowder, "Democracy, Solidarity, and the Rule of Law: Lessons from Athens," 62 *Buffalo Law Review* 1 (2014).

30 See Aristotle, *The Constitution of Athens* LXIII–LXV.
31 See James Surowiecki, *The Wisdom of Crowds: Why the Many Are Smarter Than the Few and How Collective Wisdom Shapes Business, Economies, Societies and Nations* (2004).
32 Thus, the trial was a two-step process, requiring two speeches from each party. Plato's *Apology* is the only example we have of someone giving a third speech after condemnation. After the failure of Socrates' defense, his accusers demand death by hemlock. Socrates proposes a counter-penalty: that he be fed at public expense the way champions at the Olympic games are. He laments that he did not have another day to persuade the jurors but reasserts that he will not go into exile and he will not cease his activities in the city. Yet, since a fine does not harm him (presumably, he means it does not harm his soul), he proposes a fine of one silver mina. He then raises the amount to 30 minas at the urging of others (including Plato), who guarantee its payment. Whether Socrates' counter-proposal was meant as a 'final outrage' or a deliberate provocation has been debated for centuries. See Thomas C. Brickhouse and Nicholas D. Smith, *Socrates on Trial* (1990), pp. 214–215. In Xenophon's version, Socrates refused to propose a counter-penalty and forbade his friends from doing so.

In Diogenes Laertes' "Life of Socrates" (written in the 3rd century C.E.), the jurors vote to condemn Socrates by an even wider margin than they convicted him – 360 to 141 – which supports the view that Socrates provoked the jurors. In Plato's *Apology*, there is no indication that more jurors voted for the death penalty than the initial conviction. His proposal to be given free meals at the Prytaneum could be seen as a provocation (or, perhaps, as an unsuccessful jest?), but the monetary counterproposal is more problematic. Some see one mina as a paltry sum; others as a substantial one. In the *Nicomachean Ethics* (1134b21), Aristotle mentions one mina as a conventional ransom for one prisoner. Certainly, given his avowed poverty, it was a substantial fine for *Socrates*, and 30 minas is without doubt a substantial sum – for why would Socrates' friends also offer a half-hearted counter-penalty? By contrast, earlier in the *Apology* (20b9), Socrates notes it was claimed that Evenus of Paros received five minas for teaching human excellence, which Socrates exclaims is a 'modest' sum for such a lesson. But, then again, what is the price of human excellence?
33 Alcibiades incurred the disfavor of the Athenians when he was accused of desecrating sacred statues (*hermai*) throughout the city, which is what led him to flee into exile.
34 Readers of Attic Greek can find a number of puns on the accusers' names in Plato's *Apology* (for example, on "Meletus" at 24d7–9, 25c, and 26b1–2) and even a pun on Plato's own name in the first few lines (17c5) (*plattonti logous* – fabricating speeches or Plato-izing speeches). This, in turn, raises questions on the extent to which Plato is merely reporting the trial or fictionalizing it. See Donald Morrison, "On the Alleged Historical Reliability of Plato's Apology."
35 Scholars differ on whether the number of jurors/judges had to be odd to avoid a tie. Aristotle indicates that a tie vote meant acquittal (*The Constitution of Athens* LXIX).
36 See, generally, Gabriel Danzig, "Apologizing for Socrates: Plato and Xenophon on Socrates' Behavior in Court," 133 *Transactions of the American Philological Association* (2003), pp. 281–321, which argues that Plato and Xenophon each craft an account of Socrates' defense to answer post-trial perceptions of the faults Socrates displayed.
37 We need not go so far as those who argue that philosophers have a duty to conceal the truth lest the masses be disturbed in the 'noble lie' of their 'opinion.'
38 To belabor the point: The oracle in Plato's version does not claim Socrates is the 'wisest' – only that no one else is wiser unlike Xenophon's version, which simply proclaims Socrates the 'wisest.'
39 An untranslatable Greek word that means something along the lines of custom, lawfulness, order, and nature. The gist is that lying is not something the god does. At the

very least, it is unwise to assume so; and, rhetorically speaking, Socrates can appeal to the jurors' 'pious' assumption that the oracle does not lie.

40 And here the strangeness of Chaerophon's actions must not be downplayed – what prompted him to question the oracle if Socrates was not already engaged in his 'philosophizing' activities beforehand? Did Socrates begin questioning his fellow citizens as a result of the oracle's statement? If so, why did Chaerephon think he was wise – and consult the oracle about it? Had Socrates been teaching or questioning his fellow citizens prior to the consultation with the oracle? If so, how could he have been doing so in obedience to the god? It is also worth noting that there is no other reference to the oracle anywhere in Plato's writings. It appears only in the apologies written by Plato and Xenophon – and there as a piece of new information. See Gabriel Danzig, "Apologizing for Socrates: Plato and Xenophon on Socrates' Behavior in Court," p. 304. If the oracle was so crucial for Socrates' behavior, why is there no other mention of it? Was this when he was teaching about things natural and supernatural?

41 Miles Burnyeat, "The Impiety of Socrates," in Rachana Kamtekar (ed.), *Plato's Euthyphro, Apology, and* Crito: *Critical Essays* (2004).

42 He swears 'by Zeus' and 'by Hera' at certain points in the text.

43 For a summary of the various scholarly views on the nature of Socrates' *daimonion*, see Bridger Ehli, "Rationalizing Socrates' *daimonion*," 26(2) *British Journal for the History of Philosophy* (2018). Broadly speaking, the options are that the *daimonion* is a metaphor for Socrates' rational reflections, a description of some form of conscience, or a reflection of his genuine religious belief.

44 Traditionally, this has been interpreted as conflicting with Socrates' claim in the *Crito* of the necessity of obeying the laws.

45 This is the implication of Descartes' evil demon in his *Meditations on First Philosophy* (1641).

46 Compare the argument of Christian apologists that Christianity must be true. Otherwise, the early martyrs would not have been willing to die for it.

47 It is interesting that, in Robert Bolt's *A Man for All Seasons*, Thomas More engages in such a gambit when he swears that Richard Rich is lying – based on the proof that, if More did not take oaths seriously, he would not be on trial in the first place. We find another variation on this in Arthur Miller's *The Crucible*.

48 Although Socrates does refer in the abstract to *dikastai* at 34c2 and 35c, he is not addressing the jurors. At the beginning of his speech, he stated that the 'excellence' (*arête*) of a juror (*dikastou*) was to attend to whether he spoke 'justly' (18a5–6)

49 Outside the *Apology*, Socrates' *daimonion* is only briefly mentioned in the *Euthyphro* 3b, the *Phaedrus* 242b, the *Euthydemus* 272e–273a, the *Republic* 496a, and the *Theatetus* 151a, as well as the *Theages* 128e (attributed to Plato).

50 In the classic film of a jury trial, *Twelve Angry Men* (1957), we observe how jury deliberations are turned from the conclusion that the defendant is guilty to the conclusion that he is not guilty by an argument by one juror (Juror 8) that they must take their oaths seriously to examine the evidence impartially. We are provided narrative satisfaction that an injustice was avoided. Yet, we never learn as viewers or in the film's narrative whether the defendant was *actually* guilty or innocent. (We shall pass over in silence Juror 8's misconduct in the jury deliberations.) See Charles D. Weisselberg, "Good Film, Bad Jury," 82(2) *Chicago-Kent Law Review*: Symposium: The 50th Anniversary of 12 Angry Men (13 April 2007).

51 Compare Jacob Howland, "Plato's 'Apology' as Tragedy," 70(4) *The Review of Politics* (Fall, 2008), pp. 519–546.

52 Too extensive a topic to handle here, but it is worth noting that, throughout the Platonic canon, Socrates struggles with the ethical and moral problems Greek polytheism raises – see, for example, his remarks in Book II of the *Republic* that stories of the

gods doing evil should not be taught. One reading of Sophocles' *Antigone* is that the tragedy arises because Kreon obeys the sky gods while Antigone obeys the chthonic gods. Similarly, Aeschylus' *Oresteia* may be read as an attempt to resolve a conflict between sky gods and chthonic gods. One way of interpreting Plato's Socrates is that he is attempting to create a new theology – whether monotheism or atheism – that resolves such dilemmas.

References

Allen, R. (1980). *Socrates and legal obligation.*
Berlin, I. (1969). Two concepts of liberty. *Four Essays on Liberty.*
Brickhouse, T. C., & Smith, N. D. (1990). *Socrates on trial.*
Burnet, J. (Ed.). (1979 [1924]). *Plato's Euthyphro, Apology of Socrates and Crito.*
Burnyeat, M. (2004). The impiety of Socrates. In R. Kamtekar (Ed.), *Plato's* Euthyphro, Apology, *and* Crito: *Critical Essays.*
Collingwood, R. G. (1978 [1939]). *An autobiography.*
Danzig, G. (2003). Apologizing for Socrates: Plato and Xenophon on Socrates' behavior in court. 133 *Transactions of the American Philological Association* 281.
de Strycker, E. & Slings, S.R. (2004). Plato's Apology of Socrates. In R. Kamtekar (Ed.), *Plato's Euthryphro, Apology, and Crito: Critical Essays.*
Ehli, B. (2018). Rationalizing Socrates' *daimonion*. 26(2) *British Journal for the History of Philosophy* 225.
Gowder, P. (2014). Democracy, solidarity, and the rule of law: Lessons from Athens. 62 *Buffalo Law Review* 1.
Hansen, M. (2010). The concepts of *demos, ekklesia*, and *dikasterion* in classical Athens. 50 *Greek, Roman, and Byzantine Studies* 499.
Hooper, A. (December, 2013). The greatest hope of all: Aristophanes on human nature in Plato's *Symposium*. 63(2) *Classical Quarterly* 567.
Howland, J. (Fall, 2008). Plato's 'Apology' as tragedy. 70(4) *Review of Politics* 519.
Kahn, C. H. (1981). Did Plato write Socratic dialogues? 31(2) *Classical Quarterly* 305.
Lowenthal, D. (1985). *The past is a foreign country.*
MacDowell, D. (1978). *The law in classical Athens.*
Morrison, D. (2000). On the alleged historical reliability of Plato's *Apology*. 82 *Archiv f. Gesch. d. Philosophie* 235.
Plutarch (1914). *Parallel lives of the noble Grecians and Romans.* Loeb Classical Library.
Popper, K. (1945). *The open society and its enemies.*
Reeve, C. D. C. (1989). *Socrates in the Apology: An essay on Plato's Apology of Socrates.*
Saxonhouse, A. (1984). The net of Hephaestus: Aristophanes' speech in Plato's *Symposium*. 13(1) *Interpretation* 15.
Skinner, Q. (1998). *Liberty before liberalism.*
Surowiecki, J. (2004). *The wisdom of crowds: Why the many are smarter than the few and how collective wisdom shapes business, economies, societies and nations.*
Vlastos, G. (1971). The paradox of Socrates. In G. Vlastos (Ed.), *The philosophy of Socrates.*
Vlastos, G. (1991). *Socrates: Ironist and moral philosopher.*
Weisselberg, C. D. (13 April 2007). Good film, bad jury. 82(2) *Chicago-Kent Law Review* 717. Symposium: The 50th anniversary of 12 Angry Men.

Chapter 2

Cicero and the Trial of Gaius Verres (70 B.C.E.)

'Civic Corruption,' the Rule of Law, and the Analogy of Republican Rome

Another potential pitfall in the reading of ancient documents is that we often fit them into historical narratives we impose from without or fail to see that their authors conceived of their work within the premises of an historical narrative of which we are unaware or do not acknowledge the relevance. Indeed, we often swim in conceptions of history without thinking about where they come from and make judgments based on assumptions about history we have not examined critically.[1] Many of us, for instance, work with an implicit idea that history is more or less linear and that it 'progresses' – the notion that, over time, there is a steady, general improvement in the human condition. So-called Whig history[2] and Hegel's philosophy of history are the most prominent and influential versions of this conception. And it is a comforting one even if the causal mechanism behind it is not exactly clear. The ancient Greek and Roman concept of the 'cyclical' nature of history is rarely taken seriously these days[3] – at least, not at a conscious level. Yet, when we talk about the 'decline and fall' of some society or 'history repeating itself,' we are leaning on a 'cyclical' view of history. We may shrug and say these are mere figures of speech, but can we honestly say they have no influence on our thinking? Otherwise, why invoke them? And to what extent do they affect us even when we are conscious of their limitations? For example, when we parrot the saying attributed to Mark Twain that history may not repeat itself but it rhymes? Why study history at all if we are not supposed to learn 'lessons' from it?

I have chosen to focus this chapter on Cicero's prosecution of Gaius Verres for a number of reasons. For one thing, it provides a nice contrast between the role democratic institutions played in ancient Athenian trials and the role the mixture of aristocratic and democratic institutions played in trials in republican Rome. Thus, it serves a comparative purpose in our understanding of how law is interpreted and implemented in different systems.

It also provides an easy-to-understand illustration of how an analogy may become so pervasive in our cultural/historical imagination that it shapes our reckoning (consciously or unconsciously) of law and society. In this case, it is our understanding of the history of ancient Rome, which we almost always embed in a 'cyclical' interpretation of history from which we derive 'lessons' to

DOI: 10.4324/9781003302971-4

be learned. This cyclical interpretation is generally traced back to the ancient historian of Rome Polybius, but it is Niccoló Machiavelli's reinterpretation of Polybius[4] that had the greatest impact on modern thinking and provided a robust modern justification for the 'rule of law,' a justification that also played a central role when the principles of American constitutional government were being debated during the 18th century. And these 'lessons' are still being applied (often as a warning) in assessments of the contemporary United States,[5] as illustrated in Robert Harris' retelling of the life of Cicero, *Imperium* (2006), the artistic focus of this chapter.[6] Harris' selection of Cicero for his allegory of American politics is not accidental. It is as though a metaphor has attached itself to our understanding of ancient Rome, and we cannot resist applying it elsewhere.

If we pay attention to the way the 'cyclical' analogy has been used over the course of time, we may better be able to comprehend how our thinking can be affected by such intellectual structures and demonstrate the strengths and weaknesses of the reasoning we use to defend the 'rule of law' generally. For example, if we accept a 'cyclical' version of history, then shouldn't our understanding of the way law is implemented and how we advocate its interpretation take account of where we are in the cycle?

Why care about Cicero?

The Roman orator, consul, philosopher, and all-around busybody Marcus Tullius Cicero[7] had something of a revival a number of years ago, thanks (among other things) to the HBO series *Rome* and especially the popular trilogy of novels by Robert Harris fictionalizing his life. We are presented there with a physically slight, somewhat sickly, hyper-ambitious intellectual who is NOT the stereotypical Miles Gloriosus[8] military type we associate with ancient Roman virility. Yet, this most unmartial of Romans had as great an impact on Western civilization as any of the military men.

He was acclaimed as the supreme orator of his day, setting the standard for excellence in public speaking. His writings were revived as the model for good rhetoric during the Renaissance,[9] and they have exerted disproportionate influence ever since – at least, until the 19th century (when his ornate syntax and extravagant language gradually fell out of fashion). His treatise on duties (*De officiis*) may well have had more influence on Western European thinking than any other ethical writing from ancient times except the Bible – exceeding any other Roman writer and even Plato and Aristotle, most of whose works were unknown or known only in truncated form in Western Europe through much of the Middle Ages.[10] It is thanks to his philosophical writings that we know as much as we do about many ancient schools of thought.[11] Most importantly, he presented the definitive articulation of republican government (albeit from a very conservative point of view) that became the basis for much republican theorizing in the early modern era – in Machiavelli, Harrington, Montesquieu, and Rousseau (not to mention, Madison and Hamilton). It is only barely an exaggeration to say that our modern political worldview is Cicero's rhetorical invention; we merely occupy its spaces.

And it was Cicero's prosecution of Gaius Verres in Rome's extortion court that, as much as anything, set him on the path to fame and glory. That alone makes the case worthy of our attention – even if it were not such a good story in itself. The trial of Gaius Verres dominates the first half of Robert Harris' *Imperium*, where it serves to introduce Cicero's political career and set the baseline in the novel for the 'health' of the Roman republican system. Thanks to Harris' (relative) fidelity to historical accuracy, his account also provides a vivid re-creation of the workings of Roman legal and political structures. Tellingly for our purposes, *Imperium*'s narrator, Cicero's slave Tiro, says of Cicero's opening statement in the Verres trial: "this was to be one of the most decisive moments in the history of our Roman law – indeed, in the history of all law, everywhere, I should not wonder" (p. 207).[12]

The structure of Roman republican government

Like Athens, Rome began as a small city-state and later grew (usually through conquest) into a huge empire encompassing virtually the whole of Western Europe, the Middle East, and northern Africa. Whereas the predominant form of government in Athens was democracy, an aristocracy (the so-called patricians) dominated Rome ever since the overthrow of its kings.[13] However, Roman government was based upon a series of checks and balances: governmental offices and their functions were designed to avoid tyranny, to prevent the domination of power by a single person. As discussed below, these checks and balances were achieved by the structure of a 'mixed' government that was composed of elements of each of the classical forms of regime: rule by the one, the few, and the many.

For example, the highest magisterial office (limited to one year) consisted of two consuls who served simultaneously, each with veto power over the other. This functioned as a 'limited' version of the classical monarchy. To prevent too much power from accumulating with the patricians, the office of tribune of the plebeians was instituted. There were 10 tribunes of the plebs, and any one of them could veto actions of the magistrates, the Senate, or any other assembly. This functioned as a sort of 'limited' rule of the many. The Senate (representing the form of rule by the few), which originated under the kings, passed decrees called *senatus consulta*, which acted as "advice" to magistrates, usually obeyed unless conflicting with a law (*lex*).[14] The list of senators was controlled by the censors (two of them), who also conducted the population census and property assessments.[15] Election to a magistracy meant automatic inclusion in the Senate.

Moreover, magistrates were elected by different assemblies. Quaestors (20) and curule aediles (two) were elected by the *Comitia Tributa* – or the 35 tribes[16] of Rome, four urban and 31 rural, consisting of both patricians and plebs. The tribunes of the plebs and the plebeian aediles (two) were elected by the *Concilium Plebis* (i.e., only by the plebs as a subgroup of the *Comitia Tributa*). However, censors, praetors, and consuls were elected by the *Comitia Centuriata*, which was made up of soldiers organized into classes by wealth (so that the wealthier 'centuries' dominated). As Cicero put it, the structure of Roman republican government reflected a balance of "power (*potestas*) in the magistracies, authority (*auctoritas*) in the preeminent counselors [i.e., the Senate], and liberty (*libertas*) in the people" (*De re publica*, 2.57).

The tension between the patricians and the plebeians provided the dynamic for many of the conflicts in the Roman Republic. Things came to a head in 134 B.C.E. when a tribune of the plebs, Tiberius Gracchus, tried to implement a more equitable land redistribution and was murdered by a mob of patricians (even though his person was sacrosanct, thanks to his office). Not long afterwards, civil war broke out in Rome with Lucius Cornelius Sulla leading the patriciate interests and Gaius Marius representing the popular faction. Sulla eventually defeated Marius' army and was appointed dictator of Rome by the Senate around 80 B.C.E. (without the traditional six-month limit to that office). The 'dictator' was an irregular office of the Roman republic. In times when it was thought necessary, the Senate could pass a *senatus consulta* appointing a dictator who could rule with absolute authority but only for six months. The practice of appointing a dictator fell out of use after the Punic Wars with Carthage (264–146 B.C.E.) until Sulla revived it. Sulla initiated a series of reforms along with a 'reign of terror' that set the precedent for what would become Julius Caesar's dictatorship. The takeaway is that, while the Roman Republic had significant checks on the power of the patricians, the patricians were still the dominant force, which meant that the administration and implementation of law in Rome was rather oligarchical in nature and tended to favor the aristocracy – a fact any go-getting politician or advocate would prudently take into consideration.

The *Cursus Honorum* and Cicero's political career

Although he was extremely ambitious politically, Cicero's gifts did not lead him in a military direction (apart from brief stint in Sulla's army), the usual way to gain a reputation for political advancement. The best way for him to put himself in the public eye was to act as an advocate in prominent cases – especially criminal cases. Cicero notoriously began his career by representing an accused parricide, which apparently displeased Sulla. As a result, around 79 B.C.E., Cicero went to Greece to study rhetoric and philosophy. Sulla died the following year.

Cicero then prepared to embark upon the traditional Roman *cursus honorum* – the 'course of offices' – through which aspiring politicians rose to greater and greater power in the Roman Republic. One only became eligible for each office at a certain age (although this rule was sometimes violated), and it was considered the height of success to have held each office at the earliest possible age.[17] Cicero's election as quaestor in 75 B.C.E. made him a 'new man' (*homo novus*), a person whose ancestors had not previously achieved senatorial status. It was rare for a 'new man' to climb all the way to the top post of consul. The last person to have done it was Gaius Marius, a fact that did not endear 'new men' to the aristocracy.

Cicero's plan was to run for the plebeian aedileship (the second rung on the *cursus honorum*) in 70 B.C.E.[18] He knew, however, that gaining the aedileship alone would not provide him the political foothold he needed to fulfil his ambition of becoming consul. Cicero was known for his conservative 'middle of the road' views. He was not a 'true' patrician but not a rabble-rouser, either. He liked Rome the way it was – he just wanted a little less corruption and more room at the top for him to advance. Yet, as a 'new man,' he needed something to make him stand out in the eyes of the people (*populares*), for he certainly could not count on the support of many patricians.

Then, a case made to order fell into his lap, the case against Gaius Verres. Verres had been the praetorian governor of Sicily, a wealthy province ripe for the picking, and Verres had apparently picked it rather clean (engaging in bribery, plundering temples, naval mismanagement, extortion, and murder). Verres' judicial immunity would dissolve in 70 B.C.E. at the end of his praetorship, but few believed he could be prosecuted successfully, thanks to his ties to the aristocracy. For one thing, he would be tried by a jury of his fellow senators, many of whom had indulged in practices much like the ones of which Verres was accused in Sicily (and, many believed, such senators were susceptible to bribes – in contrast to Athenian juries).[19]

Still, in many ways, the case was ideal for Cicero. Cicero had served his quaestorship in Sicily and had served well. He knew the island and its people. It was natural, therefore, for the Sicilians to turn to him to prosecute Verres. In addition, Cicero had previously only acted as a defense attorney. If he now acted as a prosecutor, it would prove his determination to fight civic corruption in a case that was sure to gain him notoriety and popularity among the plebeians (who were the constituency for the plebeian aedileship). Best of all, if Cicero won a conviction against Verres, he would gain Verres' seniority in the Senate, which Cicero would not otherwise attain until he was elected praetor. A strict rule of seniority prevailed in the Roman Senate. When a motion was debated, senators of consular rank could speak first, then senators of praetorian rank. Senators of lower rank often did not get to speak at all.[20] By assuming Verres' praetorian seniority, Cicero would greatly enhance his political prestige and ability to influence policy.[21] Moreover, by besting Verres' advocate Hortensius, the so-called 'king of the law courts,' his reputation as an orator would be supreme. All these factors weighed into Cicero's decision to prosecute Verres.

The Roman criminal law system

Roman law generally distinguished between 'private law'[22] and 'public law.' Public law included criminal law, which came to include extortion, embezzlement, murder, and forgery, among other things (at least, if they involved the upper classes). Beginning in the second century B.C.E., separate courts (really, standing juries, known as *quaestiones perpetuae*) were established to try criminal offenses.[23] In Cicero's day the juries consisted of senators, drawn from a list of names that were included in an annual pool of jurors.[24] The procedure for determining juries for individual trials (at least, at the time Cicero was prosecuting Verres) was that all persons related to the defendant were excluded from the list. From the names that remained in the pool, the accuser nominated 100. From these, the defendant chose 50.[25] Verdicts were determined by majority vote. Trials were observed by the general public, whose function was to act as a watchdog to make sure nothing untoward happened.[26]

As in Athens, there were no state prosecutors in Rome. All prosecutions were initiated by private citizens. The would-be prosecutor would seek permission from the praetor to proceed. If more than one person sought to prosecute a case, there was a preliminary hearing[27] in which a jury would decide which person would do a better job of pursuing the case. 'Lawyers' as such, i.e., in a professional sense, did not exist in Rome. However, there were jurisconsults, who were experts in legal matters and would provide advice in response to questions, consult at trials, or draft legal documents. Advocates, on the other hand, were orators who could represent the litigating parties.[28] Their strength was not in their knowledge of the law but their expertise in the art of persuasion.[29] The role of the advocate introduced an element that had not been present in Athenian trials. For one thing, advocates brought their own personalities and reputations with them to the trial, which – as in the case of Cicero – often had a significant impact.[30] Thus, the outcome of a case might depend on the ability to hire a talented orator on your behalf (as it is today in many places), illustrating yet another way in which the aristocracy had advantages in ancient Rome.

Breaking the cycle: The rule of law and the 'mixed' regime

I pointed out in the last chapter how Plato's *Apology* exposed (or was, at least, thought to have exposed) the weaknesses of Athenian democracy, bringing that form of regime into disrepute for centuries. Plato himself theorized on these weaknesses in a more general context when he described the decline of regimes in Books VIII and IX of the *Republic*. Each good form of regime declines (through what we would call psychological or sociological causes) into its opposite. For example, he opines that tyranny springs from democracy because the masses are so susceptible to manipulation by demagogues (*Republic* 562b–569c).

The idea of a so-called cycle (*anakuklosis*) of regimes was not unique to Plato. Herodotus had provided a version of it in Book II of his *Histories*,[31] but the most powerful description by far was the 'cycle' of regimes implicit in Book V of Aristotle's *Politics* – that there are three basic forms of government by the one, by the few, and by the many, each of which has a good form (for the common interest) and a bad form (for the interest of the ruler). Any 'pure' form of a regime is necessarily unstable: kingship declines into tyranny, replaced by aristocracy which declines into oligarchy, replaced by what Aristotle calls polity (*politeia*), which declines into democracy.[32] Aristotle suggests that one way of avoiding (or slowing down) this decline is to create a regime that combines all three (good) forms of the one, the few, and the many.[33] In order for such a 'blended' regime to function, Aristotle says, the rule of law must be preferred to the rule of men. Therefore, people in such a regime must be on guard against transgressions from the law (*Politics*, 1507b30). Thus, one justification for the 'rule of law' (an answer to the question 'why obey the law?') is that it allows for the 'stabilization' of government through the mixed regime.

What was implicit in Aristotle was made explicit by the Greek historian of Rome Polybius. Polybius wrote a disquisition on the cycle of regimes in Book VI of his *Histories* and purported to demonstrate how the Roman Republic, as the exemplar of a 'mixed' regime with its checks and balances, was able to achieve remarkable stability and dominate the 'known' world.[34] Polybius was never explicit about whether the Roman Republic must also eventually decline like other regimes. We know that Polybius' version of the cycle influenced Cicero's thinking.[35] For Cicero, the agonistic features of the Roman Republic's political and legal institutions made it the 'best' regime because it spurred greatness by allowing ambition to flourish while keeping it in check for the common good. However, Cicero was aware that these same agonistic features had the potential to tear the Republic apart through polarization and civil war. Thus, for him, a statesman's highest duty and 'civic virtue' was to ensure harmony and concord among the political orders.[36]

This would only be of antiquarian interest except that Cicero's articulation of 'civic virtue' (taken up by other Roman writers) and Polybius' seductive view of history and the institutional safeguards that protect 'civic virtue' from 'civic corruption' had tremendous influence on the intellectual framework behind the construction of modern republics. This ancient vision of 'civic virtue' was revived in the Renaissance.[37] However, Renaissance thinkers knew something Cicero and Polybius did not: despite the stability of its mixed regime, the Roman Republic did indeed 'fall' into an autocracy with the Caesars.[38] Why this happened obsessed a number of thinkers but particularly Niccolò Machiavelli, who radically reconceived in his *Discorsi* (1531) the idea of 'civic virtue' by which he revitalized the republican tradition for the next three centuries with a reinterpretation of Polybius filtered through an analysis of the ancient Roman historian Livy.

What was a moral imperative for the statesman in Cicero became an historical/political imperative for Machiavelli. Like Cicero, Machiavelli emphasized that the greatness of Rome's mixed regime was to be attributed to the retention of Roman *virtù*,[39] which depended on the stability provided by the adherence of Rome's citizens to its republican modes and orders (*modi e ordini*), often congealed into its laws (*leggi*).[40] The Republic declined, according to Machiavelli, to the extent that its leaders and citizens through their personal flaws or ambitions deviated from the established modes and orders (what Machiavelli refers to as 'civic corruption'). The Republic thrived to the extent it had great leaders who brought it back to the regime's first principles (as he had reconceived them).[41] The 'greatness' of the regime depended on its leaders recognizing that it was drifting from republican modes and orders (and the 'rule of law') and discerning how to correct the course of history.

Machiavelli's commanding conception of the history of the Roman Republic (and his sources) had a profound impact on republican theorists in the 16th, 17th, and 18th centuries but especially on the founders of the American republic such as James Madison, Alexander Hamilton, and John Adams.[42] The all-consuming question for these men, like Machiavelli, was why the Roman Republic 'fell' (that is, became an 'autocratic empire' instead of a 'republican empire') and how to structure the new American republic to prevent a similar 'fall.' But Machiavelli detected another even more radical solution to the problem of 'corruption,' which shaped their conversation in a way that still affects (consciously or subconsciously) the American view of popular government today.

In addition to the elements of 'mixed' government and separation of powers in the US Constitution, the historically expansionist policies of the US government were in line with Machiavelli's idea of republican imperialism. The great debate after Machiavelli wrote the *Discorsi* was whether republics must be small or whether they could (or should) encompass a large territory. For theorists such as Guicciardini, Montesquieu, and Rousseau, republics must be small and homogeneous to be successful (like Venice). For Machiavelli, the answer was that, like Rome, republics must continue expanding (and become more and more heterogeneous) or collapse from factional strife. David Hume and James Madison (famously, in *Federalist* 10) agreed with Machiavelli: republics could be large if they were sufficiently heterogeneous and extensive to avoid lethal binary factions (which always seemed to kill republics). In this view, the westward expansion of British America was not a bug but a feature of the American form of government.[43] Thus, the Machiavellian solution to the 'cyclical' vision of Roman republican decline became 'baked' into the American conception of government. In theory, a republican government could avoid 'civic corruption' by retaining its 'civic virtue' through fidelity to its 'first principles' in a mixed balance of powers as it continually expanded to avoid factionalism. Given this premise, the question for us is whether the American founders succeeded in creating a stable government by avoiding what they deemed to be the mistakes of Cicero and other Roman republicans. It is unlikely any of the founders believed they had discovered a permanent solution.[44] One of the issues for us today is whether 'corruption' can be staved off if/when the republic ceases to expand and whether its statesmen are able to discern early enough the effects of 'corruption.'

Robert Harris' novel *Imperium* was intended to be an examination of these questions and to provide us with a subtextual warning that, perhaps, the same forces that brought down the Roman Republic (as analyzed by Machiavelli) are at play in today's America. In the novel, we can see the Polybian/Ciceronian view of 'civic virtue' and 'civic corruption' manifested in Harris' account of the trial of Gaius Verres: not only in his reproduction of Cicero's trial advocacy but in the 'between-the-lines' critique of American democracy Harris weaves into his novel. This, in turn, can give us insight into how the 'cyclical' analogy still penetrates our thinking today.

Harris' *Imperium* and the decline of republican Rome

Robert Harris is best known for his historical novels set in, *inter alia*, ancient Pompeii,[45] Nazi Germany,[46] and *belle epoque* France.[47] The novels are meant to be consumed by a wide audience and are not intended to be 'high art.' Although the Cicero novels are relatively historically accurate in comparison to other such genre novels, Harris was not trained as an historian, and he employs a venerable if somewhat ingenuous methodology. For example, he once said in an interview:

> I always take the belief that human beings don't change.... We're not really different from the Romans. There was the same proportion of geniuses to psychopaths 2,000 years ago. A successful society keeps the psychopaths out of power. When there's a breakdown and those people get control – as they are possibly in the US – that's the time to worry.[48]

Clearly, Harris makes no bones about finding ancient parallels to modern life. Although the Cicero trilogy was completed prior to the election of Donald Trump as president of the United States, Harris insists that the same forces were at work in Trump's America as in the ancient Roman Republic.[49] Moreover, Harris had observed British politics very closely as a confidante of British Prime Minister Tony Blair with whom Harris later became disillusioned after Blair's decision to assist the United States in its invasion of Iraq in 2003. Thus, while Harris goes to pains to reproduce (within reason) historical authenticity, he consciously intends the reader to draw comparisons with and lessons for today. In particular, he demonstrates to a popular audience how law and politics are inextricably intertwined – especially in a courtroom trial.

The law is a running theme throughout *Imperium*. The title itself refers to the legal authority to which Cicero ultimately aspires, described in the book as "official, political power ... the power of life and death, as vested by the state in an individual" (p. 4), its highest embodiment in the office of consul. Early in the book, we find Cicero already on the first rung of the *cursus honorum*, having served as quaestor in Sicily. Harris follows rather faithfully the sequence of Cicero's actual career. Cicero acts like a normal politician – clever and somewhat jaded.[50] Cicero is concerned for his clients but within the limits of his own interests. In some ways, Harris' account of the Verres trial, the centerpiece of the first half of the book, shows the system functioning 'normally' – within bounds. That is, Verres' corruption is treated as 'normal' corruption – an indication that the system is imperfect, has flaws, but is basically sound. In other words, as Harris presents him (and, perhaps, as he actually was), Cicero believes that the system is not so wholly corrupted that he cannot succeed in his prosecution of Verres.[51]

Thus, in the 'discovery' phase of the prosecution when Cicero goes to Sicily to collect evidence, we as readers are entertained by Cicero's skillful legal tactics, much as we would be by a well-written legal procedural on television (at least, one that takes the trouble to have a consulting lawyer on the writing staff). It is all the more satisfying to know that the legal 'tricks' Cicero employs in Harris' novel are derived from the actual historical record of the trial passed down to us so meticulously by Cicero himself.[52] Harris takes the factual details and gives them depth and context – often providing missing motivation – to indicate the complexity of the political situation in Rome.

But Cicero discovers that he is up against forces he had not reckoned with. He has been naïve and outflanked by clever maneuvering in the extortion court. He will have insufficient time to present his case in the traditional manner (days of elaborate oratory) before a series of games will interrupt the court's business for months on end. Then, new officials aligned with Cicero's enemies will be in power, and an already tainted jury will be better able to hide their malfeasance. Cicero overcomes this obstacle by following his wife's advice: make your speech shorter.[53] Cicero's strategy is now simply to shame the jury[54] – even a jury with enemies on it – into finding Verres guilty lest they expose to the people (who are spectators)[55] how debased the Senate has become. His opening words (Harris' paraphrase of Cicero's actual speech) are pointedly directed at the jury:

> there has been offered to you, not through man's wisdom but almost as the direct gift of heaven, the very thing you most need – a thing that will help more than anything else to mitigate the unpopularity of your order and the suspicion surrounding these courts. ... that these courts, with you senators as the jury, will never convict any man, however guilty, if he has sufficient *money*.
>
> (*Imperium*, pp. 207–208)

This is neat legal jiu-jitsu on Cicero's part. The rhetoric works because the senators know they are in disrepute for their 'corrupt' behavior and would not wish to be so nakedly exposed as protecting one of their *own*. It works because it is tailored to a moment in political history that is only on the cusp of grave corruption. Cicero succeeds by simply presenting the evidence of Verres' crimes and allowing the evidence to speak for itself – rather compellingly. And to put the final rhetorical cherry on the sundae, Cicero ends the case-in-chief with an emotional (nostalgic) appeal to patriotism: testimony that Verres was so depraved he crucified someone who claimed to be a Roman citizen without even attempting to discover the truth of the claim.[56] This shocking breach of a privilege[57] so basic to Roman identity prompts a mob to rush the court after Cicero's harangue, and Verres barely escapes (and then flees into exile).[58] For Cicero, the Verres trial shows that the Republic is not entirely debased – yet. Cicero can see that it is tottering but does not view the situation as unredeemable. The 'popular' check on the power of the patricians is still functional. But this is precisely where Cicero's own cleverness is a danger to him. He feels confident in his cynicism. He can see through the corruption, decadence, and ambition of others but not the rot that goes even deeper.

We then discover that, to make sure his tactics in the Verres case would work, Cicero entered into a deal with Pompey the Great (because the praetor presiding at the trial was in Pompey's entourage). As a result, the Sicilians are compensated far less than they might otherwise have been, a fact Cicero breezily dismisses. Moreover, Cicero has now aligned himself (perilously) with the Pompeian faction against the wealthy Crassus. While his success in the Verres trial has provided Cicero with a crucial stepping stone to ultimate power, it has also entangled him in ways he does not suspect in Rome's corruption. Cicero's moral integrity (already challenged) is almost immediately put to another, even more serious test in Harris' narrative.

The harbingers of republican decline

When a series of pirate attacks is carried out in Roman territory, Pompey comes up with a scheme to concentrate power into his hands to deal with the 'emergency.' The proposal undoubtedly has something to do with Pompey's ego, but it at least has the advantage of protecting the Republic from brigands. Therefore, while Cicero may deem it inadvisable and recognizes it as "a naked grab for power dressed up as patriotic necessity" (*Imperium*, p. 270), he does not seem to view it as a serious threat to the Republic itself. Indeed, Cicero believes it is merely a ploy to allow Pompey to replace another rival commander of the Eastern legions (which is probably the limit of both Pompey's ambition and imagination) (*Imperium*, p. 271).

However, Harris makes sure we understand the danger of Pompey's proposal – indeed, he shows us how the fall of the Republic may be read as a handbook for the rise of fascist regimes. It is today a political commonplace that fascists exploit 'emergencies' to take over democracies. Adolf Hitler famously used the so-called *Reichstag* fire to invoke Article 48 of the Weimar

Constitution, which allowed him to assume dictatorial powers.[59] In addition, Harris tells us that Cicero is clever enough to deduce that the proposal is not likely to have been Pompey's idea but Julius Caesar's – although Cicero has not yet worked out how such a thing could bring Caesar advantage. We readers, however, know all too well what is coming when Caesar later becomes dictator for life (exploiting the exception made by Sulla years before and following a ploy used by Cicero, explained below).

Moreover, Pompey's proposal resonates with concerns many American and European devotees of the rule of law had when *Imperium* was published in 2006: specifically, the dangerous 'emergency' measures put into place after the horrific attacks in the United States on 11 September 2001. Pompey's proposal requires nations throughout the Mediterranean (basically, the 'civilized' world at the time) to take arms against the pirates and their ships: "All captured pirates are to be handed over to Roman jurisdiction. Any ruler who refuses to cooperate will be regarded as Rome's enemy. Those who are not with us are against us" (p. 269). These words echo what President George W. Bush said in a joint address to Congress on 20 September 2001 in preparation for the US invasion of Afghanistan:

> Every nation, in every region, now has a decision to make. Either you are with us, or you are with the terrorists. From this day forward, any nation that continues to harbor or support terrorism will be regarded by the United States as a hostile regime.[60]

The parallels between the pirates and Al Qaida terrorists are fairly obvious: no state would dare to attack Rome just as no state would dare to attack the US, but shadowy, non-state actors are something else entirely.

One may agree or disagree about the seriousness of the threat terrorist groups such as Al Qaida present to the United States or Western civilization in general. It is indisputable, however, that a cadre of powerful politicians believed the attacks merited a response that broke, ignored, or reinterpreted laws and norms applicable prior to 9/11. To mention just a few examples: the attempt to create a 'law-free' zone in Guantanamo (Cuba), the reinterpretation/abrogation of anti-torture provisions to permit acts previously classified as torture, the secret widespread surveillance of citizens, etc. As Vice-President Dick Cheney observed at the time, the gloves were to come off – by which he meant that the West could no longer afford to indulge in previously sacrosanct human rights and civil rights protections. The measures taken to deviate from such protections were deeply controversial and condemned by many as corrosive of democratic principles. Often, they were implemented by secret executive actions or other *sub rosa* breaches or subversions of norms and laws.[61]

For Harris, such deviations were harbingers of a potential disaster. The lesson of *Imperium* seems to be that we should take note of what happened in Rome and be wary of our own times. Harris illustrates the path to autocracy by showing how Cicero, step-by-step, becomes complicit in shadier and shadier acts. One such act is his legal and tactical advice to Pompey's cabal here.

The proposal against the pirates stands no chance if Pompey is too obvious in his desire to be 'supreme commander' (another sign that the Republic is still not too far gone). Cicero counsels diversion. The proposed legislation (to be named the *lex Gabinia*) is more palatable if the commander is not designated. Therefore, Pompey takes some risk (by not explicitly asking for the command) in order better to secure his position (for which he is still the most obvious candidate). Another problem is more serious. Pompey's proposal is to be implemented through legislation by the Plebeian Council, an assembly convoked by the Tribunes of the Plebs. However, as Cicero astutely observes, the legislation could be vetoed by any one of the tribunes, at least two of whom were Crassus' agents. How to get around this problem is tricky and requires a bold and unorthodox approach to precedent.

One technique common in the rise of fascist states and presaged by the fall of the Roman Republic is the use of populist rhetoric and fear tactics. Mimicking the heavily media-covered legislative hearings of today, one of Pompey's maneuvers described in Harris' book is to drag the outgoing consul before an assembly of the people to grill him about security lapses and elicit testimony that inflated the numbers and exaggerated the threat of the pirates. This whips up an atmosphere of popular unrest and a clamor for action. Harris implicitly empathizes here with critics who claimed the US acted rashly in its military responses in Afghanistan and Iraq, panicking over what was, after all, not an existential threat to the nation. In Harris' book, when Roman senators object that "ancient liberties were not to be flung aside merely because of some passing scare about pirates" (*Imperium*, p. 286), Caesar responds that the 'Roman' way is to act like 'real men' – to grab them up and crucify them – echoing authoritarian voices over the centuries that advocate 'tough,' violent action as the 'only' way to deal with scoundrels.

However, Cicero supplies the crucial move to ensure the passage of the legislation: a dodgy legal ploy. He dredges up an example from the past, a tactic Tiberius Gracchus used when a fellow tribune of the plebs voted against a measure he was proposing. There, Gracchus halted polling of the tribunes, claimed the dissenting tribune was failing in his sacred duty to uphold the interests of the people, and began calling on the tribes, one by one, to vote him out of office. The same tactic is used when a tribune vetoes the *lex Gabinia*. The tribune is immediately voted out of office. When a second tribune tries to veto the legislation, however, it is too late in the day to carry out another vote. The speaker simply turns his back to the dissenting tribune, ignoring the attempted veto, and declares the legislation passed.

For the remainder of the book, as Cicero becomes praetor and prepares his campaign to run for the consulship, he is confronted by ever more devious schemes. He almost agrees to defend the notoriously corrupt and violent Catalina (who will play a significant role in the second volume of the trilogy) in a prosecution by the notoriously corrupt and decadent youth Publius Clodius (who will also appear prominently later). Cicero demurs primarily because Catalina has already bribed the jury to acquit him (and the evidence of Catalina's guilt is crystal clear). In effect, Catalina wants Cicero's skill as an advocate to veil the ludicrousness of his exoneration.

Then, Cicero learns of a plot that is even more dastardly, involving not only Catalina but Crassus and Caesar as well (among others): to use bribery to sweep all the major offices of the Republic – both consulships, all the tribunates, and even a number of praetors. More importantly, they would push a great land reform bill that would establish a commission headed by Crassus and Caesar to redistribute land to the urban plebs. Cicero calls it somewhat anachronistically "a *coup d'état* disguised as an agrarian reform bill" (p. 437). In Cicero's estimation, this is as serious a plot against the state as the Republic has ever faced. It also places Cicero in a dilemma: he realizes that "the people who stand to benefit the most from this are *my* supporters" (p. 439). Cicero must reluctantly admit that the only way to foil the plot is to enlist the support of the aristocrats who are most threatened by it, and he exposes it to the Senate. Yet, there is one good outcome for Cicero: as a result, enough aristocratic centuries vote for Cicero in the election to ensure him the consulship and prevent Catalina from assuming the second post.

Thus, Cicero achieves the power he has desired his whole life but has had to align himself with the aristocrats to do it. He is now in their debt. We see him acting like any other 'prudent' politician – that is, like politicians we see every day and to whom we have grown accustomed in the major democracies, switching allegiances as the times dictate, all the while telling themselves that it is for the greater good.[62] Yet, every episode in the novel (and its two sequels) reveals a new degradation, a new aberration in the rule of law. Cicero is intelligent enough to discern the danger of some of them; others he is not. Thus, using the Polybian/Ciceronian paradigm, Harris succeeds in illustrating very concretely how a republic declines and falls by deviating more and more from its laws and customs. The satisfaction of the novel comes from affirming a collective image we carry with us of the decline of the Roman Republic as a universal law, so to speak, and something we can learn from today: a demonstration that, without vigilance, "it can happen here."[63]

Notes

1 See Peter Gordon, "Why Historical Analogy Matters," *New York Review of Books* (7 January 2020). For an interesting analysis of a specific use of historical analogy, see Jeffrey Record, *The Specter of Munich: Reconsidering the Lessons of Appeasing Hitler* (2007).
2 See Herbert Butterfield, *The Whig Interpretation of History* (1931).
3 As a proponent of a 'cyclical' view of history, Giambattista Vico (1668–1744) is a lonely figure in the pantheon of modern Western historians with only a few followers such as Benedetto Croce (1866–1952) and the author James Joyce, who incorporated

Vico into his *Finnegans Wake* (1939). Yet, the cyclical view remained robust (in different forms) in the 18th century in the 'decline and fall' writings about Rome by Montesquieu, *Considérations sur les causes de la grandeur des Romains et de leur decadence* (1734), and Edward Gibbon, *The History of the Decline and Fall of the Roman Empire* (1776–1788).

4 Machiavelli ruminates on Polybius early in his *Discorsi* (1531). Yet, how Machiavelli knew Polybius is still something of a mystery. See J.H. Hexter, "Seyssel, Machiavelli, and Polybius vi: The Mystery of the Missing Translation", 3 *Studies in the Renaissance* (1956), pp. 75–96. For more recent thinking, see John Monfasani, "Machiavelli, Polybius, and Janus Lascaris: The Hexter Thesis Revisited," 71(1) *Italian Studies* (February, 2016), pp. 39–48.

5 See, for example, Mark Storey, *Time and Antiquity in American Empire: Roma Redux* (2021), Mike Duncan, *The Storm before the Storm* (2017), Cullen Murphy, *Are We Rome?: The Fall of an Empire and the Fate of America* (2007), and Michael Hardt and Antonio Negri, *Empire* (2000), to illustrate the variety of ways the analogy of Rome has been used to understand contemporary American politics and law. For an interesting recent use of 'cyclical' history with respect to the law, see Jack Balkin, *The Cycles of Constitutional Time* (2020). Balkin identifies three kinds of cycles in American constitutional history: the cycle of regimes (party domination), the cycle of polarization, and the cycle of constitutional rot. The cycle of constitutional rot has parallels in this chapter.

6 *Imperium* (2006) is the first volume of Robert Harris' so-called Cicero trilogy, which chronicles the political career of the orator from his entry into public life until his untimely death. *Imperium* tells of Cicero's rise through the *cursus honorum* until he is elected consul; *Lustrum* (in the US, *Conspirata*) (2009) recounts the events surrounding his consulship; *Dictator* (2015) describes the rise of Julius Caesar and Octavian (Augustus) and the fall of the Roman republic. All three volumes are narrated by the character of Cicero's slave Tiro, an actual historical figure who wrote a (now lost) biography of Cicero and invented a form of shorthand, aspects of which are still used today.

7 Cicero was born in 106 B.C.E. as the son of a well-to-do member of the equestrian order. In Roman convention, your *praenomen* (e.g., Marcus) is your personal name; your *nomen* (e.g., Tullius) is your hereditary name, indicating your tribe; and a *cognomen* could be one or the other or a combination of both, often to distinguish yourself in a large family. The *cognomen* was only used by the upper class. Cicero's *cognomen* derives from the Latin word for 'chickpea' (*cicer*) – either because his nose resembled a chickpea (according to Plutarch's "Life of Cicero") or because his family was involved in the trade of chickpeas – whichever it was, Marcus Tullius embraced the moniker. In many older texts about Cicero, you will find him referred to as 'Tully.'

8 The Roman soldier satirized in Plautus' comedy of the same name, also known as 'The Swaggering Soldier.'

9 On Cicero's influence, see, for example, Jerrold Siegel, "'Civic Humanism' or Ciceronian Rhetoric," 34 *Past and Present* (1966). On these topics generally, see also *Renaissance Civic Humanism: Reappraisals and Reflections*, ed. by James Hankins (2000), and Quentin Skinner, *The Foundations of Modern Political Thought* (1978).

10 Until the 12th and 13th centuries with the Latin translations of William of Moerbeke, only two works by Aristotle were in general circulation in Latin Europe, the *Categories* and *On Interpretation*. Similarly, in the Middle Ages, only parts of Plato's *Timaeus* were available in Europe outside of Byzantium. Most were not widely available until the 15th century. By contrast, many of Cicero's writings were in constant circulation.

11 This turns out to be something of a methodological problem. A great deal of what we know about Cicero and the Rome in which he lived comes from the writings of the man himself.

12 References are to Robert Harris, *Imperium* (2009, paperback ed.).
13 Legend has it that, around 510 B.C.E., Rome's last king, Tarquin, was overthrown by aristocrats led by Lucius Junius Brutus, prompted by the rape of the noble woman Lucretia by Tarquin's son. Brutus became one of the original consuls, founding the Roman republic. 'Patricians' were originally descendants of the original Senate appointed by Romulus, Rome's first king. A loose distinction between patricians and plebeians continued throughout the existence of the Roman republic – hence, the abbreviation we still see today on sewer covers in Rome: SPQR, *senatus populusque Romanus*, the Senate and people of Rome. It is worth noting that one of the first acts of Romulus (who murdered his brother Remus to become king) was to order the rape of the Sabine women.
14 Legislation was passed by assemblies of the Roman people (Curiate, Tribal, and Centuriate). The configuration of their powers changed over time. Any legislation here was subject to veto by a tribune of the plebs. Laws passed by the *Concilium Plebis* (Plebeian Council), known as *plebiscita*, were binding on all Roman citizens after 287 B.C.E. (the *lex Hortensius*).
15 Once you were elected as a magistrate, the censors appointed you to the Senate for life. The censors could also impeach you. Originally, under the kings, the Senate was made up only of patricians.
16 In Cicero's time, these were essentially geographical divisions, similar to voting districts today.
17 Traditional Magistrates: *Cursus Honorum* and Cicero's Rise

Office	Main function	Earliest eligible age	Cicero's age
Quaestor (20)	administration of state treasury, administration of provinces	30	31
Aedile (4)	supervised public buildings, games, grain supply, etc.	36	37
Praetor (8)	presided over lawsuits, etc.	40	40
Consul (2)	chief magistrate	43	43

18 The Roman historian Cassius Dio, writing in the 2nd century C.E., says that Cicero sought the aedileship instead of the tribuneship to gain favor with the conservative aristocracy (Dio, *Roman History* 36.43.4–5). Robert Harris in his novel suggests that the tribuneship was considered a political dead end because the aristocracy would block any attempt to rise from there.
19 In 80 B.C.E., for example, Verres had served the governor of Cilicia (southern Turkey), Gnaeus Cornelius Dollabella. Dollabella had also been tried in the extortion court for pretty much the same behavior and had been acquitted. Moreover, Verres would be defended by Quintus Horentius Hortalus, who was generally acknowledged as the preeminent orator in Rome at that time. Verres also had the support of the Metellus family – a powerful aristocratic force in Roman politics.
20 This is illustrated at the beginning of Robert Harris' novel when Cicero tries to protect the Sicilian who seeks his help from being condemned *in absentia* (Harris, *Imperium*, pp. 39–47).
21 Lily Taylor, *Party Politics in the Age of Caesar* (1961), p. 113.
22 For civil cases during the Roman republic, there were two systems of civil procedure that dominated. In the early republic, the system of *legis actiones* was in force. In this system, a plaintiff could request (or, if need be, compel) a defendant to come to court. In the first stage of the litigation, a hearing was held before a praetor (the *in iure* stage) to isolate the issues for trial, and a judge was appointed by consensus from a list of

senators called the *album iudicum*. Then, a trial was held before the judge (the *apud iudicem* stage) with witnesses and evidence, and a judgment was given. The *legis actio* procedure was a very strict and formal method of identifying claims. There were five approved general forms for seeking redress. In the preliminary stage, the trick was to hang your claim onto one of these pegs, which might require some creative pleading. By Cicero's time, the system of *legis actiones* had largely been replaced by a formulary procedure, which was a bit more flexible. The agenda for the litigation was expressed as a 'formula,' a brief statement of a few dozen words addressed to the judge. Here, too, the formula was determined at a preliminary hearing before a praetor. A formula only awarded monetary damages. For example, one ancient example of a formula, describing an action called a *condictio certae pecuniae*, a personal claim for a particular sum of money, read:

> C. Blossius Celadus shall be the judge. If it appears that C. Marcius Saturninus ought to give 18,000 sesterces to C. Sulpicius Cinnamus, which is the matter in dispute, C. Blossius Celadus, the judge, shall condemn C. Marcius Saturninus for 18,000 sesterces in favour of C. Sulpicius Cinnamus; otherwise he shall absolve.
> (E. Metzger, "Actions," in E. Metzger (ed.), *A Companion to Justinian's Institutes* (1997), p. 213)

23 The 'extortion court' (*quaestio repetundarum*) was probably set up in 149 B.C.E. through the *Lex Calpurnia*, which was to curb abuses by provincial governors. But see J.P.V.D. Balsdon, "The History of the Extortion Court at Rome, 123–70 B.C.," 14 *Papers of the British School at Rome* (1938), pp. 98–114.

24 This changed over the course of the Republic and Principate. At times, senators were forbidden from juries; at other times, only equestrians could be members. At other times again, there was a mix of senators and non-senators. There were also other legal and political ways of pursuing or dealing with criminals. Sulla changed the system to allow only senators and excluded *equites* from juries. This caused resentment among the equestrian class and was a bone of contention just as the Verres trial was taking place. Cicero alludes to the controversy in his speeches in the Verres case; and, shortly after Verres' trial, the senatorial monopoly on criminal jurisdiction was ended.

25 The number of jurors in Verres' trial is much disputed – ranging from 50 to 25 (sometimes, even fewer). William C. McDermott, for example, surmises that the jury was originally composed of 50 and, after the litigants had eliminated certain jurors, the final jury numbered somewhere over 40. See William C. McDermott, "The Verrine Jury," 120 *Rheinisches Museum für Philologie* (1977), pp. 64–75; Andrew Lintott, "Legal Procedure in Cicero's Time," *Cicero the Advocate* (2004), p. 70.

26 See Shane Butler, *The Hand of Cicero* (2002), pp. 61–62, quoting A.N. Sherwin-White, "The Political Ideas of Gaius Gracchus," 72 *Journal of Roman Studies* (1982), p. 21.

27 The *divinatio*, so-called because the procedure did not have to do with determining the facts but with something to be done in the future. Otherwise, *divinatio* has to do with knowledge of future things.

28 As they could not in Socrates' Athens, although Greek orators often wrote the speeches the parties gave.

29 Obviously, some jurisconsults could be great orators and some orators were learned in the law. Nevertheless, the (potential) conflict between the two was notorious in Rome – which did not lack for its own version of 'lawyer' jokes. Good orators thought of jurisconsults as 'failed' advocates, but advocates might miss important points of law. Cicero tells of a case in which the plaintiff's advocate demanded more compensation than the *legis actio* on which the case was based allowed. However, rather than letting the case proceed and potentially fail on technical grounds, the defendant's advocate kept protesting that the size of the plaintiff's claim was too large (*De oratore*, 1.167).

30 In Harris' novel, the corrupt Catalina tries hire Cicero for his defense with "the full Ciceronian production" of oratorical effects: "I want Carthage and Troy to be conjured before us, and Dido and Aeneas" (*Imperium*, pp. 376–377). Of course, Virgil's classic version of the tale, the *Aeneid*, had yet to be written.

31 It is debated whether Herodotus and Plato intended to describe a natural 'cycle' of regimes as opposed to providing merely a handy schema for thinking about them.

32 I hasten to add that Aristotle's discussion of this is also quite nuanced and certainly does not imply any mechanical repetition of the cycle. Indeed, he critiques the mechanistic understanding that Socrates seems to propose in the *Republic* (*Politics*, 1316a–b). In fact, much of my discussion of the 'cycle of regimes' here suffers from oversimplification for the sake of clarity, but it is important to understand the broad strokes of the theory.

33 Rule by the many gets different names in different versions. Polybius substitutes 'democracy' for Aristotle's 'polity' and the term 'ochlocracy' (or 'mob rule') for Aristotle's 'democracy.' In his *Discorsi*, Machiavelli (apparently working from Polybius' version) calls the legitimate form of rule by the many the *'stato popolare'* and the illegitimate rule 'anarchy' (*'la licenza'*).

34 Polybius demonstrates how Rome followed Aristotle's declension of regimes in the development of its republican institutions. The city-state began as a monarchy, which became tyrannical, ending with the overthrow of the Tarquins by the aristocracy, which established the consulship. As the aristocracy grew gradually more arrogant, the people eventually revolted and demanded the creation of the tribune of the plebs. This created a balanced 'mixture' of regimes that led to the stability and greatness of Rome.

35 Especially in *De re publica*, but most of this work was unavailable in Western Europe until the 19th century. For an overview of Polybius' influence on Cicero, see Elizabeth Asmis, "A New Kind of Model: Cicero's Roman Constitution in 'De republica,'" 126(3) *The American Journal of Philology* (Autumn, 2005), pp. 377–416.

36 Cicero, *De re publica*, 2.69; see Joy Connolly, *The Life of Roman Republicanism* (2015), esp. chap. 1.

37 The classic overview is Hans Baron, *The Crisis of the Early Italian Renaissance* (1955), but compare Siegel, "'Civic Humanism' or Ciceronian Rhetoric," and see James Hankins, "The 'Baron Thesis' after Forty Years and Some Recent Studies of Leonardo Bruni," 56(2) *Journal of the History of Ideas* (April, 1995).

38 The 'fall' of the Republic was a theme for the ancient Roman historians Tacitus and Suetonius (on whom Robert Graves relied heavily in his novels *I, Claudius* and *Claudius the God* (1934–1935)). They were extremely critical of the Roman imperial regime (under which they also lived). These historians chronicled the scandals of Roman emperors, which later readers contrasted with legends of the superiority of republican virtues. They helped to create a mental pattern – the 'tragedy' of the fall of the Republic – that still holds sway over us today. To pick but one well-known (should we not say ubiquitous?) example, we recognize this pattern in George Lucas' *Star Wars* universe, which depicts, painted on a broad canvas, the fall of a 'republican' form of government and the rise of an autocratic 'empire.' Tellingly, the early films extol the virtues of the 'republic' within the context of an already victorious 'empire' – just as Tacitus and Suetonius did. Compare Isaac Asimov, *Foundation Trilogy* (1951–1953).

39 The Roman concept of *virtus,* like the Greek concept of *arête*, had powerful overtones of 'manliness' and martial ability and became the cornerstone of Niccolò Machiavelli's political theory. On Machiavelli's reworking of the concept of *virtus*, see John Geerken, "Homer's Image of the Hero in Machiavelli: A Comparison of *Areté* and *Virtú*," 14 *Italian Quarterly* (1970–1971) and Russell Price, "The Senses of *Virtú* in Machiavelli," 3 *European Studies Review* (1977) as well as Isaiah Berlin, "The Originality of Machiavelli," in Myron P. Gilmore (ed.), *Studies on Machiavelli* (1972).

40 Machiavelli and Cicero had different ideas about the extent to which 'goodness' in statesmen was necessary (and what that means). In many ways, Machiavelli is critiquing and subverting both Cicero's ideas and the previous 'humanist' tradition of the early Renaissance in which these 'republican' sentiments flourished. Machiavelli's *Principe* is constructed, in part, both as an homage to and as a satire of Cicero's *De officiis*. "What [Machiavelli] is repudiating is nothing less than the Ciceronian vision of the *concordia ordinum*." Quentin Skinner, "Machiavelli's *Discorsi* and the Pre-humanist Origins of Republican Ideas," in Gisela Bock, Quentin Skinner, and Maurizio Viroli (eds.), *Machiavelli and Republicanism* (1990), p. 136; see Marcia L. Colish, "Cicero's *De Officiis* and Machiavelli's *Prince*," 9(4) *The Sixteenth Century Journal* (Winter, 1978), pp. 80–93. The scholarship on this is voluminous; but, briefly, in Machiavelli's view, the Roman republican institutions did not necessarily maintain stability by promoting the personal moral virtue of citizens or statesmen. Rather, Machiavelli toyed with an approach much more like Bernard Mandeville's virtue through competing vices. See Bernard Mandeville, *The Fable of the Bees or Private Vices, Public Benefits* (1714); compare Publius (James Madison), *Federalist Paper* 51 ("Ambition must be made to counteract ambition") and Albert O. Hirschman, *The Passions and the Interests: Political Arguments for Capitalism before Its Triumph* (1977).

41 A position that turned out to be consonant with Cicero's theory of the Roman constitution. See generally Elizabeth Asmis, "A New Kind of Model: Cicero's Roman Constitution in 'De republica,'" pp. 377–416. Needless to say, Machiavelli's position is more complicated than indicated here.

42 For the most influential tomes on the republican conceptions behind the US Constitution, see Bernard Bailyn, *The Ideological Origins of the American Revolution* (1967), Gordon Wood, *The Creation of the American Republic, 1776–1787* (1969), and J.G.A. Pocock, *The Machiavellian Moment: Florentine Political Thought and the Atlantic Republican Tradition* (1975). For a more general take, see Thomas Ricks, *First Principles: What America's Founders Learned from the Greeks and Romans and How That Shaped Our Country* (2020). For an alternative view, see also Joyce Oldham Appleby, *Liberalism and Republicanism in the Historical Imagination* (1992) (dissecting the 'liberal' and 'classical republican' influences on American constitutionalism).

43 As Bishop Berkeley put it: "Westward the course of empire takes its way" (George Berkeley, *Verses On the Prospect of Planting Arts and Learning in America* (1728)). This is why, in part, the so-called 'closing' of the western frontier in the United States was deemed to be a crisis. See Frederick Jackson Turner, "The Significance of the Frontier in American History" (1893), a lecture delivered to the American Historical Association and published as *The Frontier in American History* (1920). Admittedly, Turner was making a different kind of argument. A counter-example to this argument about Rome is that the external threat of Carthage kept the Republic unified. The destruction of that city then led to ruinous factionalism within the Roman state. On the strength of this analogy, some thinkers have warned about the effect the fall of the Soviet Union may have (or has had) on the American republic.

44 For example, at the end of the convention in Philadelphia, Benjamin Franklin gave a qualified endorsement of the proposed Constitution:

> I agree to this Constitution with all its faults, if they are such; because I think a general Government necessary for us, and there is no form of Government but what may be a blessing to the people if well administered, and believe farther that this is likely to be well administered for a course of years, and can only end in Despotism, as other forms have done before it, when the people shall become so corrupted as to need despotic Government, being incapable of any other.
>
> (2 *Records of the Federal Convention of 1787*
> (Max Farrand, ed.) (17 Sept. 1787), p. 642)

45 This novel, *Pompeii* (2003), was intended as an allegorical satire of American culture after Harris reached the artistic conclusion that it was impossible to satirize the contemporary United States directly.
46 *Fatherland* (1992), an alternative history depicting the world if Germany won World War II.
47 *An Officer and a Spy* (2013) on the infamous Dreyfus affair.
48 Charlotte Edwardes, "Author Robert Harris on Donald Trump, Theresa May and the new super-elite," *Evening Standard* (6 February 2017). Compare, for example, David Hume's vision of history in his *An Enquiry concerning Human Understanding* (1978 [1777]), p. 65: "Mankind are so much the same, in all times and places, that history informs us of nothing new or strange in this particular."
49 Edwardes, id.
50 Tiro explicitly warns us against viewing Cicero as a hero: "Power brings a man many luxuries, but a clean pair of hands is seldom among them" (p. 4).
51 For example, Harris chooses to tell us that, when challenged, Cicero wins the right to prosecute Verres in the *divinatio* thanks to the abstention of a patrician, Catulus, who because of familial and political ties could not vote outright in favor of Cicero but was insufficiently corrupt to vote against him, inspiring others to follow his lead in abstaining (p. 141).
52 For example, the stories of the Sicilian records in which the name Verres was changed to Verrucius (p. 174) and Cicero's joke about the sphinx (p. 237) are culled from Cicero's voluminous collected speeches against Verres, *The Verrine Orations* (*In Verrine*). Except for the *divinatio*, which won him the right to pursue the prosecution (the only such speech we have preserved from antiquity), Cicero only gave his first speech (or portions thereof) before the court at the first hearing, the so-called *actio prima*. Apparently, the evidence presented by Cicero in the *actio prima* was so damning that Verres fled the city before the trial was finished. The material Cicero prepared for the second hearing, the *actio secunda*, he later published in all its gory detail, organized as five undelivered orations (utilizing the fiction that Verres is still present at the court).
53 Plutarch says of the case that Cicero won not by speaking but by not speaking. "Life of Cicero" 7, *Parallel Lives of the Noble Grecians and Romans,* Loeb Classical Library (1911). However, in actuality, Cicero's tactic was slightly different. As Ann Vasaly explains:

> What Cicero claims is *novum* about his method, then, is not that he will eschew a long speech and introduce witnesses immediately, since others have done this in the past. What is *novum* is that he will treat each charge as a miniature case, with its own small-scale introductory oration, followed by corroborating witnesses; the only difference between his procedure and what is normally done, therefore, will be that in the latter, the oratorical treatment of all the charges (*omnia*) precedes the introduction of the witnesses, while in Cicero's method witnesses to each particular issue (*in singulas res*) will follow introduction of that charge.
> (Ann Vasaly, "Cicero, Domestic Politics, and the First Action of the Verrines," 28(1) *Classical Antiquity* (April, 2009), p. 111)

54 A similar strategy was employed in the US Supreme Court by attorneys opposed to policies of Donald Trump: known colloquially as the 'shaming John Roberts' strategy. John Roberts is Chief Justice of the US Supreme Court, appointed by a conservative Republican president, George W. Bush. The 'shame John Roberts' strategy was used when Donald Trump's legal position deviated so far from the norm of Supreme Court precedent and practice that John Roberts would be exposed as an institutional hypocrite if he voted to support the administration's position. See, for example, *Dept. of Commerce v. New York et al.* (2019) (denying the inclusion of a 'citizenship question' on

the 2020 census because of clear evidence that it was included only as a tactic to suppress voting) and *June Medical Services L.L.C. v. Russo* (2020) (striking down a Louisiana restriction on abortion rights identical to a law struck down just 4 years before). Of course, this only worked when the Court was in equipoise between conservative and liberal factions.

55 As mentioned, one of the major checks on corruption in the Republic was the fact that prosecutions took place in public, which meant 'the people' could witness what happened in a trial and see whether or not it was corrupt. In many ways, Harris' depiction of the Verres case offers a nice contrast with Plato's *Apology*. For Plato, the danger was too much democracy; for Cicero, the danger was too much aristocracy – for a 'mixed regime' must maintain a balance between the interests of the patricians and the plebs in order to remain stable.

56 And without benefit of trial, but since Roman citizens were not crucified, it is a redundant point.

57 It also evokes the pride many people take in claiming American or British citizenship, which they presume guarantees them certain inalienable rights – another sentiment Harris clearly plays on.

58 After a bloody civil war that took the lives of Cicero's greatest contemporaries – including Julius Caesar, Pompey the Great, Marcus Brutus, and Cato the Younger – henchmen of Mark Antony murdered Cicero on 7 December 43 B.C.E., not long after they had murdered Gaius Verres in Marseilles. It is said Verres refused to surrender some *objets d'art* to Antony – art Verres may well have plundered from Sicily. Some years later, Mark Antony would commit suicide in Egypt, and the last vestiges of the Republic would be swept away by Rome's first emperor, Augustus.

59 It is reported that General Mark Milley, chairman of the Joint Chiefs of Staff, applied this historical analogy when he warned of a "Reichstag moment" just before the 6 January insurrection after President Donald Trump lost his reelection bid in 2020.

60 "President Bush Addresses the Nation," *The Washington Post* (20 Sept. 2001).

61 For a contemporary, critical overview, see, for example, Charlie Savage, *Takeover: The Return of the Imperial Presidency and the Subversion of American Democracy* (2007) or Jane Mayer, *The Dark Side: The Inside Story of How the War on Terror Turned into a War on American Ideals* (2008).

62 As an aide to Chancellor Bethmann Hollweg in World War I Germany observed: "politics is really the art of doing evil and attaining the good" (quoted in Fritz Stern, *The Failure of Illiberalism: Essays on the Political Culture of Modern German* (1971 [1955]) p. 88).

63 See Sinclair Lewis, *It Can't Happen Here* (1935) (a fictional account of the rise of a fascist regime in the United States). Compare Philip Roth, *The Plot Against America* (2004). Compare also Jack Balkin, "Constitutional Rot," in Cass R. Sunstein (ed.), *Can It Happen Here?: Authoritarianism in America* (2018).

References

Asmis, E. (Autumn, 2005). A new kind of model: Cicero's Roman constitution in 'De republica.' 126(3) *American Journal of Philology* 377.

Bailyn, B. (1967). *The ideological origins of the American revolution*.

Balkin, J. (2018). Constitutional rot. In C. R. Sunstein (Ed.), *Can it happen here?: Authoritarianism in America*.

Balkin, J. (2020). *The cycles of constitutional time*.

Balsdon, J. P. V. D. (1938). The history of the extortion court at Rome, 123–70 B.C. 14 *Papers of the British School at Rome* 98.

Baron, H. (1955). *The crisis of the early Italian renaissance.*
Berkeley, G. (1728). *Verses on the prospect of planting arts and learning in America.*
Berlin, I. (1972). The originality of Machiavelli. In M. P. Gilmore (Ed.), *Studies on Machiavelli.*
Butler, S. (2002). *The hand of Cicero.*
Butterfield, H. (1931). *The Whig interpretation of history.*
Colish, M. L. (Winter, 1978). Cicero's *De officiis* and Machiavelli's *Prince.* 9(4) *Sixteenth Century Journal* 80.
Connolly, J. (2015). *The life of Roman republicanism.*
Duncan, M. (2017). *The storm before the storm.*
Edwardes, C. (6 February 2017). Author Robert Harris on Donald Trump, Theresa May and the new super-elite. *Evening Standard.*
Farrand, M. (Ed.) (1911). *Records of the Federal Convention of 1787 (3 vols.).*
Geerken, J. (1970–1971). Homer's image of the hero in Machiavelli: A comparison of *areté* and *virtú.* 14 *Italian Quarterly* 45.
Gordon, P. (7 January 2020). Why historical analogy matters. *New York Review of Books.*
Hankins, J. (April, 1995). The 'Baron thesis' after forty years and some recent studies of Leonardo Bruni. 56(2) *Journal of the History of Ideas* 309.
Hankins, J. (Eds.) (2000). *Renaissance civic humanism: Reappraisals and reflections.*
Hardt, M., & Negri, A. (2000). *Empire.*
Harris, R. (2009 [2006]). *Imperium.*
Hexter, J. H. (1956). Seyssel, Machiavelli, and Polybius vi: The mystery of the missing translation. 3 *Studies in the Renaissance* 75.
Hirschman, A. O. (1977). *The passions and the interests: Political arguments for capitalism before its triumph.*
Hume, D. (1978 [1777]). *An enquiry concerning human understanding.*
Lewis, S. (1935). *It can't happen here.*
Lintott, A. (2004). Legal procedure in Cicero's time. In J. Powell & J. Paterson (Eds.), *Cicero the advocate.*
Mayer, J. (2008). *The dark side: The inside story of how the War on Terror turned into a war on American ideals.*
McDermott, W. C. (1977). The Verrine jury. 120 *Rheinisches Museum für Philologie* 64.
Metzger, E. (1997). Actions. In E. Metzger (Ed.), *A companion to Justinian's institutes.*
Monfasani, J. (February, 2016). Machiavelli, Polybius, and Janus Lascaris: The Hexter thesis revisited. 71(1) *Italian Studies* 39.
Murphy, C. (2007). *Are we Rome?: The fall of an empire and the fate of America.*
Plutarch (1911). *Parallel lives of the noble Grecians and Romans.* Loeb Classical Library.
Pocock, J. G. A. (1975). *The Machiavellian moment: Florentine political thought and the Atlantic republican tradition.*
Price, R. (1977). The senses of *virtú* in Machiavelli. 3 *European Studies Review* 315.
Record, J. (2007). *The specter of Munich: Reconsidering the lessons of appeasing Hitler.*
Ricks, T. (2020). *First principles: What America's founders learned from the Greeks and Romans and how that shaped our country.*
Roth, P. (2004). *The plot against America.*
Savage, C. (2007). *Takeover: The return of the imperial presidency and the subversion of American democracy.*
Siegel, J. (1966). 'Civic humanism' or Ciceronian rhetoric. 34 *Past and Present* 3.
Skinner, Q. (1978). *The foundations of modern political thought.*

Skinner, Q. (1990). Machiavelli's *Discorsi* and the pre-humanist origins of republican ideas. In G. Bock, Q. Skinner & M. Viroli (Eds.), *Machiavelli and republicanism*.
Stern, F. (1971 [1955]). *The failure of illiberalism: Essays on the political culture of modern Germany*.
Storey, M. (2021). *Time and antiquity in American empire: Roma redux*.
Taylor, L. (1961). *Party politics in the age of Caesar*.
Turner, F. J. (1920). *The frontier in American history*.
Vasaly, A. (April, 2009). Cicero, domestic politics, and the first action of the Verrines. 28(1) *Classical Antiquity* 101.
Wood, G. (1969). *The creation of the American republic 1776–1787*.

Chapter 3

The Trial of Jesus (30/33 C.E.[1])

Law, Narrative, and *Nomos* in the *Gospel according to Mark*

The trial of Jesus is, undoubtedly, the most famous trial in Western history – one of the crucial elements of the passion[2] of the Christ with which every professing Christian and every person educated in the Western tradition (and many who were not) are broadly familiar. What we know about it historically, however, is even more tentative than what we know about the trial of Socrates. The accounts provided in the New Testament (to limit ourselves to the canonical gospels – excluding, for example, the Gospels of Thomas, Peter, and Judas) are contradictory in fundamental ways – or, at the very least, the narratives they provide are not easily reconcilable, and the legal basis for the trial is hopelessly muddled in all the accounts (see Appendix 1). Moreover, the historical accuracy[3] and integrity[4] of the gospels as they have been handed down to us are doubtful. We do not, for example, have any two manuscripts of any gospel that are exactly the same although the seriousness of the discrepancies varies from the trivial to the decisive. If our task is to assess the gospel accounts of the trial of Jesus in light of the other historical evidence available to us, then the challenge is daunting indeed. Yet, such an approach might miss the most important aspect of any gospel's account: the reason the author presented his narrative in the way that he did.

In one of the foundational documents of the law and humanities movement, Robert Cover argued:

> No set of legal institutions or prescriptions exists apart from the narratives that locate it and give it meaning. For every constitution there is an epic, for each decalogue a scripture. Once understood in the context of the narratives that give it meaning, law becomes not merely a system of rules to be observed, but a world in which we live.[5]

This context of narratives that give law meaning constitutes a *nomos*, according to Cover. By invoking the Greek term *nomos*, Cover did not intend the narrow meanings of 'law' or 'custom' by which it is usually translated but the broader framework from which those meanings derive: the entire normative worldview in which a living community gets its sense of right and wrong.[6]

DOI: 10.4324/9781003302971-5

An account of Cover's subtle and sophisticated theory is beyond the scope of this chapter.[7] I merely want to suggest that we might fruitfully utilize some of Cover's ideas (by turning them inside out, so to speak) to illuminate how the gospel account of the trial of Jesus fits within the broader narrative context in which it is set.

My proposal in this chapter is to bracket or abandon any attempt to reconcile the various accounts of the trial of Jesus and, utilizing Robert Cover's insights, to try to make sense of the legal issues raised in light of the overall narrative provided by a single author, the author of the *Gospel according to Mark*. The presumption here is that each author of each gospel had his own reasons for presenting the narrative in the way he did and his own interpretation of the events of Jesus' life.[8] However, to make clear what is unique in Mark's narrative, I shall occasionally make comparisons to the other gospels.

On the historicity of Jesus

When one creeps into the minefield of biblical interpretation, it behooves one to tread cautiously. And – to mix metaphors – it is undoubtedly best to lay one's cards on the table at the beginning. I am agnostic as to whether there actually was a trial of Jesus of Nazareth though I am certain that it could not have taken place as described in all four of the canonical gospels. The variations in their stories are simply too great to be reconciled – which is not to say (necessarily) that any or all of them are deliberately deceptive. Eyewitnesses will often differ on significant details of an event; but, of course, eyewitnesses are not among the best sources of evidence, thanks to the dynamic forces at work in human memory.[9] Nor – the scholarly consensus agrees – were any of the gospels written by an eyewitness.[10] Even the evidence that Jesus existed is razor-thin in the end, for it must be acknowledged that the Jesus mythicists – those who believe Jesus is simply a fictional character – have a point: all the written sources for the existence of Jesus could be made-up stories or evidence of a tradition handing down the made-up stories – as we have for Achilles or Hercules or, perhaps, even Socrates. By the same token, this is not evidence that Jesus did not exist.

To my mind (and it is hardly original to me), the one detail in the story of Jesus of Nazareth that seems to speak for the existence of an historical figure behind it is the crucifixion. All the stories of Jesus contain at least two inescapable details: that Jesus was thought (by some, at least) to be the messiah[11] of Jewish tradition and that Jesus was crucified. In the Jewish tradition, the messiah was supposed to be a great earthly leader who would defeat the enemies of Israel. Yet, Jesus, rather than liberating the Jews from the Romans, wound up being killed by them. If, as the mythicists claim, Jesus is 'only' a fictional character, then why invent someone who died in the most ignominious manner possible in the ancient world? Naturally, the mythicists cannot be completely discounted: one can imagine circumstances in which such a character might be invented in order to disseminate a 'new' cult. However, we can also imagine this situation: that an itinerant preacher has gathered a certain following who believe he will instigate some revolutionary reform of society or lead them to a new form of enlightenment. Against all their expectations, this leader is arrested and executed by the authorities for insurrection (whether justified or not). His death might have destroyed the cult altogether; but, if it did not, we can also imagine that the cult might produce a new explanation of why the leader died in this manner. We must weigh the probabilities as they seem best.[12]

The narrative in the *Gospel according to Mark* fits well within this hypothesis. Mark ends with a Jesus abandoned and in despair. He is mocked by both the men crucified beside him and by others who witness his death. Even his last words of lament are misunderstood by bystanders, who think Jesus is calling for Elijah instead of wondering why God has forsaken him.[13] Yet, Mark does not allow the reader (who is presumed already to be a follower of Jesus or someone the author hopes to persuade to be) to despair. No, despite how things may have looked in this life, the narrative tells us, Jesus really was who he claimed to be – just not in the way people thought.

On Jesus and divinity

Of course, who Jesus really was is the $64,000 question, as they say. Each of the gospel writers, drawing on other oral or written sources, provides his own unique and varying narrative and interpretation of the story of Jesus. None of the canonical gospels fails to include the crucifixion. All need to explain how Jesus reaches that end – and, perhaps, to explain what it means. I do not reject a comparative approach but believe we are best served first to try to understand what each author intended to convey from the way he presented the story. I bracket any general theological or christological discussion and focus on what Mark tells us.

And the question of Jesus' divinity is tricky enough in Mark because the author, like many first-generation Christians, most likely believed Jesus was divine (though how and in what way is uncertain). Nevertheless, a case can be made that he did *not* believe Jesus was divine (or, at least, he believed that Jesus did not exhibit divinity while on earth), and this in itself tells us something about what the author wanted to convey. Mark states in the very first line that he is relating the gospel of Jesus Christ, "the son of God."[14] But the phrase 'son of God' need not refer to someone divine.[15] That Mark relates stories of Jesus performing miracles does not necessarily demonstrate his belief in Jesus' divinity, either, since God may work miracles through mere mortals.[16] Joshua brought down the walls of Jericho and stopped the sun in the sky. Elisha cleansed the pottage of poison and fed a hundred men with twenty loaves. More importantly, we get no clear statement in the Bible from Jesus himself claiming divinity until the Gospel of John, written after the Synoptic Gospels.[17] Therefore, I want to leave open, at least, the possibility that the historical Jesus never claimed to be divine (or even understood himself to be divine) but that this was a conclusion reached by his followers after his death.

Indeed, the lack of divine claims by Jesus in the earliest gospels may count as indirect evidence of an historical Jesus. If the historical Jesus had claimed to be divine, then this fact would certainly never be omitted from the stories about him, but it would also not distinguish the narrative from fiction. If Jesus is entirely fictional, invented in order to found a new religion or reform one, then why would the authors have hesitated to claim or have Jesus claim that he was divine? However, the presentation makes sense if the historical Jesus never made such a claim, but his followers came to believe it later.[18]

A similar difficulty arises with the phrase 'son of man.' The phrase is used 14 times in Mark, but it is unclear what the term means. It might simply mean 'human being.' At 3:28, Mark says that the "sons of men"[19] will be forgiven of their sins, including blasphemy,[20] but sometimes Jesus seems to use the term about himself (although each instance can – with a stretch – be interpreted as referring to a third person who is not Jesus). This allows for the possibility that, while Mark means for the reader to understand that at least some of the references are to Jesus, the character of Jesus himself might not be aware of it.

My hypothesis here is that the author of Mark is trying to reproduce in his text the experience of the disciples, who did not understand the nature of Jesus' messiah-hood until after his death. He is trying to give the reader the same experience as the disciples, to allow the reader (or listener) to come to their belief in the same way the disciples did. Therefore, (most of) the ambiguities we find in the text are there deliberately. The author intends the reader to puzzle over them – just as the disciples did when Jesus was walking the earth. To my mind, this makes the *Gospel according to Mark* a rather superbly executed piece of literature. But if there is one thing the author of Mark does make clear, it is that what Jesus means by his messiah-hood is different from the traditional view of the messiah.

The general style of the *Gospel according to Mark*

The *Gospel according to Mark* is the shortest of the four canonical gospels. It begins with the Greek word for 'beginning' (Ἀρχή) with John the Baptist appearing in the wilderness and ends in mid-sentence (apparently) with three women fleeing in fear from the empty tomb.[21] The narrative is presented in a dynamic writing style. Its sentences are often short and very often linked by the Greek word *kai*, which means 'and' (among other things) but could be accurately rendered in English in most contexts in Mark as 'and then.' So, the reader gets a sense of a narrative that is moving forward at a brisk pace (sometimes called an 'apocalyptic style' since it is rushing toward the end). It is reasonably speculated that this style was to aid the oral reception of the book – after all, most early Christians were illiterate and had to rely on oral traditions to learn the story of Jesus.[22] There are other indications that the book was specifically aimed at introducing the story of Jesus to Greek speakers (whether they engaged with the written text or listened to it being read aloud). For example, when Mark occasionally mentions Aramaic terms, he immediately explains them.[23] Many New Testament scholars have also agreed that Mark has a distinctive structure in which events are arranged chiastically (in concentric circles as in Homer's *Iliad*)[24] or in a sandwich framing, which may affect how certain passages are to be interpreted.[25] However, one biblical scholar famously described the gospel of Mark as a "passion narrative with an extended introduction."[26]

Unlike Matthew and Luke, Mark does not begin with the birth of Jesus but *in media res* with his baptism as an adult. Admittedly, this may be interpreted as a birth of another kind, but it signals very clearly that the gospel is *not* a biography of Jesus. Immediately thereafter, Jesus calls his first disciples. Thus, the reader's experience of Jesus' story is almost identical to (some of) the disciples. The first half of the book deals with Jesus' ministry, and around a third of Mark takes place during the last week of Jesus' life. Yet, while Mark makes reference to Jesus' resurrection, the author does not depict the miraculous event in the text. Rather, the book ends with a young man dressed in white, found sitting in the empty tomb, who says to the three women who came to anoint the corpse that Jesus is risen. He orders them to tell the disciples to go to Galilee, where they will see Jesus, but the women flee in fear and say nothing to anyone (Mark 16:7–8).

Assuming we have the complete text, this ending is remarkable for the questions it raises. Why does the author depict a futile attempt of the women to anoint the body? Is it because Jesus had already been anointed as the messiah? If the women tell no one, how do we know about this part of the story? Unlike the other gospels in which the disciples indeed meet with the resurrected Christ and, thus, see it with their own eyes,[27] the author of Mark does not deem this important to include in the story. Does this mean that such a meeting did not happen and the later gospel writers made it up? Or that Mark did not know about this part of the story? Or that it was included in a part of the manuscript that was lost? Whatever the case may be, the narrative is consistent with an author who wanted the reader to do the work of constructing a faith; it is not the work of an author who simply hands out dogma. The author leaves the text open and implies a meaning beyond the bare bones of the story of which the story's participants were not aware at the time. Indeed, the silence of the women echoes a theme that runs throughout the gospel.

The messianic secret

One of the most notorious aspects of the *Gospel according to Mark* is the so-called 'messianic secret.'[28] Nowhere in the Synoptic Gospels does Jesus claim to be divine. But, in Mark especially, there seems to be a pattern in which Jesus also tries to conceal being the 'messiah.' If we assume that Mark believed in the divinity of Jesus, the 'messianic secret' is entangled with the fact that no one understands that Jesus is divine. This may include Jesus himself, which would explain why his final words are ones of despair! When Jesus calms a storm, the disciples ask, "Who is this that even the wind and sea obey him?" (4:41). In the very next chapter, however, a demon called Legion recognizes Jesus and worships him as "son of the God of the most high" (5:7).[29] At the beginning of Mark, another unclean spirit says to Jesus, "I know who you are, sacred one of [the] God" (1:24). Other 'unclean spirits' 'recognize' him as well.[30] However, no person in the gospel of Mark (including especially the disciples) ever understands who Jesus really is – even, perhaps, the Roman centurion who witnesses the crucifixion and remarks, "Truly, this man was the son of God" (15:39).[31]

Throughout the narrative, when people have cause to suspect Jesus may be the messiah (or divine), Jesus cautions them against revealing it. Early in Mark, when Jesus cures a leper, he commands him not to tell anyone (1:44), but the ex-leper does so anyway. Similarly, when Jesus heals a deaf-mute, he charges those who witnessed it not to tell anyone, but they do anyway (7:36). When Jesus heals a blind man, he tells him not even to enter the village (8:26). Is this an indication that Jesus finally figured out that people were not listening to him about keeping mum? How might this affect our interpretation of the fact that the women at the empty tomb told no one afterwards?

A crucial turning point in the 'messianic secret' narrative occurs at Mark 8:27 – literally at the center of the text. Jesus and the disciples are on their way to Caesarea Philippi, and Jesus asks the disciples:

> "Who do people say I am?" They replied, "Some say John the Baptist; others say Elijah; and still others, one of the prophets." "But what about you?" he asked. "Who do you say I am?" Peter answered, "You are the messiah." Jesus charged them not to tell anyone.

Thus, Jesus tacitly consents to the designation of 'messiah.' However, he immediately begins to explain that the "son of man" must suffer many things including being rejected by elders, chief priests, and scribes, that he will be killed, and that after three days he will rise again. Peter immediately objects to this, and Jesus rebukes him: "Get behind me, Satan!" (8:31–33). It is uncontroversial that this incident shows that Peter still conceived of the 'messiah' as the great leader who would save Israel from its earthly enemies. Jesus, however, has a different vision of what it means to be a 'messiah,' and this is where he announces that vision. Still, it is anything but clear to those around him.

Torah and the kingdom of God

To illustrate the nature of Jesus' messiah-hood, the author interweaves two themes that have a bearing on the charges later brought against him at his trial: the proper interpretation of Jewish law and the coming of the kingdom of

God.[32] The author scatters throughout the text repeated comparisons of Jesus to Moses and Elijah. Like Moses the Lawgiver, Jesus wanders in the wilderness (but only for 40 days, not 40 years). The prophet Elijah also traveled 40 days and 40 nights to the place where Moses received the law, but Elijah preached repentance for failure to follow God's commandments.[33] When Jesus is transfigured, Moses and Elijah appear on the mountain with him. The invocation of these personages must surely indicate that the author of Mark sees Jesus as somehow altering or bringing a new law and that this message is connected to the theme of repentance for failing to live up to God's word.

Throughout the gospel, Pharisees in particular accuse Jesus and the disciples of flouting Jewish law. But Jesus argues that the law must be interpreted in accordance with circumstances.[34] The Pharisees object to the disciples plucking grain on the Sabbath, but Jesus retorts that David and Abiathar violated the rule when circumstances warranted. The Sabbath is for people, not people for the Sabbath (2:27), Jesus explains. Jesus heals a withered hand, daring the Pharisees to opine that it is impermissible to do good on the Sabbath (3:4). Moreover, when the Pharisees and scribes complain that Jesus' disciples are eating with unclean hands, Jesus accuses them of paying lip service to the law while not keeping it in their hearts. Nothing from the outside, Jesus says, makes one unclean, only that which is in one's heart (7:6–9, 15).

Mark depicts Jesus not as rejecting the Torah but as interpreting it humanely. To use Robert Cover's terminology, Jesus advocates the interpretation of the law within a 'redemptive' *nomos*.[35] Christians would later split on the issue of whether they were required to keep the law or whether they were free to ignore it. The author of the *Gospel according to Matthew* seems to believe that Christians must continue to obey the law (Matthew 5:17–20), but the apostle Paul disagrees (Galatians 3:19–23). Matthew views Christianity as Judaism as it ought to be practiced, and Mark does not appear to disagree. Certainly, the two gospels are reconcilable on this issue. The Law continues in effect, but obeisance to every jot and tittle is not as important as other things.[36]

Interwoven into Jesus' ministry (up until chapter 8) are references to the kingdom of God, first mentioned in chapter 1 when Jesus called his earliest disciples. The parable of the sower (who sows the word of God among the people) in chapter 4 is to explain the mystery of the kingdom of God. While it remains a parable to outsiders, the author says, the disciples are supposed to understand it by now. But they still don't catch on, and Jesus has to explain the parable to them.

In chapter 8, Mark has Jesus announce explicitly to the disciples the coming of the kingdom of God. Jesus is then transfigured on a mountain (where Moses[37] and Elijah appear), and a voice proclaims, "This is my beloved son. Listen to him."[38] Jesus admonishes the disciples present (Peter, James, and John) not to tell anyone of this until the 'son of man' rises from the dead. The secret of who Jesus really is (at least, with respect to the rest of the world) continues. The disciples keep the secret (though there is still no indication that they understand him to be divine) but discuss among themselves what it means "to rise from the dead" (9:10). So, even after all that, those closest to Jesus still do not understand what he is up to. Nevertheless, with the admonition to secrecy, Mark explains in the narrative why the 'true nature' of Jesus was not revealed to the world until after his death – the disciples were sworn to secrecy and did not really understand it anyway.

For the rest of the book, Jesus consistently teaches the coming of the apocalypse[39] and that glory must be preceded by suffering. How we are to interpret this teaching is notoriously difficult, if not outright impossible. Theologians have battled about the nature of the predicted apocalypse and its relative imminence. At one point, Jesus says that "even the son of man did not come to be served but to serve and to give his *psyche*[40] as a ransom for many" (10:45). What this means is opaque at best. Early Christians differed on the theory of salvation it ostensibly espouses. Some considered Jesus' death as a ransom paid to Satan (for example, Origen of Alexandria and Augustine of Hippo), others theorized later that it was an atonement to God for the sins of mankind (or Adam) (for example, Anselm of Canterbury and Martin Luther, etc.).

Related to this puzzle is the 'culpability' for Jesus' death – particularly as it relates to Judas. The paradox is well-known.[41] If Jesus' sacrifice is necessary for salvation, then Judas' act of 'betrayal' was also necessary for the good of mankind. Is Judas then a good or an evil character? In the non-canonical Gospel of Judas, Judas is the only disciple who actually understands what Jesus is up to. Remarkably, the *Gospel according to Mark* is not inconsistent with this interpretation. In Mark, no motivation is given to Judas for his actions, and no punishment is described in the text. In the other canonical gospels, some sort of motivation or explanation is indicated (thirty silver pieces or possession by Satan). In Matthew and the *Acts of the Apostles*, Judas suffers punishment. Yet, all these details raise the question: Are the betrayal and suffering predicted by Jesus inevitable; and, if necessary, are they wrong?

Mark provides no definitive answer. His word choice seems to avoid the question deliberately. For example, just before entering Jerusalem, Jesus takes the disciples aside and explains to them privately that the "son of man" will be "handed over" (παραδοθήσεται) to the chief priests and scribes. They will condemn him to death and then "hand him over" (παραδώσουσιν) to the Gentiles (10:33).[42] When Judas 'betrays' Jesus with a kiss, the word 'betray' is not used. Rather, Judas is described as "the one handing [him] over" (ὁ παραδιδοὺς) (14:42, 44). The neutrality of the word is striking. No culpability is attached anywhere. It allows for a sense that these are things that are supposed to happen and are not to be resisted. It is the same verb one would use in discussing the 'handing down' of a tradition. Of course, here, it could be said that a new tradition (or, at least, a new interpretation of tradition) is being forged.

The neutrality and ambiguity of the author of Mark continue as he takes the narrative to the passion story and the Jewish and Roman trials. A narratological problem to be raised with respect to the trials is that the author gives us no indication of the source for his account – he places no disciples there to witness them. Whence then does the account come (in terms of the narrative)?

The charges against Jesus and the Sanhedrin trial

The Synoptic Gospels (unlike the *Gospel of John*) place the story of the driving of the moneychangers from the Temple at the end of Jesus' career. For many interpreters of the trial of Jesus, it is this act that seems to provide the motive for Jewish authorities to arrest and try him[43] although they have clearly been hostile to him all along. Mark tells us that the chief priests and scribes heard of the driving out of the moneychangers and then sought a way to kill Jesus because they were afraid of his popularity. The story itself raises questions of credibility. If it happened, why didn't the authorities arrest Jesus at once? But, at least, Mark provides a ground for Jesus' later arrest (which, after all, was not long afterwards in the Synoptic Gospels) and one that explains why he would be brought before Jewish authorities. Still, this is not the issue upon which the trial before the Sanhedrin turns in Mark.

In the telling of the trial before the Sanhedrin (a Jewish judicial and administrative council composed of local elites), Mark makes sure the reader (or listener) knows that the authorities are judging Jesus unjustly. The author seems to assume the reader has some familiarity with the Jewish law of evidence. In capital cases under Jewish law (although not stated explicitly in Mark), two witnesses were required (Deuteronomy 19:15) or a confession. The Sanhedrin seeks testimony against Jesus but can find none. Mark says that many bore false witness against Jesus, but none agreed on their story (Mark 14:58). Thus, there was insufficient evidence for the Sanhedrin to convict Jesus on any charge, much less one regarding the hubbub at the Temple. Only confession was left. The high priest asks Jesus whether he had an answer to the many charges the witnesses made (perhaps, as a way to elicit a confession), but Jesus does not reply.

Harking back to Peter's answer in chapter 8 (using almost the exact words but in the interrogatory), the author has the chief priest ask, "Are you the messiah, son of the blessed?" Here, unlike in the other gospels, Jesus says, "I am."[44] Thus, the 'messianic secret' is out (albeit still behind the closed doors of the high priest's residence). Dramatically speaking, Jesus is admitting his messiahhood even as Peter is outside denying him. In the narrative crosscutting, the author presents the fulfillment of Jesus' prophecy even as Peter is realizing its meaning.[45] This is just one of many ironies. When Peter acknowledges Jesus as the Christ in chapter 8, he does not believe this is to be tied to suffering. When the high priest asks whether Jesus is the Christ, it is in order to instigate the suffering Jesus believes he must undergo.

Jesus also replies to the high priest, "you will all see the son of man sitting at the right hand of Power and coming with the clouds of heaven,"[46] whereupon the priest tears his mantle and asserts there is no more need for witnesses since they have heard Jesus' blasphemy, i.e., Jesus's statement is the equivalent of a confession. Yet, nothing Jesus says is blasphemous under Jewish law. It might only be blasphemous if Jews accepted the nature of the messiah as divine, which they do not and did not. So, it is a nice irony that, for the Jews, the Sanhedrin's claim of blasphemy is false (so they themselves are committing a crime) but, for later Christians, Jesus' divinity is true (and the Sanhedrin's accusation might be legally accurate). Yet, in the text, the Sanhedrin never explicitly condemns Jesus. They merely agree that he is "deserving of death."[47] Moreover, stoning was the appropriate punishment for blasphemy,[48] and anyone who knows anything about Jesus knows that he was crucified, a Roman punishment. So, the narrative must somehow get Jesus into the hands of the Romans.

The respected legal historian Alan Watson argues that the author of Mark provides a plausible account of Jesus' trial (perhaps, the only plausible account).[49] Regardless of whether the Sanhedrin did or did not condemn Jesus that night, the next morning, the chief priests consult with the elders and scribes[50] and decide to hand Jesus over to the Romans. The text is silent as to why. Watson has speculated that, if a condemnation did take place, the Sanhedrin has realized that they violated the law by condemning Jesus at night and reverse themselves. On the other hand, they might have realized that there was no legitimate charge of blasphemy against Jesus. Yet, they still want to get rid of the troublesome rabbi. So, they pass him on to Pontius Pilate.

What is the author's point in including the narrative of the Sanhedrin trial – particularly, if it winds up being irrelevant to Jesus' death? The answer may be as simple as this: it is what happened to the historical Jesus (assuming he existed). But it is also consistent with the themes the narrative has been pushing. As depicted in Mark, Jesus' problem is not with the Torah but the way it is interpreted. The author of Mark has presented the Sanhedrin trial in such a way as to preserve the legitimacy of the law while condemning the powers that administer it – which is exactly what Jesus seemed to be doing in his ministry. To use Robert Cover's terminology, he is establishing a 'redemptive' *nomos* in which law is interpreted in accordance with higher (or, at least, different) ideals. Thus, the attack in Mark is on corruption, on perverse or inhumane interpretations, not the law itself. The trial narrative reinforces that point.

The Roman trial

The author of Mark does not explain Roman legal thinking any more than he does Jewish legal thinking. Apparently, he could assume his audience would sufficiently understand the situation without more context. In Mark's narrative, Jesus is just as laconic with Pilate as he was with the Sanhedrin – more so, in fact. From a narrative perspective, this lack of defense is surprising[51] unless we see it as part of Jesus' belief that his suffering is inevitable and necessary. Any defense might lead to acquittal – and it almost results in that anyway as the gospels depict it. Yet, Jesus has already intimated that he knows he will die by crucifixion. The first mention of the cross in Mark is just after his assent to the disciples that he is the messiah at 8:34, where Jesus turns and exhorts the nearby crowd to take up the cross (even though they could not possibly know what that meant yet). Certainly, the author intends this to foreshadow Jesus' death at Roman hands.

As readers, we may assume that the Sanhedrin has informed Pilate of the charges against Jesus. The author tells us at any rate that they charged him with many things (15:3). However, Pilate begins by saying, "You are the king of the Jews [or Judeans]?" The question mark is an interpretation because there was no equivalent of a question mark in ancient Greek and Latin until around the 8th century C.E. Whether something was a question had to be determined by context in written texts. Therefore, Pilate's statement could just as easily be an assertion. Is he inquiring, or is he mocking Jesus? How to interpret the tone here is crucial but probably impossible to determine definitively. It is the first time in the text the title has been attributed to Jesus, and it is highly relevant since the Roman authorities would presumably care if some imposter claimed to be king of the Jews. Who rules the Jews is (ultimately) a Roman decision. Still, it is interesting that the presumption behind Pilate's statement is not that Jesus *claims* to be king of the Jews[52] but that he *is*. Nevertheless, we readers feel comfortable it is an accusation.

Where does this accusation come from? In terms of Mark's text, it may be linked to the proclamation of the coming kingdom of God and Jesus' (implied?) role as its king. Nowhere in the gospel of Mark does Jesus explicitly make such an assertion,[53] but the conclusion would not be difficult to deduce from his statement to the Sanhedrin that the son of man would sit at the right hand of Power. As already indicated, it is not entirely unreasonable for the Sanhedrin to assume that Jesus used the term 'son of man' to refer to himself. More likely, however, is that, since Jesus confessed to being the 'messiah' to the Sanhedrin, they logically concluded that he meant the term to refer to some sort of earthly kingship – as it had always been understood before. The reader (or listener) reasonably assumes this meaning was conveyed to Pilate.

Jesus replies to Pilate enigmatically, "You say so" – although the Greek could also be translated as a question, "Are you saying so?"[54] Jesus makes no further reply to Pilate, which – we are told – astonishes him. The author of Mark has created a significant ambiguity. Is Jesus tacitly admitting to the charge, sarcastically denying it, or sincerely inquiring into its source?

The ambiguity of this story in Mark is compounded by the paucity of information the author provides. We must ask what narrative purpose it serves. Even though there are 'many' charges against Jesus, we do not get a sense of what they are or their relevance to Pilate. Certainly, blasphemy against a Jewish god is not a charge that would concern Roman authorities.

We are told that Pilate knows the chief priests are bringing their charges from 'envy,' but we are not told how he knows that or why the priests are 'envious.' Envy is not necessarily the first emotion the reader would ascribe to them in this situation. Yet, Pilate only concerns himself with the issue of whether or not Jesus claims to be 'King of the Jews.' Whereas the Sanhedrin explicitly accused Jesus of blasphemy (although it is unclear whether they actually condemned him or not), we are not told what *Pilate's* charge against Jesus ultimately is. We are only guessing that it must have been sedition or insurrection of some kind.

This is complicated by the fact that, when Pilate uses the term 'King of the Jews' later, he seems to concede the title – although he could be (is most likely) speaking ironically or sarcastically. He asks the crowd whether he should release the 'King of the Jews' (15:9) and what he should do with the man "you call the King of the Jews" (15:12) even though he does not know what crime he has committed (15:14). This is made even more problematic when Pilate agrees to release Barabbas, who (Mark explains) committed murder during an uprising. Is this an irony like those we have seen before? What, too, are we to make of the fact that the name Barabbas means 'son of the father' in Aramaic but the author does not explain what the name means to his Greek audience? That Mark was unaware of the meaning or that he expected his audience already to know it (or to find out for themselves)? Ultimately, the text tells us, Pilate – wanting to please the crowd – had Jesus scourged and sent off for crucifixion.

Does this mean that Pilate never convicts Jesus?[55] In the *Gospel according to Luke*, Pilate renders a judgment to grant the crowd's request – which may be interpreted as a sort of verdict even though it makes hash out of the legal concept.[56] However, the author of Mark does not explicitly indicate that there was a judgment of any kind. Still, a reader might infer that, because Jesus mounts no defense, the accusation is proven by default. Or one might conclude that Jesus' reply ('you say so') is sufficient to count as a confession to the accusation of insurrection. Certainly, the reader would be encouraged to reach this conclusion by the sign naming the charge (ἡ ἐπιγραφὴ τῆς αἰτίας) nailed above Jesus' head on the cross: King of the Jews (15:26). But the author is never explicit. Why?

With the trial before Pilate, the author of Mark has created a masterpiece of ambiguity. It may be read in a multitude of ways, depending on how one interprets the syntax and/or the tone of the Greek. Pilate may be seriously concerned about Jesus' guilt but weak-willed in asserting Roman authority. Or he may be wickedly indifferent to guilt or innocence and annoyed at having to deal with a mob. Why would the author of Mark be so vague? It is a commonplace among New Testament scholars that the gospels to a greater or lesser extent downplay Pilate's role in Jesus' death as an attempt to placate Roman authorities. Typical is Haim Cohn's assessment that it was a "vital interest of the Christians, at that time, to represent the contemporary Roman powers-that-be as favorably inclined to the Christ, his activities and teaching, and with no hand at all in his trial and its sequel."[57] The author of Mark allows for this reading of the text.

However, the vagueness of his phrasing also allows the reader (or listener) to draw a different conclusion. In other words, a reasonable reader of the text may conclude that Pilate condemns Jesus unjustly – that he knows Jesus has committed no crime.[58] Pilate is thus culpable in Jesus' death to that extent. Indeed, the discerning reader may even conclude that Pilate is a feeble, despicable character. Yet, if questioned by Roman authorities, the same reader could claim that the real responsibility must be placed upon the Jews, who chose Barabbas over Jesus. Moreover, because Pilate found Jesus guilty of no crime, Christianity violates no Roman norms, and there is no reason to persecute Christians.

More importantly, we should notice how these ambiguities play into the narrative strategy of the author. The author of Mark does not supply us with dogma. The reader is not simply told what to think about the text but is required to do the work of interpretation – to see the varieties of meaning and choose among them or refrain from choosing. This reflects the work the author himself has done to interpret the meaning of Jesus' mission. The author re-creates that experience for the reader (listener) and does not let him (or her) off the hook in terms of the responsibility to make the choice. But the author is not going to tell us the right answer.[59] In a similar vein, while analyzing the abrupt ending at the empty tomb in Mark's gospel, Gabriel Josipovici says of the author: "A lesser writer, one with a thesis to propound, would have had the women rejoice at the news; Mark seems merely to tell us how it was: the most joyful tidings are also the most frightening."[60] The author of Mark also seems to say: here is the story as it appeared, make of it what you will – but the stakes are high.

Notes

1 None of the sources provide us with a definitive date for the birth or death of Jesus. The consensus of scholars estimates that the date of Jesus' trial (if it took place) must have been 30 C.E. or 33 C.E. This is based on guesses from ambiguous data – e.g., we can calculate the dates on which Passover fell during Jesus' lifetime, but the New Testament gospels apparently disagree on whether Jesus died on the day of Passover or the day before.

2 'Passion' here derives from the Greek word for 'suffering.' Church tradition has selected four accounts of the life of Jesus to be deemed "authoritative": the Gospels of Matthew, Mark, Luke, and John. The gospels were assigned names by the tradition. There is no evidence who any of the authors were or what their specific connection to the Christian religion was. Each gospel provides a version of the trial and death of Jesus. The so-called Synoptic Gospels (Matthew, Mark, Luke) provide a roughly similar account (with a variety of major and minor deviations), while the Gospel of John diverges more significantly from the other three. 19th-century German scholars also speculated that, because roughly a quarter of their accounts contains common content that differs from Mark, Matthew and Luke might have had access to a different source about Jesus' life, called Q (*Quelle* = source). John, on the other hand, appears to derive from a different tradition and shows signs of having had several hands in

its composition. Biblical scholars have painstakingly pored over the manuscripts and agonized over whether individual passages were or were not part of the "original" *koine* Greek text (and whether or not the Greek text had even earlier Aramaic – or other – origins) or whether they were the result of a scribal error, interpolation, or forgery. The earliest evidence we have for any of the gospels are fragments of John and Matthew from ca. 150–200 C.E. We do not have examples of complete (or even mostly complete) gospels prior to ca. 250 C.E. Scholars generally believe that the Gospel of Mark was written first and John last.

3 To take a single example: early in the Gospel of Luke (chapter 2), it is said that Caesar Augustus sent out a decree that a census should be taken of the whole world for tax purposes and everyone had to return to their home village to be enrolled. Hence, Joseph and Mary were required to travel to Bethlehem (the city of David) – because Joseph was of the house of David, who (if he existed) is thought to have lived around 1000 B.C.E. This certainly did not happen as related. There is no other evidence whatsoever of a 'worldwide' census like this occurring under Caesar Augustus. If there is a kernel of truth to the story, it is that, in 6 C.E., a regional census of property for tax purposes was initiated by Quirinius, the governor of Syria (who is mentioned in Luke but apparently did not become governor until after the death of Herod the Great in 4 B.C.E. during whose reign Jesus was supposedly born – implied even in Luke). Quirinius' census was the result of the Roman deposition of Herod the Great's son Herod Archelaus in that year and the creation of Iudaea as a Roman province in which case the census would probably not have affected Nazareth in Galilee (which remained a separate client state). Of course, whoever the gospel writers were, they were not primarily interested in conveying an historically accurate account of the life of Jesus but in proclaiming what the gospels and German theologian Rudolf Bultmann called the *kerygma*, the 'good news' or religious teaching of the life of Jesus as Christ. It is plausible that the author of Luke wanted to link Jesus' birth to a supposed prophecy in Micah 5:2 of the birth of a messiah in Bethlehem and needed a reason to get Joseph and Mary from Nazareth to Bethlehem.

4 By integrity, I mean how pristine the text is – that is, whether or not the text has been corrupted over time. To give one example: There is a famous story in John 7:53–58:12 of a woman taken in adultery. The scribes and Pharisees bring her to Jesus, and they ask him what should be done with her. It is a trap, which Jesus escapes by suggesting that he who is without sin should cast the first stone at her. This is a great story, but it is not found in the earliest and best manuscripts of the Gospel of John and has a different style, including words and phrases alien to the rest of the Gospel. It is thought by scholars that the story was originally a marginal note that was incorporated into the text by later scribes. See Bart Ehrman, *Misquoting Jesus* (2005), pp. 63–65.

5 Robert Cover, "*Nomos* and Narrative," 97 *Harv. L. Rev* 4 (1983–1984), p. 4.

6 Comparable to what Thomas Kuhn meant by a scientific 'paradigm.' Id., p. 6. See Thomas Kuhn, *The Structure of Scientific Revolutions* (1962).

7 Cover himself offers an example of how the interpretation of Deuteronomy 21:15–17 (providing that the first-born son must be preferred even if he is the son of a hated wife) is nuanced by stories in the Old Testament of younger sons being preferred, e.g., Cain and Abel, Ishmael and Isaac, Esau and Jacob, Adonijah and Solomon. "Life in the normative world of the Bible," Cover observes,

> required a well-honed sense of where the rule would end and why.... To be an inhabitant of the biblical normative world is to understand, first, that the rule of succession can be overturned; second, that it takes a conviction of divine destiny to overturn it; and third, that divine destiny is likely to manifest itself precisely in overturning this specific rule.
>
> (p. 22)

70 Ancients

8 It is assumed throughout here that the authors were men – for which we have no evidence except the already dubious evidence for the traditional names we ascribe to each gospel. There are good reasons to choose Mark's account of the trial narrative to analyze. The gospel attributed to Mark is thought to be the first of the canonical gospels to be written. Therefore, interpretive issues regarding its difference from or reliance on the other gospels may be more easily bracketed. Moreover, as will be argued below, Mark's gospel may be the most satisfying account of the trial of Jesus in terms of legal accuracy, but the scantiness of the evidence limits any historical reconstruction. So the focus here will be on the narrative purposes of the author rather than whether particular details may or may not be historically accurate. For convenience, I shall refer to the author of the *Gospel according to Mark* as 'Mark,' but it should be emphasized that we do not know who wrote this gospel.

9 To cite randomly just three studies among many, see G.L. Wells, "Eyewitness Testimony," *The Encyclopedia of Crime and Punishment* (2002), Dan Simon, *In Doubt: The Psychology of the Criminal Justice Process* (2012); Joyce W. Lacy and Craig E.L. Stark, "The Neuroscience of Memory: Implications for the Courtroom," 14(9) *Nat. Rev. Neurosci.* (2013).

10 The best guess is that the *Gospel according to Mark* was written just before the destruction of the Temple in Jerusalem in 70 C.E. – primarily because it does not assume the destruction of the Temple has taken place as the gospels of Luke and Matthew seem to do.

11 'Messiah' means 'the anointed one.' In Greek, the 'Christ.' Hebrew kings were anointed and, hence, sometimes called God's 'messiah.' See also Isaiah 45:1, where the Persian emperor Cyrus is called the anointed one, i.e., the messiah, for delivering the Jews from their Babylonian Captivity. Quotations from the Greek text are taken from David Robert Palmer (trans.), *The Gospel of Mark* (2021), which includes a fine translation. However, translations from the Greek in this chapter are my own and may vary from Palmer's.

12 On the historicity of Jesus generally, see Bart Ehrman, *Did Jesus Exist? The Historical Argument for Jesus of Nazareth* (2012) (offering other evidence for this conclusion and arguments against the so-called mythicist position).

13 This is quite a contrast to the way the Gospel according to Luke describes the crucifixion. However, the reference to Elijah should not go unnoticed.

14 In Greek, some versions have "υἱοῦ θεοῦ" (son of [a] god), and some versions have "υἱοῦ τοῦ θεοῦ" (son of [the] god).

15 In passages in the Old Testament, the phrase 'son of God' may be interpreted as referring to angels, or the Jewish people as a whole, or a Davidic king: for example, Genesis 6:4 (angels), Deuteronomy 14:1 (the Jews), Psalms 2:7, 89:27 (Davidic kings). In the Beatitudes in Matthew 5:9, the 'peacemakers' are called 'sons of God.' Of course, all these passages may be interpreted in different ways, and many Christians do. My point is only that the phrase may bear a non-divine interpretation.

16 Similarly, the reference to the resurrection in Mark 8 need not point to Jesus' divinity. Lazarus, for example, is raised from the dead but is not divine (John 11), but the story of Lazarus is not told in Mark. Mark provides a story early on about the daughter of Jairus, who is ill but (the story says) dies before Jesus can get to her. It is usually thought that Jesus then raises her from the dead. If that is the case, there is evidence in Mark itself that being raised from the dead is not a sign the person being raised is divine. However, in Mark's version of the story, Jesus himself says that the girl is not dead but only sleeping (5:39). Most Christians interpret this metaphorically, but we cannot rule out the possibility that Mark is not relating the story of a miracle here.

17 Even the ability to forgive sins is not inherent in him, Jesus says, but such authority has been given ("ἐξουσίαν ἔχει ὁ υἱὸς τοῦ ἀνθρώπου," Mark 2:10) – just as Catholic priests today have the authority to dispense forgiveness of sins without being divine. Neither

does the power to drive out demons or 'unclean spirits' indicate divinity since Jesus himself gives this authority to his disciples (3:15).
18 I owe much of this argument to Bart Ehrman's scholarship – especially *How Jesus Became God: The Exaltation of a Jewish Preacher from Galilee* (2014) – but also to many other biblical scholars.
19 "τοῖς υἱοῖς τῶν ἀνθρώπων."
20 A foreshadowing of the charges against him later? See also Mark 2:28 (the 'son of man' is the lord of the Sabbath). One of the possible sources for the term is Daniel 7:13, which seems to indicate that it means 'human being.' This also seems to be the most logical readings of the use of the phrase in the Book of Job (16:21, 25:6, 35:8).
21 Therefore, it may be we have an incomplete text. To fill this lacuna, later scribes added verses, including the twelve verses with which readers of the King James translation are familiar but which do not exist in the earliest manuscripts.
22 See Werner Kelber, *The Oral and Written Gospel: The Hermeneutics of Speaking and Writing in the Synoptic Tradition, Mark, Paul, and Q* (1983). See also Joanna Dewey, "Oral Methods of Structuring Narrative in Mark," 53 *Interpretation* (1989), pp. 32–44; Christopher Bryan, "Was Mark Written to Be Read Aloud?" Part 2 of *A Preface to Mark: Notes on the Gospel in Its Literary and Cultural Settings* (1993); Elizabeth Struthers Malbon, *Hearing Mark: A Listener's Guide* (2002).
23 In Mark 14:36, Jesus asks to have the cup of suffering taken from him and the author has him address God as '*Abba*,' which is immediately translated into Greek as 'ὁ πατήρ' – 'father.' And, most famously, Jesus' last words (of despair) in Mark are '*Eloi, Eloi, lama sabachthani*,' which is explicitly translated into Greek as "Ο θεός μου ὁ θεός μου, εἰς τί ἐγκατέλιπές με' – 'My God, my God, why have you forsaken me' (Mark 15:34). Interestingly, in the earliest manuscripts of Mark, when Jesus 'resurrects' the young girl in chapter 5, he says in Aramaic '*Talitha, koum*,' translated as 'little girl, stand up' in the Greek. However, '*koum*' is the singular imperative masculine form in Aramaic. Later manuscripts correct it to '*koumi*.' See David Robert Palmer (trans.), *The Gospel of Mark* (2021), note 39. Does this mean the author of Mark or the copyist was not that fluent in Aramaic? Or that there was an error in the early manuscripts?
24 See Cedric Whitman, *Homer and the Homeric Tradition* (1958) (on the geometric structure of the *Iliad*).
25 For example, the notorious parable of the fig tree frames the story of the cleansing of the Temple in Mark 11. See also Mark 13:28. Scholars dispute how extensive or consistent the structure is. See, for example, Kevin W. Larsen, "The Structure of Mark's Gospel: Current Proposals," 3:1 *Currents in Biblical Research* (2004).
26 Martin Kähler, *The So-called Historical Jesus and the Historic, Biblical Christ* (1964 [1896]), p. 80 n. 11.
27 Or feel it with their own fingers like doubting Thomas (John 20:27).
28 Investigated by the German theologian William Wrede in *Das Messiasgeheimnis in den Evangelien: Verständnis des Markusevangelium* (trans. as *The Messianic Secret* (1901)).
29 But see the remarks above on the phrase 'son of God' with respect to Jesus' 'divinity.' If the author of Mark accepts Jesus' divinity, the demon recognitions in the gospel are no problem. They have access to knowledge ordinary human beings do not. On the other hand, just because the demons recognize him as divine, it does not mean that *Jesus* recognizes himself as divine.
30 Jesus heals a number of other people as well but stops the demons he expels from speaking ostensibly because they know who he is.
31 The fact that it is a *Roman* who makes this final statement raises all kinds of questions about how it should be analyzed: Would a Roman mean the same thing as a Jew when he uses the idiom? Does the centurion intend to imply a monotheism? He says in

Greek, 'Ἀληθῶς οὗτος ὁ ἄνθρωπος υἱὸς θεοῦ ἦν.' Interestingly, the Greek could also be translated as 'a son of a god.' Moreover, the centurion makes no bones that the man being crucified is a 'human being,' an *anthropos*. So, what is it he is trying to say? The author of Mark once again remains ambiguous.

32 Many other scholars, including Albert Schweitzer, have also seen two threads of 'radical ethics' and 'apocalyptic predestinarianism' in the canonical gospels. See Gabriel Josipovici, *The Book of God: A Response to the Bible* (1988).
33 Elijah is also the prophet who performed the first resurrection in the Bible. The reference also echoes the 40 days and 40 nights of Noah's flood, which led to a complete renewal of the world.
34 Compare the rule Robert Cover cites on favoring first-born sons in footnote 7 above.
35 Cover distinguishes between an 'insular' and a 'redemptive' *nomos*. People may isolate themselves within their own distinctive *nomoi*, but they may also come together to transform themselves within a *nomos* (Cover, pp. 33–35). For example, in a 'redemptive' paradigm, the proper interpretation of a law would be one that realized an ideal promoted within the paradigm – the way Abraham Lincoln interpreted the 'silver frame of the Constitution' in the light of the 'golden apple of the Declaration of Independence.' 'Redemptive' paradigms assume that the current reality is 'unredeemable' and must be replaced by another. See the discussion of this in the Epilogue.
36 This is bolstered by other aspects of the Gospel of Mark with respect to Gentiles. While Jesus ministers to Gentiles on rare occasions, his focus is not on them. For example, when he relieves the demoniac (who is most likely Gentile) of the 'legion' of unclean spirits in Gerasa, he refuses to allow him among the disciples. On this episode, see Alan Watson, "Jesus and the Gerasene/Gaderene Demoniac (Mark 5.1–20)" (lecture 4), *Authority of Law; and Law: Eight Lectures* (2003).
37 In the *Gospel according to Luke* (9:31), this is even explicitly connected to the 'exodus' of Jesus to Jerusalem.
38 The parallels here to what happens around Jesus' baptism are striking. This episode can be interpreted in many different ways – one of which is that this is the moment at which Jesus becomes divine, but the author gives no explanation of what sort of 'metamorphosis' Jesus underwent.
39 Which will come before some of the disciples have tasted death (Mark 9:1). For more on Jesus as an apocalyptic preacher, see Bart Ehrman, *Jesus: Apocalyptic Prophet of the New Millennium* (1999); compare Albert Schweitzer, *The Quest for the Historical Jesus* (1906).
40 Usually translated as 'life' but literally in Greek 'soul' or 'breath' (τὴν ψυχὴν).
41 Jorge Luis Borges played with this idea in one of his short stories, "Three Versions of Judas" (1944).
42 The phrasing is repeated when Pilate 'hands over' Jesus to be crucified (15:15). In the gospel of John, Jesus 'hands over' his spirit in death (John 19:30). See William Klassen, *Judas: Betrayer or Friend of Jesus?* (1996) (arguing that the use of the Greek term supports the view that Judas did not betray Jesus), pp. 47–49.
43 Bart Ehrman sees the attack at the Temple as a symbolic display illustrating Jesus' apocalyptic message that those who did not accept his message (Pharisees, Sadducees, Essenes, etc.) would be destroyed as would the Temple (which actually happened in 70 C.E.) (Ehrman, *Jesus: Apocalyptic Prophet*, pp. 208–209).
44 It is irresistible to note that Jesus' reply in Mark – 'I am' – is a variation of the name God gives to Moses in Exodus 3:14.
45 See Mary Ann Beavis, "The Trial before the Sanhedrin (Mark 14:53–65): Reader Response and Greco-Roman Readers," 49(4) *The Catholic Biblical Quarterly* (October, 1987), pp. 581–596.

46 It is probably only this statement that even has a hint of blasphemy: sitting at the right hand of Power *could* be interpreted as implying a divine status, but this is at best ambiguous. See Edith Z. Friedler, "The Trial of Jesus as a Conflict of Laws?" 32 *Irish Jurist* (1997), p. 415n.83.
47 "'οἱ δὲ πάντες κατέκριναν αὐτὸν ἔνοχον εἶναι θανάτου" (Mark 14:64).
48 Since my analysis focusses solely on Mark, I omit any considerations on the claim in the *Gospel according to John* that Jews were forbidden from exercising the death penalty at that time. See Appendix 1.
49 Watson, *The Trial of Jesus*, p. 73.
50 And under Jewish law, a second meeting is required in a capital case. Mishnah Sanhedrin 5.5.
51 This may explain why in the *Gospel according to John* (written later) Jesus is almost chatty with Pilate by comparison. See Appendix 1.
52 Compare the *Gospel according to John* 19:21 (when the Jews object that the sign on the cross does not make explicit that Jesus only *claims* to be king).
53 Although, in chapter 10, the disciples James and John vie for who will set on Jesus' right and left hand in the kingdom of God, which at least implies some kind of a kingship.
54 See Jonathan Schwiebert, "Jesus's Question to Pilate in Mark 15:2," 136(4) *Journal of Biblical Literature* (2017), pp. 937–947.
55 Giorgio Agamben makes much of the claim that Pilate may not formally have condemned Jesus, arguing (citing Dante) that killing without judgment means Adam's sin was not punished in Christ's death. Agamben, *Pilate and Jesus* (2015). But see D.L. Dusenbury, "The Judgment of Pontius Pilate: A Critique of Giorgio Agamben," 32(2) *Journal of Law and Religion* (2017), pp. 340–365.
56 Luke 23:24: "Καὶ Πιλᾶτος ἐπέκρινεν γενέσθαι τὸ αἴτημα αὐτῶν" ("And Pilate passed sentence for this to be done"). Famously, Luke's Pilate declares that he finds in Jesus no crime deserving of death and, therefore, will release him after scourging him. The question arises: then, why scourge him? Some have speculated that simply not answering Pilate's questions would have been sufficient for punishment – even the death penalty.
57 Haim Cohn, *The Trial and Death of Jesus* (1967), p. xvi.
58 This is why the author of Matthew has Pilate wash his hands of the matter (Matthew 27:24).
59 We may also speculate about the author's motives here. It might be that the author's style reflects a desire to encourage the reader to come to his or her own decision, but it could also be out of fear of punishment if the author is too explicit about his message.
60 Gabriel Josipovici, *The Book of God* (1990), p. 231.

References

Agamben, G. (2015). *Pilate and Jesus*.
Beavis, M. A. (October, 1987). The trial before the Sanhedrin (Mark 14:53-65): Reader response and Greco-Roman readers. 49(4) *Catholic Biblical Quarterly* 581.
Bryan, C. (1993). Was Mark written to be read aloud? *A preface to Mark: Notes on the Gospel in its literary and cultural settings* (Part 2).
Cohn, H. (1967). *The trial and death of Jesus*.
Cover, R. (1983–1984). *Nomos* and narrative. 97 *Harvard Law Review* 4.
Dewey, J. (1989). Oral methods of structuring narrative in Mark. 53 *Interpretation* 32.
Dusenbury, D. L. (2017). The judgment of Pontius Pilate: A critique of Giorgio Agamben. 32 *Journal of Law and Religion* 340.
Ehrman, B. (1999). *Jesus: Apocalyptic prophet of the new millennium*.

Ehrman, B. (2005). *Misquoting Jesus*.
Ehrman, B. (2012). *Did Jesus exist? The historical argument for Jesus of Nazareth*.
Ehrman, B. (2014). *How Jesus became god: The exaltation of a Jewish preacher from Galilee*.
Friedler, E. Z. (1997). The trial of Jesus as a conflict of laws? 32 *Irish Jurist* 398.
Josipovici, G. (1988). *The book of God: A response to the Bible*.
Kähler, M. (1964 [1896]). *The so-called historical Jesus and the historic, biblical Christ*.
Kelber, W., Ong, W. J., & Rust, R. (1983). *The oral and written gospel: The hermeneutics of speaking and writing in the synoptic tradition, Mark, Paul, and Q*.
Kuhn, T. (1962). *The structure of scientific revolutions*.
Lacy, J. W., & Stark, C. E. L. (2013). The neuroscience of memory: Implications for the courtroom. 14(9) *Nat. Rev. Neuroscience* 649.
Larsen, K. W. (2004). The structure of Mark's gospel: Current proposals. 3(1) *Currents in Biblical Research* 140.
Malbon, E. S. (2002). *Hearing Mark: A listener's guide*.
Palmer, D. R. (trans.) (2021). *The gospel of Mark*. Retrieved from https://bibletranslation.ws/palmer-translation/.
Schweitzer, A. (1906). *The quest for the historical Jesus*.
Schwiebert, J. (2017). Jesus's question to Pilate in Mark 15:2. 136 *Journal of Biblical Literature* 937.
Simon, D. (2012). *In doubt: The psychology of the criminal justice process*.
Watson, A. (1995). *The trial of Jesus*.
Watson, A. (2003). Jesus and the Gerasene/Gaderene demoniac (Mark 5.1–20) (lecture 4). *Authority of law; and law: Eight lectures*.
Wells, G. L., & Olson, E. A. (2002). Eyewitness testimony. *Encyclopedia of crime and punishment*.
Whitman, C. (1958). *Homer and the Homeric tradition*.
Wrede, W. (1901). *Das Messiasgeheimnis in den Evangelien: Verständnis des Markusevangelium* (trans. as *The Messianic Secret*).

Part II
Moderns

Chapter 4

The Trial of Thomas More (1535)
Authentic Selfhood and Procedural Law in *A Man for All Seasons*

The trial of Thomas More has loomed larger in the modern popular imagination ever since Robert Bolt's successful play *A Man for All Seasons*. Bolt first crafted *A Man for All Seasons* as a radio play in 1954 – partially in response to the McCarthyite 'witch hunts' that were taking place at the time in the United States. Eventually, he reworked it into a theatrical piece, which premiered in 1960. In 1966, the play was made into an Academy Award-winning film, largely shorn of its Brechtian *Verfremdung*[1] features (such as the character of the 'Common Man,' who regularly breaks the so-called 'fourth wall' and makes comments on the action of the play).[2] By contrast, the filmitization set the standard for 'realistic' historical films, replicated in such movies as *Anne of the Thousand Days* (1969), *Cromwell* (1970), and even *Le Retour de Martin Guerre* (1982).[3] Indeed, the film version has become a pop culture source of quotes for pundits and politicians about the 'rule of law' (see below).

More is portrayed in the drama as a worldly-wise man of conscience, trying to remain true to his religious convictions as he attempts to navigate the shoals of political intrigue in the royal court of England's Henry VIII. Henry VIII famously broke with the Catholic Church and declared himself head of the new Church of England – all so he could divorce his wife, Catherine of Aragon, and marry another courtesan, Anne Boleyn. More failed to evade the wrath of his king and was, in the end, beheaded.[4] Bolt portrays More as a champion of freedom of conscience. He depicts the king's privy councillor, Thomas Cromwell, as a Machiavellian villain. Recently, readers (and viewers) of Hilary Mantel's *Wolf Hall* (2009)[5] have found the roles of Cromwell and More reversed. Mantel paints Cromwell as a hero of Protestantism, tolerance, and modern administration and presents a much darker view of Thomas More – More the fanatic, the heretic hunter, the misogynist.[6]

Thomas More has always been a controversial and polarizing figure – by turns, a saint who met his fate with admirable aplomb or a man obsessed with death, whose famous wit was a sublimation of an intense self-loathing.[7] Ever since Marie Delcourt's 1936 essay "Recherches sur Thomas More,"[8] it has been fashionable to say that there are (at least) two Mores. Delcourt discerns

DOI: 10.4324/9781003302971-7

a Latin More (witty, erudite, tolerant) and an English More (fierce, dogmatic, ascetic), but there are many such divides in the way he is seen. This makes the historical issues raised by the trial of Thomas More and their transformation into fiction all the more intriguing for us. Since Robert Bolt based his play on historical research, modelling speeches on passages from contemporary sources such as More's prison letters to his daughter and the biography of More written by his son-in-law William Roper, it may be useful to recount some of the history in order to assess Bolt's interpretations and deviations from it.

More as humanist

As the son of John More, a prominent lawyer and judge, Thomas More received a classical education steeped in the 'new learning' of Renaissance humanism – the cry to return to ancient texts and understand them in their own light even if that light was pagan. The 'new learning' was spurred (in part) by the (re)discovery in the 14th and 15th centuries of hitherto unknown ancient works (at least, to Latin Christendom) by such authors as Plato, Aristotle, Cicero, and Lucretius, which in turn led to deep inquiries into the nature of language, politics, rhetoric, and history. Indeed, humanism invented the very concept of critical scholarship, the notion that we must understand texts as historical documents, created at specific historical times for specific historical purposes. Through a rigorous application of the principles of historical linguistics, for example, Lorenzo Valla around 1439 was able to demonstrate as a fraud the so-called 'Donation of Constantine' (a document that purported to give the Catholic Church secular dominion over the western Roman Empire – a major point of contention throughout the Middle Ages). In some ways, the conflict between Henry VIII and Thomas More may be seen as the last great battle in this dispute. More's great friend, Desiderius Erasmus of Rotterdam, compiled a critical edition of the Greek New Testament to which all editions and translations of the New Testament are indebted today. Erasmus himself wrote some of the most famous essays of the sixteenth century – including *In Praise of Folly*, whose original title *Moriae Encomium*[9] is considered an oblique tribute to Thomas More.[10]

More studied at Oxford and became a barrister in 1502 although he was also powerfully drawn to monasticism and the spiritual life. Elected to Parliament in 1504, More gradually rose in office, eventually serving under Henry VIII's Lord Chancellor, Cardinal Wolsey. It was around this time that More wrote his most famous work, *Utopia* (1516),[11] and his *History of Richard III* (circa 1513), which was to have such an impact on William Shakespeare's version of the hunchbacked king. More's erudition also attracted the attention of Henry VIII, and More became an intellectual advisor to the monarch. By this time, Martin Luther had sparked the Protestant Reformation in Germany, and More struggled mightily to prevent this heterodoxy from infecting England. He is thought to have had a hand in writing the king's treatise entitled *Defence of the Seven Sacraments* (1521), an anti-Lutheran tract for which the Pope granted Henry the title 'Defender of the Faith.' One of the great puzzles in understanding More as a person is the relationship between his humanism and his religious faith. Some scholars believe these two sides of More are marvellously integrated; others argue that the religiously-fanatic older More betrayed the humanist principles advocated by the younger More.[12] How Robert Bolt walks this tightrope is one of the allures of the play.

The political dilemma of Henry VIII

Henry VIII has become a familiar character to most of us – usually in caricature form as the gouty, corpulent tyrant who decapitates wives with one hand while munching turkey legs with the other. We know him from iconic performances by Charles Laughton and Keith Mitchell as the monarch, from popular TV series such as *The Tudors* and Damien Lewis' uncanny interpretation in the televised version of *Wolf Hall*. Yet, we must understand the real problems Henry faced if we are to understand the trial of Thomas More.

Henry VIII was undoubtedly a narcissist and a megalomaniac – as one might expect from the man who introduced the 'divine right' of kings to English politics. However, he also had to grapple with a serious political situation. His legendary rages often vented frustration at his impotence to influence crucial aspects of his reign. Henry was the second son of Henry VII, who established the Tudor dynasty in England after the bloody civil war we know as the War of the Roses. Henry's older brother Arthur[13] was supposed to succeed to the throne, but he died of a fever not long after wedding Catherine of Aragon, a marriage arranged to secure an alliance with Spain, the greatest power on the European continent at the time. Thus, Henry came to the throne without proper preparation in the arts of kingship, but the manner of his succession taught him better than anything else the importance for the State of having an heir to the throne – preferably, more than one. In order to preserve the alliance with Spain, Henry was granted papal dispensation to marry Arthur's widow, Catherine. Catherine, unfortunately, was unable to provide Henry with a male heir. She lost four children (3 boys) in a row before giving birth to a girl, Mary, who would later become Queen of England and be given the sobriquet 'Bloody Mary' by her Protestant opponents.

By 1525, Henry had become enamored of Anne Boleyn, the daughter of one of Henry's favorite courtiers. Anne, unlike her sister (Mary), refused merely to become the king's mistress and insisted on marriage before engaging in the ultimate carnal act. The king was by this time 34 years old, and the average lifespan at this time in 16th-century England was around 38. In his mind, Henry owed a duty to his kingdom to produce an heir. Otherwise, there was a danger that the country would slip back into civil war, an evil to be avoided at any cost. Henry and his advisors explored various alternatives. The option most attractive to the king was to wed Anne, which meant he must have his marriage to Catherine annulled. Henry tasked his Lord Chancellor, Cardinal Wolsey, to resolve the 'King's Great Matter.'

Henry argued through his advisors that his marriage to Catherine violated the prohibition of Leviticus 20:21[14] and that the Pope did not have the ability to grant dispensation from it. Wolsey ultimately failed in his attempts to get an annulment – perhaps, in part, because, in 1527, the Holy Roman Emperor, Charles V (who was Catherine's nephew and King of Spain), captured Rome and the Holy See, massacring 1,000 people in the Vatican alone.[15] This may have disinclined the Pope to rule against the Emperor's aunt. As a result, Wolsey fell[16] (the king charged him with treason, pardoned him, and charged him again). Wolsey died in 1529 before he could be tried.

The treasons of Thomas More

Thomas More succeeded Wolsey as Lord Chancellor, the first lawyer to hold the post. This move has puzzled many since More made no secret of his opinion about the divorce. Some have said that the king promised not to draw More into his 'great matter.' Yet, the evidence shows that, after his appointment, the king regularly pressed More for his opinion and that More gave it candidly, if circumspectly.[17] Still, More's legal background made him a logical choice for the post since the main formal duty of the Lord Chancellor was to hear appeals from the common-law courts.[18] More also used his office to ward off the Protestant threat. More had put to death (and may have tortured) a number of Protestant 'heretics' (at least, six) and, perhaps, had a hand in the death of William Tyndale (whose English translation of the Bible became the foundation for the King James Bible).[19]

About the same time, the king appointed Thomas Cromwell (who had secured a seat in Parliament) to the Privy Council. Cromwell gradually became one of the king's most important legal and parliamentary advisors.[20] During the so-called Reformation Parliament (1529–1536), a series of laws was passed that revolutionized the English form of government, the effect of which was to transfer power over religious affairs to the king and to establish the principle of sovereignty known as the Crown-in-Parliament.[21] More resigned his office in 1532 after Parliament passed laws preventing clergy from being tried by canonical courts and forbidding individuals convicted of a crime to appeal to an authority outside England, an attack on the independence of the clergy, including their independent right to determine matters of heresy.[22] Because More believed in the supremacy of the spiritual sword (the Church) in these matters, he could no longer serve in secular office without violating his conscience. Yet, it is also true that the king and others placed constant pressure on More to support Henry in the matter of his marriage to Anne Boleyn.

One conventional interpretation of the events that followed is that, when More resigned, he promised to retire from public life and, in compliance with his oath of office, not to oppose Henry's policies publicly. Nevertheless, More continued to publish writings that supported positions of the Catholic Church and undermined positions taken by Parliament. Was this a violation of More's oath of office? Some scholars have concluded that he was as good as his word, while others believe he was "working behind the scenes to muster support for the old church in Parliament."[23] So, once again, it is a matter of contention whether More's actions after his resignation justified or, at least, motivated the charges against him later. Certainly, More's deliberate absence from Anne Boleyn's coronation in 1533 did not help his cause.[24] Whatever the king's position was at the time of More's resignation, "now, early in 1534, the cloud of uncertainty over the new polity and the succession made More's unyieldingness intolerable."[25]

Wherever the truth may lie, it is clear that More finally became entangled in two statutes passed by Parliament in 1534: the Act of Succession, which required an oath on penalty of treason to recognize the legality of the marriage of Henry VIII and Anne Boleyn and the legitimacy of their offspring, and the Act of Treasons, enacted some months later. More first ran afoul of the Succession Act. This statute provided that 'to obstinately refuse' to take the oath would be deemed 'misprision of high treason,' a lesser offense than 'high treason.'[26] On 13 April 1534, More and others (More was the only layman) were summoned to Lambeth (in London) to take the oath. In a letter to his daughter Margaret, More recounts that he asked to see the oath and the statute. After perusing them both, he related, "I would not deny to swear to the succession, yet unto the oath that there was offered me I could not swear, without the iubarding [jeopardizing] of my soul to perpetual damnation."[27] Thomas Cranmer, the Archbishop of Canterbury, who was present, argued that More's doubt must be uncertain (since he did not condemn others who took the oath) while his allegiance to the king was a certainty. "And therefore are ye bounden to leave off the doubt of your unsure conscience in refusing the oath, and take the sure way in obeying of your prince, and swear it."[28] However, More refused. Nor would he explain to which part of the oath he objected or why. It was upon this 'silence' that More pinned his hope of averting disaster.

The Act of Treasons made it high treason "maliciously ... to deprive [the king's most royal person, the queen's, or their heirs apparent of] their dignity, title, or name of their royal estates." One of Henry's titles was Supreme Head of the Church of England, conferred on the king by the Act of Supremacy of 1534.[29] The Act of Treasons also made 'maliciously speaking' against the king an act of high treason but said nothing about a silent refusal to take an oath.

The importance of procedural law

A Man for All Seasons is often construed as a simplified variation on the themes of Sophocles' *Antigone* (at least, as *Antigone* is traditionally and frequently interpreted). That is, it illustrates, depending on your preferred formulation, the conflict between natural law and positive law or between law and morality or between God's law and manmade law, centering on Thomas More's religious objections to Henry VIII's divorce from Catherine of Aragon.[30] Although he is a dutiful servant of the king, Thomas More (it is argued) must choose to remain faithful to God's commandments rather than the king's directive to take the Oath of Succession. Like *Antigone*, the play is purported to be a 'tragic' conflict between two 'valid' realms of law.[31]

However, the drama of the play does not turn on the conflict of substantive law. The substantive dispute is a given; and, if it is given that the conflict is between God's law and man's law, then, of course, God's law must be preferred – in other words, no drama there. Nor does Thomas More ever express doubt in the play about the substance of his position – so that the drama might turn on whether More might change his mind and reconcile with the king.[32] Rather, the drama turns on procedural points. Will or won't Thomas More be condemned for his piety? It depends on whether More can cleverly evade (by legal maneuver) the repercussions of his (inward) disagreement with the king's actions. On the whole, the play works as a meditation on the importance and the purpose of procedural law. As first-year law students in the US are forced to learn early and all too well,[33] the difference between substantive and procedural law can sometimes be difficult to determine but is frequently crucial to the outcome of a case.[34]

Perhaps, the most widely-cited and recognized passage in Bolt's *A Man for All Seasons* is this:

Roper: So, now you give the Devil the benefit of law!
More: Yes! What would you do? Cut a great road through the law to get after the Devil?
Roper: Yes, I'd cut down every law in England to do that!
More: (roused and excited): Oh? (*Advances on Roper*) And when the last law was down, and the Devil turned 'round on you, where would you hide, Roper, the laws all being flat? This country is planted thick with laws, from coast to coast, Man's laws, not God's! And if you cut them down, and you're just the man to do it, do you really think you could stand upright in the winds that would blow then? Yes, I'd give the Devil benefit of law, for my own safety's sake![35]

This excerpt is aptly quoted in op-eds during times of emergency when calls for suspension of the rule of law are regularly and predictably made – such as after 9/11 when certain forms of torture were 'legalized' in the United States and attorneys who defended accused terrorists were labelled 'traitors.'[36] The (often frantic) justification is always that the danger to the state is far too urgent to bother with observing 'mere' legalities.

Some argue that epistemological uncertainty is the primary philosophical foundation for procedural law, and More's remarks above are consistent with that view. We cannot simply 'know' whether or not someone is guilty of a crime, for example. Therefore, we must establish fair procedures by which to determine whether someone should be held criminally liable for an act or omission. The whole point of procedural law is to slow down the process of judgment, to make sure we are determining things on solid and defensible evidentiary grounds.[37] Yet, procedure acknowledges that we may never arrive at the noumenon, the *Ding an sich*, of any event. We have no windows into men's souls, and the law cannot peer into them.

Indeed, it might not even be expedient for the law to do so. This is illustrated in another exchange between Thomas More and his (still prospective) son-in-law Roper just before the dialogue cited above. Roper, ever excitable, has switched from enthusiastic Church reformer to protector of the purity of the Church, and his rhetoric is getting away from him, bordering on treason. More stops him short, asking him to remember More's office. Roper retorts, "Oh, if you stand on your office." To which More replies, "I don't stand on it, but there are certain things I may not hear!"[38]

Thomas More surmises full well what Roper means to say, but he also believes that he is only compelled to act in his capacity as Chancellor if Roper actually utters the words. One may suspect hypocrisy on More's part here because it is also treason to harbor treasonous thoughts. One could argue that, because More is cognizant of potential treason in Roper's mind, it should trigger action against Roper. However, in this instance, the form *is* the substance. As long as Roper is silent, More cannot be *legally certain* Roper's intent is criminal and, therefore, need not take action against him. A legal nicety, some would say.[39] Still, it is a procedural principle in the law of evidence upon which More himself will stand later in the play.

The self and 'authenticity'

This same principle is provided some nuance when Thomas More is informed in the play that Parliament has passed an act concerning the 'Marriage' containing a compulsory oath. More is concerned about the wording of the oath. Roper scoffs, "We don't need to know the (*contemptuous*) wording – we know what it will mean!" More replies, "It will mean what the words say! An oath is made of words. It may be possible to take it. Or avoid it" (*A Man for All Seasons*, p. 39).[40] More seems to be insinuating that one may take an oath and have a private conviction about its meaning as long as it is consistent with the words (even though that interpretation may not be compatible with the 'intent' behind the oath).[41] How does this differ from simply lying while taking the oath?

It transpires that More does not feel he is able to take the oath, and he is jailed (not explained in the play but for misprision of treason). Therefore, it is at least the case that a 'secret interpretation' of the words can only go so far.

Later in the play, More's daughter Margaret implores him to take the oath, to "say the words of the oath and in your heart think otherwise." More replies that an oath is nothing but words one says to God: "When a man takes an oath, Meg, he's holding his own self in his own hands. Like water (*cups his hands*) and if he opens his fingers *then* – he needn't hope to find himself again" (*A Man for All Seasons*, p. 87).[42] The play does not explain where to draw the line between a 'good faith' interpretation of the words of an oath and a mendacious one.

Nevertheless, the position of the fictional Thomas More makes sense in terms of the conception of self that Robert Bolt attributes to him, which almost certainly was not compatible with the views of the *actual* Thomas More. Bolt's fictional More seems to hold that belief is *personal*, that it is theoretically possible for a personal belief to be judged differently in different individuals even if the substance is the same. This is illustrated at various moments in the play. In one interrogation of More, Norfolk despairs that he (Norfolk) doesn't know whether the king's marriage was lawful or not, but he says (showing More a list of affiants to the oath): "damn it, Thomas, look at those names.... Can't you do what I did, and come with us, for fellowship?" More replies: "And when we stand before God, and you are sent to Paradise for doing according to your conscience, and I am damned for not doing according to mine, will you come with me, for fellowship?" (*A Man for All Seasons*, pp. 82–83). The point is made even clearer in a different retort to Norfolk elsewhere in the play. More says: "But what matters to me is not whether it's true or not but that I believe it to be true, or rather, not that I *believe* it, but that *I* believe it ... I trust I make myself obscure?" (*A Man for All Seasons*, pp. 56–57).

The concept of conscience to which More alludes here is wildly modern and would almost certainly have been considered heretical in More's day – except, perhaps, in matters on which the relevant religious authority had not yet taken a position. Once a position was taken on a matter of substance, however, all believers would be required to hold that position in their hearts.[43] It is why the Church permitted the use of torture in matters of heresy. How else could inquisitors plumb the depths of the soul to find out whether deviant beliefs flourished there? William Rockett puts it well: "More's theology was juristic. Matters of faith and belief were *ipso facto* matters of legality. Dogma and law were not dichotomous but continuous. The consensus of the faithful and the canonical standing of dogma were inseparable."[44] Yet, what Bolt is trying to preach, that More is a "hero of selfhood,"[45] is more in alignment with the existentialist concept of 'authenticity' outlined by thinkers such as Jean-Paul Sartre or Albert Camus.[46]

'Authenticity' here may be compared (crudely) to the courage of one's convictions. The implication of the fictional More's statement is that, if Norfolk sincerely believes in the legitimacy of the oath, he will not be condemned in the afterlife even if it turns out he was wrong; whereas, because More does not sincerely believe in the oath's legitimacy, he cannot take it and should be condemned for doing so even if it turns out the oath *was* legitimate. The due process considerations we see illustrated in *A Man for All Seasons* all swirl around the sanctity of individual belief and serve as the foundation for protections we now cherish such as the right against self-incrimination. In a way, the play provides us with a fictional 'pre-justification' for them – not as a channel for dealing with epistemological uncertainty but as the guardian of the sanctity of individual conscience.

Proof and procedure

The fictional More stands against Cromwell on the same principle by which he restrained Roper's potentially treasonous statement. Without external proof or confession, More may not be condemned for treason. This point is made quite eloquently in the play. More is perfectly willing to recognize the offspring of Queen Anne as heirs to the throne – Parliament has said so. He is even prepared to swear to it, but he will not swear to the Act of Succession – because there is more in the Act than that. Archbishop Cranmer tries to wheedle out More's objection, but More refuses to take the bait and makes no reply. Norfolk accuses him of insulting the King – More's reasons for refusing the oath must be treasonable!

More: Not must be; may be.
Norfolk: It's a fair assumption!
More: The law requires more than an assumption; the law requires a fact.
(A Man for All Seasons, pp. 81–82)

The thought process we see here is familiar to us. We are used to protections against self-incrimination and the presumption of innocence, of proof of criminal action beyond a reasonable doubt (none of which were settled in English law in the 16th century).[47] We naturally empathize with More here, but it is precisely because we feel such procedural considerations are essential not only to a just outcome but to the integrity of our 'private selves.' We have a 'right to think' – to think anything. Actions may be restricted, utterances may be forbidden, but we regard our innermost thoughts as inviolable to the intrusions of the state. It is not enough to suspect someone has treasonous thoughts; it must be proven in connection with some act. More likens the law to a "causeway upon which so long as he keeps to it a citizen may walk safely."[48] In Bolt's hands, More's resistance is a rejection of all totalitarianisms, be they Fascist, Communist, Protestant, or Catholic. At the same time, Bolt's defense of 'rule of law' procedure as protector of 'authentic selfhood' is as consistent with an atomistic conception of the 'liberal' state as it is with democratic socialism.

A question worth asking here (because it is so obvious) is why are More's prosecutors so committed to coercing him by law? Why not just spirit him away and murder him like Thomas Becket[49] if he is so dangerous? We get no answer except indirectly. In the play (but omitted in the film), after the colloquy just cited above, Cromwell contemplates his options. He fiddles with the rack, which is a prop on the stage, and opines that the King will not permit such harsh methods and that conniving More's death might bring about his own (*A Man for All Seasons*, p. 85). Moreover, as Cromwell hints elsewhere, such a 'disappearance' would serve as propaganda for the enemies of England even greater than More's imprisonment and silence. Yet, most importantly, everyone in the play acknowledges that such tactics are regarded as un-English ("this isn't Spain, you know," where the Inquisition does not shrink from coercive measures).[50] It is unacceptable for the parties to resort to (egregiously) extra-legal means. Law must be the arena to resolve the dramatic conflict between the antagonists Cromwell and More in the denouement of the play. Cromwell must either bring More to the King's side or show his recalcitrance is treasonous.

Yet, More's silence is a seemingly insurmountable barrier to the prosecution unless a procedural way may be found around it. A battle of legal wits is now engaged. This is where we get the most famous scene in the play – the trial scene, which turns on the interpretation of a presumption. Harking back to More's rejoinder to Roper about standing on his office, Cromwell accuses More of standing upon his silence. Then, he explains to the jury that there are many kinds of silence, each of which may betoken different things in different circumstances. The silence of a corpse betokens nothing. The silence of onlookers to a creeping assassin implies consent to the killing. The King's oath was subscribed by good subjects around the land, Cromwell claims, but More refused to do so. Therefore, in this context, More's silence must betoken a 'most eloquent denial' of the King's title. To which More replies with some impatience:

> Not so, Master Secretary, the maxim is 'qui tacet consentire.' (*Turns to Common Man*) The maxim of the law is (*very carefully*) "Silence Gives Consent." If, therefore, you wish to construe what my silence 'betokened,' you must construe that I consented, not that I denied.
> (*A Man for All Seasons*, pp. 96–97)

Dramatically, the scene works brilliantly. At first blush, we must feel that Thomas More, the clever lawyer, has finally stymied his foes with his superior legal reasoning. However, a moment's reflection allows us to see that Thomas More stakes his life on a technicality, the proper interpretation of a dusty legal maxim. Moreover, we must admit that Cromwell has some justice in his claim that most people would not so construe More's silence. Indeed, the very examples Cromwell uses provide a concession that ultimately undermines More's point. We cannot but accept that a dead man's silence is prelude to no intention. Witnessing a potential murder in the circumstances Cromwell describes *might* indicate consent – as the '*qui tacet*' maxim dictates. But Cromwell's point is made all the same. It is the circumstances surrounding the silence that point in the direction of an interpretation. It cannot be denied that, in certain circumstances, silence may betoken denial. More's argument puts empty formalism before substance.[51]

Yet, that is precisely the point of procedural law – and the eternal argument surrounding substance and procedure. If procedure protects the innocent, then it also protects the guilty, but isn't the point of the law (the counterargument goes) to render justice? Why should someone we 'know' is guilty get off on a technicality? So what if the arresting officer did not have a proper search warrant when she found the illegal cocaine – she *found* the cocaine! Is the law really so toothless that a criminal should go free for lack of procedural punctiliousness? In effect, More says 'yes.' If we agree with him, it is because we also agree (the logic of the play goes) that the individual conscience is a circumscribed area beyond which the state may not go (at least, not without certain safeguards and authorizations in place).

In the play, More's procedural parries seem to prevail – or, at least, put the evidence in equipoise. Therefore, Cromwell must win (and, dramatically, *can* only win) by cheating:[52] Richard Rich's perjury. Rich testifies that he witnessed More treasonably deny the king's title in the so-called 'putting of cases.' More counters Rich by swearing an oath that Rich's testimony is false, another evidentiary counterweight that, rhetorically, is even more persuasive because it is More's refusal to take an oath that has landed him in this predicament in the first place. More also asserts that there were two other witnesses to the interview, but he is told that both are abroad and have submitted depositions that they "did not hear what was said."[53] More comments on the suspicious nature of this absence. How convenient that they were not available to be cross-examined. To our modern sensibilities, the procedural flaws in the process accumulate and become more imbalanced in favor of the prosecution although More valiantly fends them off. (But remember, again, that such safeguards were not actually available to defendants in the 16th century.)

The dramatic *coup de grâce* in the procedural injustice against Thomas More is the jury's verdict. The jury (in reality, manned by enemies of Thomas More) does not even retire. Cromwell bullies them into rendering their verdict immediately[54] – which can only imply they must find the prisoner guilty. Thus, the whole point of a jury – which is to provide an impartial assessment of the evidence – is undermined, but the point of the maneuver is to give the illusion that the evidence is so clear-cut that deliberation is unnecessary. The cynicism of Cromwell's move should not go unappreciated.

The irony is that, once More has been illegitimately found guilty, he immediately removes the doubt as to his guilt, confessing that his "indictment is grounded in an Act of Parliament which is directly repugnant to the Law of God. The King in Parliament cannot bestow the Supremacy of the Church because it is a Spiritual Supremacy!" (*A Man for All Seasons*, p. 101). How are we to interpret this? Should we say that, once More was found guilty, he had nothing to lose by unburdening his mind and providing an explicit warning of the spiritual danger to his fellow citizens? If so, was Cromwell not right that

More's 'silence' concealed his 'treason' to the King? Or had this been what More was planning all along – to seek his own death[55] and unveil his opinion in the moment of his martyrdom, to magnify his message all the more? Is this what he means when he tells Margaret: "perhaps we *must* stand fast a little – even at the risk of being heroes."[56]

If so, we should contemplate the consequences of the alternative. What if the king had left More to his 'silence'? Would More be acting nobly or selfishly to maintain that course? He would be preserving (perhaps) his own soul, but is there not a danger that fellow citizens might lose theirs without the courage of his example?[57] These are probably not questions Bolt meant for us to contemplate. The integrity of your soul is ultimately your own business, Bolt seems to imply, but place no stock in your ability to affect outcomes in this life. Indeed, like Atticus Finch in *To Kill a Mockingbird*, every time More makes a prediction, he turns out to be spectacularly wrong.[58] This seems to be the point of the recitation of certain characters' fates (which occurs at the end of the film but before the denouement of the play). In the play, the Common Man reads aloud the fates of the various other characters we have encountered. Thomas Cromwell is executed for high treason; Thomas Cranmer is burned alive. Norfolk would have been executed, but the King died of syphilis before he could sign the warrant. Then, almost as an aside, the narrator says, "Richard Rich became a Knight and Solicitor-General, a Baron and Lord Chancellor, and died in his bed" (*A Man for All Seasons*, p. 79).

Bolt means for us to be shocked by the 'verdict of history,' which makes preserving the integrity and authenticity of one's 'selfhood' all the more important "for the context which we all inhabit, the terrifying cosmos. Terrifying because no laws, no sanctions, no *mores* obtain there."[59] 'Authenticity' is the only *meaning* to which one may cling in the vacuity of the universe – arguably, an artistically profound point to make in the mood of moral bankruptcy and existential despair following the Second World War but certainly not one the actual Thomas More would have endorsed.

Notes

1 A coinage of Bertolt Brecht to describe certain theatrical effects deliberately aimed at 'alienating' his audience from the action taking place on stage.
2 Quotations derive from the 1960 version of the play, but reference will also be made to the 1966 film.
3 See John M. Price, "Traces of *Utopia* in *A Man for All Seasons*," 47(1) *Literature/Film Quarterly* (Winter, 2019). The film is still regularly shown in connection with, for example, Catholic youth events, etc.
4 For his martyrdom, Thomas More was canonized by the Catholic Church in 1935.
5 Followed by the sequels *Bring Up the Bodies* (2012) and *The Mirror and the Light* (2020).
6 See, for example, Vanessa Thorpe, "Thomas More is the Villain of Wolf Hall. But Is He Getting a Raw Deal?" *The Guardian* (18 January 2015). On the charge of misogyny,

one must weigh his attitude toward his second wife Alice against his encouragement of learning among his daughters, especially Margaret.
7 More's contemporaries reported that, throughout his adult life, More regularly wore a hair shirt beneath his fine robes and engaged in self-flagellation. See Thomas Stapleton, *The Life and illustrious martyrdom of Sir Thomas More*, part III of *Tres Thomae* (1588), trans. by Philip Hellet (1928), p. 75.
8 Marie Delcourt, "Recherches sur Thomas More," *Bibliothèque de l'Humanisme et Renaissance* III (1936), pp. 22–42. For more on this, see Travis Curtright, *One Thomas More* (2012), esp. the chapter entitled "Iconic Mores on Trial."
9 On contemporary puns on More's name, see Stephanie Elsky, *Custom, Common Law, and the Constitution of English Renaissance Literature* (2020), p. 43.
10 Scholars have debated whether 'humanism' is inherently secular or compatible with religion. With Machiavelli and the *condotierri* (mercenary armies that ravaged Renaissance Italy) in mind, Jacob Burckhardt, the famous 19th-century Swiss historian of the Renaissance, called the revival of learning with its celebration of the ancients 'pagan.' However, most of the men and women whom we would identify as 'humanists' were devout Christians, who did not feel their faith was threatened in the least if they learned something from virtuous pagans – think of Dante's attitude toward Virgil, for example. Indeed, without the principles of humanism, it is difficult to imagine how Martin Luther would have been able to conceive of Protestantism's bedrock: *sola scriptura, sola fide* (scripture alone, faith alone). But, of course, More's position all along was that, while reason is important, it is not the only thing. Scripture is important, but our reason alone is too fragile a thing to grasp its meaning entirely. Scripture must also be understood through the Church in the light of tradition and the Church Fathers.
11 A large portion of More's book, one of the classic writings of the Renaissance, describes a supposedly ideal society – the title is a pun on the Greek words for 'good place' and 'no place.' *Utopia* contains many ironies when compared to More's own convictions: for example, divorce was permitted in More's Utopia and its inhabitants could follow whatever religion they liked. Some scholars have concluded that More meant *Utopia* to be a satire, not a blueprint. After all, the full title of the book is *The Best State of a Commonwealth and the New Island of Utopia* – one must take note of the 'and' that separates the title's two parts. See James Greene, "Introduction" to Thomas More, *Utopia and Other Essential Writings of Thomas More*, by James Greene and John Dolan (eds.) (1967), p. 22.
12 Compare, for example, Gerard Wegemer, *Thomas More as Statesman* (1996) with Richard Marius, *Thomas More: A Biography* (1984).
13 The hope was to bolster the Tudors' shaky claim to the throne by evoking the legend of King Arthur in the second Tudor king.
14 "And if a man shall take his brother's wife, it is an unclean thing: he hath uncovered his brother's nakedness; they shall be childless." We can never know the sincerity of Henry's conviction about this, but it is not implausible that he might actually have believed that Catherine's inability to produce an heir was an indication of God's disapproval. Nevertheless, we should take notice of the authoritative voice given to Scripture here as superseding even the authority of the Pope, a very 'Protestant' position and one not unlike the position some would take with regard to written constitutions in the 18th century.
15 Historians disagree on whether Charles V authorized the sack of Rome. It may have been a spontaneous reaction of imperial troops when the Pope allied himself with France in an attempt to free the Vatican from imperial and Spanish dependence.
16 It should be noted that More himself was vituperative in his attacks on Wolsey at this time. See Richard Marius, *Thomas More*, pp. 366–367. This plays an important role in the interpretation of More in *Wolf Hall*.

17 Marius, *Thomas More*, pp. 361–362. See, for example, William Roper, *The Life of Sir Thomas More*, G. Wegemer and S. Smith (eds.) (2003 [1556]), p. 22.
18 Marius, *Thomas More*, p. 360. On the duty of a judge's impartiality, William Roper records More's statement that even the Devil, his cause being good, should have the benefit of law (Roper, *The Life of Sir Thomas More*, p. 24). More's position also reflects an acceleration in the sixteenth century of the growing distinction between common law and equity. On this, see Samuel Gregg, "Legal Revolution: St. Thomas More, Christopher St. German, and the Schism of King Henry VIII," 5 *Ave Maria L. Rev.* 173 (2007).
19 This is a controversial point in More scholarship. John Foxe's *Book of Martyrs* (1563), which describes the suffering of Protestants at the hands of Catholics, claimed that More personally tortured people. More's biographers are divided on this. Compare Marius, *Thomas More: A Biography* (1984) with Peter Ackroyd, *The Life of Thomas More* (1999). On one hand, More wrote explicitly that he approved of burning heretics in his 1528 *Dialogue Against Heresies*. On the other hand, it cannot be said that his 'persecutions' were excessive or out of the ordinary in the context of the times.
20 G.R. Elton in his *The Tudor Revolution* (1953) transformed our view of Thomas Cromwell as an historical figure. Much of Hilary Mantel's view of Cromwell derives from Elton's work. Later scholarship may quibble with various aspects of Elton's interpretation, but there is no question now of Cromwell's importance in the reformation of the English state.
21 The Magna Carta had guaranteed the liberty of the English Church, which came to mean in practice that the Church was governed by canon law and had its own courts. Henry VIII's advisors collected a series of documents, called the *Collectanea satis copiosa*, to prove that Henry was an Emperor who could exercise supreme authority over both Church and State, which in effect meant that all English subjects, including clergy, were bound by parliamentary acts.
22 William Rockett, "The Case against Thomas More," 34 *Sixteenth Century Journal* 4 (2008), pp. 1065–1067; Peter Marshall, "The Last Years," in *The Cambridge Companion to Thomas More*, George M. Logan (ed.) (2011), pp. 116–117.
23 Marius, *Thomas More*, p. 413. Compare G.W. Bernard, The *King's Reformation: Henry VIII and the Remaking of the English Church* (2005), pp. 125–151. The interpretive theories are these: 1) The moment More resigned, the king determined to exact vengeance on him for failing to support his claims (vendetta theory). This theory comports with an interpretation of Henry VIII as an unstable, narcissistic tyrant. 2) More resigned and worked against the king behind the scenes. Therefore, the king had no choice but to execute him (conspiracy theory). This is G.R. Elton's conjecture, which is consistent with Thomas Cromwell's explanation in a letter to the Pope, justifying the executions of Thomas More and Bishop Fisher. (See G.R. Elton, "Sir Thomas More and the Opposition to Henry VIII" in *Essential Articles for the Study of Thomas More*, Richard Standish Sylvester and Germain Marchadour (eds.) (1977), pp. 79–91). 3) William Rockett recently argued that the king could tolerate More's cavils of conscience until the succession of Anne's progeny became a key issue. And, even then, it was not More's writings that were the problem. Rather, it was because the king's position had become more precarious. In 1533, Pope Clement VII had declared Henry's marriage to Anne null and void and excommunicated the King – a direct threat to the stability of the English throne. Therefore, the King could brook no hint of opposition from prominent subjects. See generally William Rockett, "The Case against Thomas More," pp. 1065–1067.
24 Roper recounts a telling anecdote about the purchase of a gown for the occasion and what can only be described as a brazen snub of the king by More. *Life of Sir Thomas More*, pp. 33–34. The 1966 film version of *A Man for All Seasons* inverts the meaning

of More's absence from the wedding, depicting Henry VIII as desperate for More's approval.
25 William Rockett, "The Case against Thomas More," p. 1085. It is also thought that Henry VIII himself had instigated the inclusion of More's name on the bill of attainder to condemn Elizabeth Barton and that Thomas Cromwell urged the king to take More's name off. See Marshall, "More's Last Years," p. 120.
26 The act specified that speaking "maliciously and obstinately" against the king's marriage was 'misprision of treason.' It became 'high treason' if anything were written or printed maliciously against the marriage. Technically speaking, 'misprision of treason' occurs when a person knows that treason is being planned or committed and does not report it as soon as he can to the proper authority.
27 Letter to Margaret Roper, 17 April 1534, in Thomas More, *Selected Letters*, Elizabeth Rogers (ed.) (1961), p. 217. We do not know the form of the oath presented to More. However, it is speculated that the oath presented by Cromwell went beyond the authority of the statute in that it required, for example, that the affiant renounce foreign powers and any previous oaths to such powers. This, at least, is what the oath required when an act specifying its content was passed in November 1534. If so, More had some legal justification to object to the oath at that time as *ultra vires*. Roper seems to confirm this, but he mixes up the different statutes in his account. See Roper, *Life of Sir Thomas More*, p. 44.
28 Letter to Margaret Roper, 17 April 1534 in *Selected Letters*, p. 221.
29 The Supremacy Act was passed in November 1534, the Treasons Act slightly later.
30 Many people read the play and film as turning on the Catholic teaching against divorce. To be fair, even the fictional More's objection is more likely to Henry VIII's claim to be Supreme Head of the Church, whether because of its challenge to papal 'infallibility' (which would be anachronistic in More's time) or its challenge to conciliarism (which would not be).
31 See, for example, Patrick J. Whiteley, "Natural Law and the Problem of Certainty: Robert Bolt's 'A Man for All Seasons'," 43(4) *Contemporary Literature* (Winter, 2002), pp. 760–783. Whiteley sees the play as dramatizing "conflicts among characters who are all at least potential heroes: Henry, Roper, and More. More stands above the other two whose certainties about divine law evade the epistemological challenges that Bolt's More faces." Id., p. 782. It is the uncertainty of Bolt's More that ennobles him according to Whiteley. While Whiteley's analysis is a sensitive reading of the character of More, More is not uncertain – at least not where it counts in this situation, as argued below.
32 Indeed, during Cranmer's interrogation of More, he says so explicitly:

> *Cranmer*: But that you owe obedience to your King is not capable of question. So weigh a doubt against a certainty and sign.
> *More*: Some men think the Earth is round, others think it flat; it is a matter capable of question. But if it is flat, will the King's command make it round? And if it is round, will the King's command flatten it? No, I will not sign.
> *Cromwell*: (*leaping up, with ceremonial indignation*) Then you have more regard to your own doubt than you have to his command!
> *More*: For myself, I have no doubt.
> *Cromwell*: No doubt of what?
> *More*: No doubt of my grounds for refusing this oath.
> (*A Man for All Seasons*, p. 83)

33 Thanks to the US Supreme Court's ruling in *Erie Railroad v. Tompkins*, 204 U.S. 64 (1938), which held that, in state law matters (usually, arising in diversity jurisdiction),

federal courts were to apply state substantive law and federal procedural law – which often requires 'angels on the head of a pin' determinations of what is substantive and what is procedural. But see Suzanna Sherry, "Wrong, Out of Step, and Pernicious: Erie as the Worst Decision of All Time," 39 *Pepperdine Law Review* 129 (2011).

34 As Supreme Court Justice Robert Jackson put it:

> Only the untaught layman or the charlatan lawyer can answer that procedure matters not.... Indeed, if put to the choice, one might well prefer to live under Soviet substantive law applied in good faith by our common-law procedures, than under our substantive law enforced by Soviet procedural practices.
> (*Shaughnessy v. United States ex rel. Mezei*, 345 U.S. 206, 224 (1953) (dissenting))

35 *A Man for All Seasons*, pp. 41–42. Interestingly, Justice Felix Frankfurter, who joined Jackson in dissent in the *Shaughnessy* case, was taken to see *A Man for All Seasons* by Australian ambassador Howard Beale in 1962. "Beale recounts that the Justice could scarcely contain his excitement during the scene just set out, and as it ended Frankfurter whispered in the dark. 'That's the point, that's it, that's it!'" ("Arms and the Man, A Man for All Seasons," *The Harvard Crimson* (15 July 1966)).

36 See, for example, Conor Friedersdorf, "Tarring Guantanamo Defense Lawyers as Traitors," *The Atlantic* (28 April 2011).

37 An excessive adherence to procedure, of course, has its own problems. As US Supreme Court Justice Antonin Scalia once remarked (thankfully, in dissent): "This Court has *never* held that the Constitution forbids the execution of a convicted defendant who has had a full and fair trial but is later able to convince a habeas court that he is 'actually' innocent" (*In re Troy Anthony Davis*, 557 U.S. 952 (2009)).

38 *A Man for All Seasons*, p. 39. In the play, More once again forbids Roper from uttering an opinion that is 'high treason' although, this time, he is no longer Chancellor (id., p. 52).

39 In England, torture was not used on suspected traitors (to get a confession of treasonous thoughts not otherwise provable) until 1540 and was justified on a theory of royal prerogative or sovereign immunity (and, hence, outside the normal common law regime). See Danny Friedman, "Torture and the Common Law," 2 E.H.R.L.R. (2006), p. 188, referencing David Jardine, *A Reading on the Use of Torture in Criminal Law of England* (1837) (arguing royal prerogative), p. 59, and John Langbein, *Torture and the Law of Proof: Europe and England in the Ancien Régime* (1977) (arguing sovereign immunity), pp. 129–131.

40 Compare Frederick Douglass' position on interpreting the US Constitution, discussed in the Epilogue.

41 The State of California obliges its public employees to sign a loyalty oath, which requires the affiant to pledge to defend the US and California Constitutions. When the oath was instituted in 1950, a number of faculty members at the University of California refused to take an oath of allegiance on principle (as a coercion that violated freedom of thought) and resigned, including the great German-American intellectual historian Ernst Kantorowicz, who had fled Nazi Germany and was an anti-Communist – presumably, precisely the kind of immigrant the California legislature wanted to encourage to become a US citizen. In 2012, Marianne Kearney-Brown, a Quaker and state college teacher, insisted on adding the word 'non-violently' to the word 'defend' when she took the oath – which she was not allowed to do and for which, failing to sign the oath, she was fired. She was later reinstated when the university issued a statement that the oath did not require public employees to bear arms or engage in violence. If Ms. Kearney-Brown had taken the oath while secretly promising to herself that she would never engage in violence to defend the Constitution (though defend

it she would – by other means), would that have violated the 'intent' of the oath or otherwise have been illegitimate?

42 It is worth noting that More stresses the notion of 'self' here and not the theological implications of perjury. See Travis Curtwright, *The One Thomas More* (2012), p. 196. However, when, for the same reason, More refuses to confide in his wife, he explicitly mentions the prospect of damnation from perjury (*A Man for All Seasons*, pp. 59–60). Elsewhere in the play, More also mentions the consequences of taking an oath for one's prospects in the afterlife.

43 As Tudor historian G.R. Elton pithily noted, Thomas More may have died for conscience but not for *freedom* of conscience (G.R. Elton, *Policy and Police: The Enforcement of the Reformation in the Age of Thomas Cromwell* (1972), p. 417). For an interesting perspective, see Brian Cummings, "Conscience and the Law in Thomas More," 23(4) *Renaissance Studies* (2009), pp. 463–485.

44 Gordon William Rockett, "Thomas More's Quarrel with Reform," 92 *Church History and Religious Culture* (2012), p. 206. Some have speculated that, out of some deep affection for Thomas More or concerns about his own soul, Henry VIII refused to have More tortured. This is the impression given in *A Man for All Seasons*, for example. However, there may have been legal reasons. Cromwell observed in his final interview with More that the former Chancellor himself had compelled heretics "to make a precise answer thereto" (*Selected Letters*, p. 251). This was a reference to the oath *ex officio* of canon law, which forced an accused heretic to answer the charge and not remain silent – a legal tool More had defended in his 1533 *Apology of Sir Thomas More*. It is speculated that Cromwell had someone in particular in mind – John Lambert, who was accused of heresy in 1531. Lambert argued that, under canon law, he could not be compelled to testify against himself, a claim Thomas More would not accept in cases of heresy. More replied that, there, he was acting in accordance with the "law of the whole corps of Christendom" as opposed to the laws of a local realm and that "the reasonableness or the unreasonableness in binding a man to precise answer standeth not in the respect or difference between heading or burning, but because of the difference in charge of conscience, the difference standeth between heading and hell" (*Selected Letters*, p. 252). The difference between beheading and burning is a reference to the different ultimate penalties available, respectively, to the State and the Church. In cases of heresy, canon law exceptionally allowed compulsion (i.e., torture) against the suspected heretic because the crime was so heinous and so difficult to prove otherwise. However, such measures were not permissible under English common law. If this is the case, it is evidence that Cromwell and his king had not entirely abandoned the principle of legality – or, at least, had not entirely thought through the implications that arose from transferring responsibility for religious matters to the State.

45 Bolt, *A Man for All Seasons*, Introduction, p. xiii. And, what is more, "a sense of selfhood without resort to magic." For an intriguing alternative analysis of More's concept of the self (or, rather, 'self-erasure'), see Stephen Greenblatt, *Renaissance Self-Fashioning: From More to Shakespeare* (1980), "At the Table of the Great: More's Self-Fashioning and Self-Cancellation."

46 Although Bolt only explicitly mentions Camus in his introduction to the play, the existentialist concept of 'authenticity' owes most of its content to Martin Heidegger's notion of "being-toward-death," that an authentic life can only be led in consciousness of its finitude – which certainly applies to Thomas More's circumstances.

47 To give a sense of it, the legal historian John H. Langbein describes the defendant's position in the early modern era this way:

> the defendant was not only locked up, denied the assistance of counsel in preparing and presenting his defense, and restricted in obtaining defense witnesses,

he was also given no precise statement of the charges against him until he stood before the court at the moment of his trial. The total drift of these measures was greatly to restrict defensive opportunity of any sort other than responding personally at trial to the incriminating evidence.

(Langbein, "The Historical Origins of the Privilege against Self-Incrimination at Common Law," 92(5) *Michigan Law Review* (March, 1994), p. 1058)

Of course, this was also Thomas More's predicament. To be fair, so was it the predicament of all defendants adjudged by Thomas More.

48 *A Man for All Seasons*, p. 97. Cromwell employs a metaphor that echoes this sentiment when he says: "now we'll apply the good, plain sailor's art/And fix these quicksands on the Law's plain chart!" (*A Man for All Seasons*, p. 94).

49 Henry II's conflict with the Archbishop of Canterbury has also been the subject of major artistic treatments such as T.S. Eliot's *Murder in the Cathedral* (1935) (adapted as a television play in 1962) and Jean Anouilh's *Becket* (1959) (filmed in 1964, constituting a sort of preparatory etude for the film version of *A Man for All Seasons*).

50 *A Man for All Seasons*, pp. 57, 64. More even chides Roper at one point in the play that he would not have lasted six months in Spain. He would have been burned during his 'heretic' period (*A Man for All Seasons*, p. 51).

51 On More's use of this maxim, see Appendix 2.

52 In the play, this issue is highlighted when More's jailer (the Common Man) is offered fifty guineas to report any of More's statements on the king's divorce, marriage, or Supremacy of the Church after he has already sworn to do so. It is the implied bribe that convinces the Jailer to experience a sudden onslaught of deafness. *A Man for All Seasons*, pp. 84–85.

53 Id., p. 100. The scene also illustrates nicely the limits of the defense in the 16th century, as described by Langbein in the quote above. There is no right to confront witnesses against you.

54 In real life, the jury did deliberate but only for a short time (15 minutes). Note the contrast with the jury in Socrates' trial, which was also to render an immediate verdict.

55 A number of different scholars have seen a 'death wish' in More's behavior. See, for example, Alistair Fox, *Thomas More: History and Providence* (1985), p. 254, and Frank and Fritzie Manuel, *Utopian Thought in the Western World* (1979), "The Passion of Thomas More," esp. pp. 138–143.

56 *A Man for All Seasons*, p. 88. Bolt here consciously evokes some lines in Bertolt Brecht's *Life of Galileo*: "Unhappy the land that breeds no heroes." To which Galileo replies: "Unhappy the land that needs a hero." Bertolt Brecht, *Galileo* (1952) (Eng. version by Charles Laughton), p. 115.

57 The same year Thomas More wrote his *Utopia* (1516), Niccoló Machiavelli was in the process of writing his *Discorsi* (*Discourses on Livy*). The two thinkers have constantly been linked and compared as polar opposites in 16th-century thought. Yet, in a letter to his friend Francesco Vettori in 1527, Machiavelli wrote, "I love my native city, more than my own soul." If he meant it, this would be quite a contrast to Robert Bolt's Thomas More. See R.W. Chambers, *Thomas More* (1935), p. 291 (comparing More as 'Utopian' and Cromwell as 'Machiavellian').

58 More assures his wife that, "when they find I'm silent they'll ask nothing better than to leave me silent; you'll see." He reassures Margaret: "There'll be no trial, they have no case." Bolt, *A Man for All Seasons*, pp. 60, 89. See the discussion of Atticus Finch in the Epilogue to this book.

59 Id., Introduction, p. xiv.

References

Anonymous. (15 July 1966). Arms and the man, A man for all seasons. *The Harvard Crimson*.
Bernard, G. W. (2005). *The King's reformation: Henry VIII and the remaking of the English church*.
Bolt, R. (1990 [1960]). *A man for all seasons*.
Brecht, B. (1952). *Galileo* (Eng. version by Charles Laughton).
Chambers, R. W. (1935). *Thomas More*.
Cummings, B. (2009). Conscience and the law in Thomas More. 23(4) *Renaissance Studies* 463.
Curtright, T. (2012). *One Thomas More*.
Delcourt, M. (1936). Recherches sur Thomas More. 3 *Bibliothèque de l'Humanisme et Renaissance* 22.
Elsky, S. (2020). *Custom, common law, and the constitution of English renaissance literature*.
Elton, G. R. (1953). *The Tudor revolution*.
Elton, G. R. (1972). *Policy and police: The enforcement of the reformation in the age of Thomas Cromwell*.
Elton, G. R. (1977). Sir Thomas More and the opposition to Henry VIII. In R. S. Sylvester & G. Marchadour (Eds.), *Essential articles for the study of Thomas More*.
Friedersdorf, C. (28 April 2011). Tarring Guantanamo defense lawyers as traitors. *Atlantic*.
Friedman, D. (2006). Torture and the common law, 2 *E.H.R.L.R* 180.
Greenblatt, S. (1980). *Renaissance self-fashioning: From More to Shakespeare*.
Gregg, S. (2007). Legal revolution: St. Thomas More, Christopher St. German, and the schism of King Henry VIII. 5 *Ave Maria Law Review* 173.
Langbein, J. (1977). *Torture and the law of proof: Europe and England in the Ancien Régime*.
Langbein, J. (March, 1994). The historical origins of the privilege against self-incrimination at common law. 92 *Michigan Law Review* 1047.
Marius, R. (1984). *Thomas More: A biography*.
Marshall, P. (2011). The last years. In G. M. Logan (Ed.), *The Cambridge companion to Thomas More*.
More, T. (1961). *Selected letters*, E. Rogers (Ed.).
More, T. (1967). *Utopia and other essential writings of Thomas More*, J. Greene & J. Dolan (Eds.).
Price, J. M. (Winter, 2019). Traces of *Utopia* in *A Man for All Seasons*. 47(1) *Literature/Film Quarterly*.
Rockett, G. W. (2012). Thomas More's quarrel with reform. 92 *Church History and Religious Culture* 201.
Rockett, W. (2008). The case against Thomas More. 34 *Sixteenth Century Journal* 4.
Roper, W. (2003 [1556]). *The life of Sir Thomas More*, G. Wegemer & S. Smith (Eds.).
Sherry, S. (2011). Wrong, out of step, and pernicious: Erie as the worst decision of all time. 39 *Pepperdine Law Review* 129.
Stapleton, T. (1928). *The Life and illustrious martyrdom of Sir Thomas More, part III of Tres Thomae* (1588), trans. by Philip Hellet.
Thorpe, V. (18 January 2015). Thomas More is the villain of Wolf Hall. But is he getting a raw deal? *The Guardian*.
Wegemer, G. (1996). *Thomas More as statesman*.
Whiteley, P. J. (Winter, 2002). Natural law and the problem of certainty: Robert Bolt's 'A Man for All Seasons'. 43(4) *Contemporary Literature* 760.

Chapter 5

The Salem Witch Trials (1692)
The Tragedy of Law in Arthur Miller's *The Crucible*

The great historian of New England Puritanism Perry Miller once wrote with exasperation about the Salem witch trials that "the intellectual history of New England up to 1720 can be written as if no such thing ever happened. It had no effect on the ecclesiastical or political situation, it does not figure in the institutional or ideological development."[1] Only much later did the witch trials become such a stain on the collective reputation of the Puritans. For someone like Perry Miller, the modern obsession with the trials is a sign of prurience, a product of sensationalism. Ironically, in the very year before Perry Miller published the second edition of his *magnum opus*, *The New England Mind*, this sensationalist view was trumpeted in Arthur Miller's play *The Crucible* (1953). With its suggestions of mass hysteria[2] and sexual repression resonant with 20th-century Freudian analysis, *The Crucible* has gripped audiences and the popular imagination ever since.

Arthur Miller (no relation to Perry) intended the play (at least, in part) to be an allegory of the Communist 'witch hunts' led by Senator Joseph McCarthy[3] and the House Un-American Activities Committee in the late 1940s and 1950s. The analogy to the Salem witch trials is (hopefully) all too clear: whether witches (or Communists in the government) actually existed is not really the issue – particularly when denouncing baseless accusations of witchcraft (or Communist sympathies) is itself deemed evidence of witchcraft (or Communist sympathies).[4] However, once the McCarthyite panic had waned, the analogy became obvious to the point of banality. So convincing do most people today find the 'allegory' that Miller's play is often criticized for being 'one-sided' and 'moralizing.' Yet, Miller did not intend *The Crucible merely* to be a political allegory. It would not stand as a work of art if it were only that.

Historians also sometimes express despair (feigned or otherwise) at the historical inaccuracies in *The Crucible*. Miller deliberately[5] fictionalized the crucial dramatic relationship in the play: he makes his hero John Proctor younger than he was in order to make plausible an affair with one of the accusers Abigail Williams (whom he makes older than she was – she was actually 11 years old in 1692).[6] But some of his other errors were inadvertent. For example, he made the slave Tituba black although she was almost certainly of Indian descent.

DOI: 10.4324/9781003302971-8

Tituba's husband, John Indian, who played a prominent role, is never mentioned. Still, Miller based his play on a conscientious (non-lawyer's) reading of the transcripts and records.[7]

One cannot help but suspect that the scoffing of historians may be, in part, an effort to mask a tacit acknowledgment that a truly satisfactory explanation of what happened in Salem in 1692 has not yet been provided.[8] Nor will one be until we can resolve two major issues. One is: what prompted the behavior of the accusing girls, what was the motivation behind it? Were they lying? Delusional? Insane? Was it a conspiracy? Adolescent hijinks that got out of hand? We shall probably never be able to answer this question in a manner that mollifies our modern sensibilities. We are simply too far removed from a mindset that accepts the existence of witchcraft as a matter of course. We demand an explanation rational to our times, not theirs. To put it in Collingwood's terms, the question we most want answered here is not a question the 17th-century New England mind (to pilfer Perry Miller's phrase) would think to ask of its legal paradigm. Therefore, any evidence we could point to would be sheer indeed – and almost certainly require speculation and an imposition of modern concepts (not that this should deter any attempt).

The other question is: what were the motivations of the judges and jurors? Were they sincere? Cynical? Deluded? Incompetent? Merely a product of their times? We do not yet have a full answer to this, but it is at least a question we can hope *may* be answered. And one component to an answer is whether or not the judges and jurors can be said to have fairly applied the law and legal reasoning as they understood it.[9]

The Crucible offers hypothetical and artistic answers to both questions. To the first question, Arthur Miller's play speculatively suggests what started and sustained the witch craze: repressed sexuality – as exhibited by the naked dance in which the girls were caught, John Proctor's frigid marriage, and Abigail William's frenzied, adolescent appetite. Nicholas Hytner, the director of the 1996 film version of the play, reflected a popular commonplace regarding the Puritans and contemporary America when he remarked that "a community that denies to its young any outlet for the expression of sexuality is asking for trouble."[10] This vision is attractive to certain contemporary sensibilities: we sophisticates all 'know' with a wink and a nod that everything is 'really' all about sex. There is a certain gratification from this acknowledgement by the play. And it has, at least, the advantage of providing *some* kind of explanation for the events in Salem.

However, *The Crucible* does not merely provide a facile psychological 'explanation' of a bizarre (to us) historical event. It also provides a deeper perspective on the role law played in the trials and how its application presented genuinely tragic choices. As such, the play is a nice companion piece to Robert Bolt's *A Man for All Seasons*, particularly since both plays were written (at least, in part) in response to the McCarthyite 'witch hunt.' Both are set in a distinct and distant historical period. Both explore what the nature of a 'hero' is. And both demonstrate the importance of settled, regular procedure that protects the rights of the accused in a courtroom setting.

The Crucible as a critique of courtroom procedure

Indeed, Miller's play usefully illustrates many of the legal weaknesses we recognize today as characteristic of the Salem witch trials – some peculiar to the time, some still with us even now. For example, it highlights the problem of lack of legal representation – as was the case with Thomas More. Anticipating a sentiment later expressed by many a police officer in an interrogation room, Judge Danforth says to John Proctor, "The pure in heart need no lawyers. Proceed as you will."[11] Almost immediately, the expert witch-hunter Reverend Hale objects, "But in all justice, sir, a claim so weighty cannot be argued by a farmer. In God's name, sir, stop here; send him home and let him come again with a lawyer" (*The Crucible*, p. 59). It is worth remembering that Miller's play was written well before the US Supreme Court cases of *Gideon v. Wainwright*, 372 U.S. 335 (1963), which established the right to legal counsel in a criminal case,[12] and *Miranda v. Arizona*, 384 U.S. 436 (1966), which held that suspects must be informed of their right to consult with legal counsel before and during police interrogation.

The play also provides examples of flaws in the way evidence is traduced in an adversarial proceeding (that is, the testimonial procedure for evincing facts). Miller has Judge Danforth explicitly opine on the unusual nature of the crime to be proven. In ordinary crimes, witnesses are called to prove the defendant's innocence:[13]

> But witchcraft is *ipso facto*, on its face and by its nature, an invisible crime. Therefore, who may possibly be witness to it? – the witch, and the victim. None other. Now we cannot hope the witch will accuse herself; granted? Therefore, we must rely upon her victims-and they do testify, the children certainly do testify.
>
> (*The Crucible*, p. 59)

As mentioned, the legal question inside the drama (as it was in the actual Salem trials) is not *whether* witchcraft exists but *who* the witch is. For spectators today, the play highlights the foolishness of the very proposition to be proved. How do we weigh evidence for and against something if the proceedings are based on an imaginary supposition?

We see this at the play's climax. John Proctor knows that Abigail Williams has falsely accused his wife Elizabeth of sorcery. The problem is how to undermine the credibility of her testimony. As Judge Danforth explains, the testimony of the victims is the royal road to the 'truth.' The judge concedes that the victim's statements may be tested; but, if spectral evidence[14] from a witness is admitted, what proof can refute it? This evidentiary problem hangs over the play as it did the actual trials. The court may also reasonably point to the confession of other witches to support the girls' claims. But, of course, the play illustrates the limitations of confessions. Relatively early in the play, John Proctor tells Reverend Hale (the 'witch expert') that Abigail Williams admitted to him that the whole affair had nothing to do with witchcraft:

HALE Nonsense! Mister, I have myself examined Tituba, Sarah Good and numerous others that have confessed to dealing with the Devil. They have confessed it.
PROCTOR (With dry, bitter humor.) And why not, if they must hang for denyin' it? There are them that will swear to anything before they'll hang; have you never thought of that?

(*The Crucible,* p. 38)

This issue of the motivation for confession has burrowed its way into the very marrow of the adversarial system – in many countries but particularly in the United States. The plea bargain has become the most frequent, ubiquitous, and criticized method for disposing of criminal cases.[15] In essence, the defendant agrees to 'confess' to a particular crime or crimes in exchange for the recommendation of a more 'lenient' sentence by the prosecution. It has become a cliché in television courtroom dramas to depict how, through the plea bargain system, 'innocent' people are sent to prison for crimes they did not commit and 'guilty' people get off with lesser punishments for crimes they did commit. We see this very dilemma acted out in excruciating detail at the end of the play when John Proctor is offered his life if he will confess.

Other traditional courtroom procedures prove equally problematic. John Proctor brings to the court his servant Mary Warren (whom he has beaten in the past, as was the norm) to attest that she and the other girls had been lying in their accusations of witchcraft. Even without the possibility that she has been coerced by Proctor, Mary's claim is open to a classic litigation ploy against a witness in this position: You have admitted you are a liar. Were you lying then or are you lying now?[16] This kind of problem is inherent in an adversarial proceeding, which we acknowledge is not necessarily a search for 'truth' but gauged to assess the evidence available.[17] One issue is how to evaluate the veracity of testimony – and, presumably, one's veracity is diminished if one admits to having lied before. But all witnesses suffer to a greater or lesser degree from flaws in their character, in their perceptions, in their attitudes. This is what the adversarial system is supposed to test, and everyone (who is honest) concedes that the adversarial system is imperfect in this. Still, many choose to believe that (like democracy) it is the 'least worst' system we have.

However, these 'ordinary' procedural imperfections are magnified if the very purpose for which the procedures are employed is delusional. Reverend Hale, for example, does not question the existence of witchcraft. For him, the issue is whether the evidence is sufficient to conclude that *these particular people* are witches. When Rebecca Nurse attempts to defend herself from the charge, Reverend Parris condemns it as an attack on the court. To which Hale replies in frustration, "Is every defense an attack upon the court?" (*The Crucible*, p. 55). Eventually, Hale is convinced that the girls are lying and quits the court in disgust (*The Crucible*, p. 71). Apparently, his belief in witchcraft is not shaken, but the cumulative effect of these 'ordinary' procedural problems is too much for him.

Yet, we today need no convincing that witchcraft does not exist. The evidence supposedly demonstrating it, we accept, is imagined, which means that the evidence needed to refute it is also elusive even if the authorities were inclined to hear it. The play demonstrates this in several ways. No Salem resident in the play questions the existence of witchcraft until they have reason to question the efficacy of the 'ordinary' procedures of proof. For example, there is this response by Elizabeth to Reverend Hale:

ELIZABETH (To Hale. Angrily.) I cannot think the Devil may own a woman's soul, Mister Hale, when she keeps an upright way, as I have. I am a good woman, I know it; and if you believe I may do only good work in the world, and yet be secretly bound to Satan, then I must tell you, sir, I do not believe it.

(*The Crucible*, p. 38)

Elizabeth even goes so far as to say that, if they think she is a witch, then there are none. What is remarkable here is not necessarily Elizabeth's blanket rejection of witchcraft because a (flawed) procedure goes against her. That would be entirely understandable on a personal level although, from an evidentiary point of view, a witness' belief in her own righteousness is not in itself probative.[18] Rather, what is remarkable is the inference the court might draw from that rejection. By questioning the existence of witchcraft, Elizabeth is suspected of rejecting the entirety of the Gospels, and such a rejection in itself (it is claimed) points to commerce with the Devil. Similarly, when John Proctor finally realizes that his effort to thwart the accusers is futile, he proclaims in a cry resonant with 20th-century intellectuals, but not 17th-century Puritans: "I say ... God is dead!" A veritable confession if the historical John Proctor had said it.

This demonstrates, however, that it would require an overthrow of the operating paradigm of the 17th-century legal system to discard witchcraft as a crime (which ultimately happened over the course of the 18th century). One is reminded of a similar problem raised by Albert Camus in *L'Etranger* (1942). In the first half of the book, the narrator Meursault describes the events leading up to his murder of an Arab. The second half describes the legal proceedings that condemn him and how the prosecutor and the defense attorney each fit the events of the first half into a particular narrative to achieve their own ends. Meursault cannot recognize himself in either narrative. A radical reading of the novel raises an interesting issue: both prosecutor and defense base their narratives on traditional premises of 'free will' and 'individual responsibility.' However, the whole point of the first half of the book is to show how little 'free will' had to do with it. What if it turns out our whole paradigm of 'free will' (on which criminal culpability in the West now relies) is mistaken? How would we assess the efforts of the lawyers in Meursault's trial? Would it be more or less like our assessment of the legal proceedings determining witchcraft?

Miller's play grapples with the implications of this insight in an interesting way. It explores the idea of 'tragedy' in a way that sheds light on the legal paradigms in which we are immersed.

The tragic vision in *The Crucible*

In his most celebrated play *Death of a Salesman* (1949), Miller famously broke with Aristotle's *Poetics* on whether a 'tragic hero' must be an 'elevated' figure[19] and declared the 'common man' to be a fit subject for tragedy. The 'common man,' he claimed, may also suffer the

> 'tragic flaw,' a failing that is not peculiar to grand or elevated characters. Nor is it necessarily a weakness. The flaw, or crack in the characters, is really nothing – and need be nothing, but his inherent unwillingness to remain passive in the face of what he conceives to be a challenge to his dignity, his image of his rightful status ... in essence the tragic hero is intent upon claiming his whole due as a personality, and if this struggle must be total and without reservation, then it automatically demonstrates the indestructible will of man to achieve his humanity.[20]

Critics have disagreed about whether Miller's plays may legitimately be classified as tragedies and, if so, what produces the 'tragic' component. Shakespeare critic Robert Heilman deemed *The Crucible* to be a 'superior melodrama' based on the assessment that Proctor was a wholly 'good man' destroyed by the forces of evil; whereas, in a tragedy, the 'hero' is 'divided,' guilt and innocence coexist. Using Heilman's own categories, Terry Otten has persuasively argued that *The Crucible* and the character of John Proctor belong in the tragic genre.[21] I agree but, as will become apparent, for different reasons than Otten. I also agree with Otten that what makes Proctor a 'tragic hero' may be usefully demonstrated by a comparison with Robert Bolt's Thomas More in *A Man for All Seasons*, which I also agree is better categorized as melodrama.

Although he abandons the 'elevated' hero, Miller retains much of a dramatic structure consistent with the so-called ontological reading[22] of Aristotle's view of Greek tragedy. However, Miller also gives us a new way of discerning the *meaning* of that structure. This ontological reading deviates from the more common 'psychological' reading of Aristotle's *Poetics* in which the *hamartia* or 'tragic flaw' of the 'hero' is some psychological defect, e.g., Oedipus' pride, Macbeth's ambition, or Hamlet's procrastination. In the ontological reading, the tragic perspective

> consists in taking council with oneself, weighing the for and against and doing the best one can to foresee the order of means and ends. On the other hand, it is to make a bet on the unknown and the incomprehensible and to take a risk on a terrain that remains impenetrable to you. It involves entering the play of supernatural forces ... where one does not know whether they are preparing success or disaster.[23]

In other words, tragedy is not the result of something the 'hero' did wrong or for which the 'hero' is to be blamed (necessarily). For example, the fate of Sophocles' Oedipus was determined long before the play begins. We watch it unfold in the drama, and we see Oedipus brought to his end through his 'virtues': his cleverness at defeating the Sphinx is to be applied to saving the people of Thebes by solving the murder of its former king. Oedipus is brought step-by-step to ruination by trying to be a good king. This is his *hamartia*, which has more to do with the idea of 'missing the mark,' as in an archer aiming for something and missing. It is also his *hubris* (in that one acts beyond what one knows), but it is not a moral failing or an inherent defect for which the character is to be condemned. In a way, Proctor is brought step-by-step to his ruination by persistent consciousness of his earlier failures. Like Oedipus, the crucial factors that determine John Proctor's fate occurred prior to the opening of the play. We watch the consequences of those events unfold during the drama. But what Miller means by the 'tragic flaw,' i.e., the "inherent unwillingness to remain passive," is illuminated better in *The Crucible* than, perhaps, any of his other plays.

John Proctor is no Thomas More

Crucial to his tragedy is what makes Miller's John Proctor a different sort of 'hero' from Bolt's Thomas More. Terry Otten has compared them quite usefully. Bolt's More himself is never in doubt about his convictions, but Miller's Proctor is in constant agony about them. "[W]hen More dies he remarks to the Headsman, 'Friend, be not afraid of your office. You send me to God.' Proctor dies with no such trust in the hereafter or God – 'I say – I say – God is dead!'"[24] Bolt's More is willing to 'risk' being a hero (albeit he says this with a certain irony). However, in the final act of *The Crucible*, Proctor is willing to do what More never was: to commit perjury to save his life. "More secures his soul by not taking the oath; in confessing, Proctor willingly offers up his 'soul,' negating any claim of transcendence."[25] Yet, he does so because he feels unworthy: "I am no *saint*. Let *Rebecca* go like a saint, for me it is a *fraud*" (*The Crucible*, p. 83).

No less than Willy Loman in *Death of a Salesman* and in contrast to Robert Bolt's rather 'elevated' Thomas More, John Proctor is an 'ordinary,' flawed man struggling to assert and maintain his dignity. As a character, Proctor oscillates between pride/integrity and guilt/shame. As his behavior toward his wife Elizabeth reveals, he is aware of his own failings and ashamed of his previous actions. Yet, he still covets his integrity, cognizant of the value of his remorse. The play does an admirable job of portraying the complexity of human emotions and incentives. Rebecca Nurse is innocent but also pious and proud enough to incite envy. Giles Corey is strong and independently-minded but also something of a naive fool — demonstrated by his petty litigiousness and concern about his wife's 'bookishness.' What Miller tried to avoid in the play was a 'black and white' melodrama of good vs. evil[26] in order to explore the moral complexities of human action (which also reflects inherent flaws in the adversarial court system). No one's character or motives are completely pure but a mixture of competing desires and goals (though the character of Abigail is admittedly less complex).[27]

Unlike Bolt's Thomas More, John Proctor displays no 'heroic' behavior (in the vernacular sense) until, perhaps, the climax of the drama. He scoffs at the witchcraft accusations but takes no direct action until he is compelled do so to save his wife, accused by Abigail. Proctor approaches the conventionally 'heroic' only after he is told that Elizabeth claims to be pregnant, thus postponing any possible death penalty for a year. Asked then whether he would continue his efforts 'against' the court, he hesitates but decides to persist on behalf of his friends. It is this attempt to do 'good,' to act for his neighbors, that leads to Proctor's downfall. He retains a certain ideal of a community and a certain illusion about his life and marriage, and the two intersect to produce disaster.

After failing with various other tactics, John Proctor is forced to confess himself a fornicator in order to undermine Abigail's credibility as a victim/witness. The gambit is that what he is saying must be true; otherwise, why would a man destroy his reputation?[28] The court, it must be admitted, is not wrong to test the claim, and Proctor asserts that his wife Elizabeth will confirm it: "In her *life,* sir, she have *never lied*. There are them that cannot sing, and them that cannot weep — my wife cannot lie" (*The Crucible*, p. 66). This is the formal climax of the tragedy. When called upon to testify, Elizabeth does indeed lie to protect her husband's name — an act of love and an understandable falsehood, as Reverend Hale immediately points out. Nevertheless, it punctures John's testimony.[29] It is John's lack of cynicism in this one instance that undermines him. He believes in and relies on his wife's integrity and honesty and is betrayed by the very nobility of her intentions, but he is also betrayed by the idea that his wife would never compromise herself for *him*, who (in his own view) proved so unworthy of her love. Nothing could better illustrate how the complexities of human perception combine to affect courtroom proceedings.

The final act of the play demonstrates the tragically 'ordinary' complexity of human interaction by juxtaposing a variety of reactions to the way the witchcraft trials developed over the course of the drama. When the number of confessed 'witches' exceeds a hundred, Judge Danforth is undeterred in his pursuit of them. He is opposed by two former supporters. Reverend Parris is afraid for his own safety if a new round of executions is carried out, which will include 'respectable' people such as Rebecca Nurse and John Proctor. Parris already knows that his niece Abigail has fled the town, casting serious doubt on her testimony, and he fears the wrath of the citizens when they realize this. Reverend Hale, on the other hand, has determined to undermine the proceedings in another way: he encourages the accused to lie their way out of the gallows. As he says to Elizabeth Proctor: "Life, woman, life is God's most precious gift; no principle however glorious may justify the taking of it.... Quail not before God's judgment in this, for it may well be God damns a liar less than he that throws his life away for pride" (*The Crucible*, p. 79). The sentiments Hale expresses here are quite familiar to modern-day secularists, based as they are on the principles of life as the *summum bonum* and the appropriateness of choosing the lesser evil. Yet, Hale also confesses more selfish reasons: to mitigate the blood on his own hands from his previous support of the trials. The complexity of motives here is noteworthy and resonates with the complexity of Proctor's own thoughts and feelings about what he should do.

John Proctor, too, values his life simply as life. He is willing to perjure himself to save it in full acknowledgement that such a confession would be evil – evil in the eyes of God and evil for the mockery it makes of society and the legal system. He also feels unworthy to die for a principle. He cannot tolerate the fraud if his death were to be considered a 'saintly' one because he knows himself to be a sinner. A fraud upon whom would be an interesting question to ask here: his friends, his wife, his fellow prisoners, himself? He is not a saint like Rebecca Nurse, but he seems to assume that those hanged will be justified later (as we spectators of Miller's play know happened historically).[30] The most powerful contending emotion in John's breast is how his confession might be used to persuade others to lie to spare their lives, a temptation to which he would not willingly subject them.

Yet, there are other, more profane concerns. At one point, Proctor expresses resentment at being *used* in this way, in a manner beneath his dignity as though he were a Tituba or Sarah Goodman.[31] This is where Miller shows how fundamental the struggle for dignity is in his tragic theory. Proctor is cajoled into signing a confession but refuses to hand it over to be made public. He insists that it is enough that God and the court have seen it. He will not have his name besmirched by his own hand. The stage directions state that even Proctor understands this is a 'childish' distinction. One can understand Judge Danforth's suspicion that Proctor is prevaricating and means to deny his confession later – against which he only has Proctor's word that he will not.

Yet, we as spectators can see that Proctor is struggling to preserve some wisp of dignity without which he will not be able to live with himself. In explanation, he cries in anguish:

> Because it is my *name*! Because I cannot have another in my life! Because I *lie* and sign myself to lies! Because I am not worth the dust on the feet of them that hang! How may I live without my name? I have given you my soul, leave me my name!
>
> (*The Crucible*, p. 86)

Miller has reproduced the moment of truth in every rebellion, slave revolt, or overthrow of oppression in drama: I will take this much but no more.[32] Proctor's death approaches from the opposite direction the issue of existential 'authenticity' raised in Bolt's *A Man for All Seasons*. Bolt's Thomas More was a 'hero of selfhood,' and his death resulted from his fidelity to his own high principles. If Miller's John Proctor is a 'tragic hero,' it is not from his adherence to principles but from his recognition that his own flaws and sins render him incapable of heroism.

But there is a rock-bottom floor of dignity below which he will not sink. Miller described the 'flaw' of his 'tragic hero' as the "inherent unwillingness to remain passive in the face of what he conceives to be a challenge to his dignity." How is this a 'flaw'? It is a flaw in the sense of *hamartia* if dignity *must* result in downfall. Despite everything in his life that conspires against the heroic, Proctor makes one final life-affirming gesture, which ensures that he will die. It is both an illustration of the ontological view of tragedy and a manifestation of what Søren Kierkegaard and Albert Camus called the Absurd, the need to seek meaning in life and the universe's apparent refusal to provide any.

The circumstances of Proctor's death may be helpfully compared to the death of Giles Corey. As in real life (though at a different time), Corey was pressed to death by stones[33] to force him to plead to the charges against him. Under the law at that time, defendants who did not plead could not be tried. It is speculated that he refused in order to prevent forfeiture of his property to the state and, thus, preserve it for his children.[34] As legend has it and Miller describes it, Corey died defiantly, asking for "more weight" (*The Crucible*, p. 81). Stephen Marino has written a fine essay on the imagery of 'weight' in *The Crucible*, starting with Reverend Parris' mention of the "weight of truth"[35] at the beginning of the play. However, he did not emphasize sufficiently (it seems to me) the crucial aspect of the metaphor: The weight is crushing. Accepting the weight is, in effect, accepting death or, perhaps, accepting the futility of the gesture. But, Miller indicates, the gesture is what gives *meaning* to the tragic. This may be what Elizabeth means when she says as John Proctor is led to his execution, "He have his goodness now. God forbid I take it from him" (*The Crucible*, p. 87). It is a Nietzschean view of meaning like the view of tragedy expressed by Camus' myth of Sisyphus. Sisyphus forever rolls the rock up the hill, only to have it roll down again, but once he says 'yes' to this: "One must imagine Sisyphus happy!"[36]

Notes

1. Perry Miller, *The New England Mind: From Colony to Province* (vol. 2) (1954 [1939]), p. 191.
2. The term is used advisedly, since it derives from a now debunked theory of a specifically 'female' mental disorder. But see Sigmund Freud, *Group Psychology and the Analysis of the Ego* (1960 [1921]).
3. McCarthy's ethically questionable tactics ultimately led to his censure by the US Senate.
4. Miller himself wrote cogently and insightfully about it:

    > In any play, however trivial, there has to be a still point of moral reference against which to gauge the action. In our lives, in the late nineteen-forties and early nineteen-fifties, no such point existed anymore. The left could not look straight at the Soviet Union's abrogations of human rights. The anti-Communist liberals could not acknowledge the violations of those rights by congressional committees. The far right, meanwhile, was licking up all the cream. The days of "*J'accuse*" were gone, for anyone needs to feel right to declare someone else wrong. Gradually, all the old political and moral reality had melted like a Dali watch. Nobody but a fanatic, it seemed, could really say all that he believed.
    > (Arthur Miller, "Why I Wrote 'The Crucible': An artist's answer to politics," *The New Yorker* (14 October 1996))

    Relating *The Crucible* more directly to his own personal experience, Miller stated:

    > What they were demanding of Proctor was that he expose this conspiracy of witches whose aim was to bring down the rule of the Church, of Christianity. If he gave them a couple of names he could go home. And if he didn't he was going to hang for it. It was quite the same excepting we weren't hanged, but the ritual was exactly the same. You told them anyone you knew had been a left-winger or a Communist and you went home. But I wasn't going to do that.
    > (Christopher Bigsby (ed.), *Arthur Miller and Company* (1990), p. 81)

    A few years after he wrote *The Crucible*, Miller himself was called before HUAC and refused "to name names" for which he was convicted of contempt of Congress. His conviction was later overturned by the US Court of Appeals, *Arthur Miller v. United States of America*, 259 F.2d 187 (D.C. Cir. 1958).
5. Miller prefaced his play with a "Note on Historical Accuracy" to prevent exactly what has, in effect, happened with *The Crucible* – that it has replaced our view of what actually happened. On historical inaccuracies, see, for example, Christopher Bigsby, *Arthur Miller: A Critical Study* (2005), pp. 147–148 and Robert A. Martin, "Arthur Miller's *The Crucible*: Background and Sources," in Dorothy Parker (ed.), *Essays in Modern American Drama* (1987), pp. 80–93.
6. For a more thorough examination of the differences between the historical John Proctor and *The Crucible*'s depiction, see William J. McGill, Jr., "The Crucible of History: Arthur Miller's John Proctor," 54(2) *The New England Quarterly* (June 1981), pp. 258–264.

7 Most of the official records of the trials themselves were lost. However, we still retain many of the court records and transcripts of many of the preliminary examinations. Thus, any reconstruction of what happened in the trials must be tentative; we cannot assume, after all, that the testimony before the grand jury was the same as that before the petty jury, but it is the best guess we have. Documents labelled as '*jurat in curia*' [sworn in court] are obviously an exception to this. The historian Edmund Morgan noted the confusion in relation to Arthur Miller's play:

> What Miller has done in *The Crucible* is to conflate the preliminary hearings, of which many records survive, with the actual trials, of which few records survive. Danforth could not actually have signed the seventy-two death warrants that Miller has him say he has done in the play. Nor could the Reverend Hale have signed the seventeen he says he did in the film. And though Parris and other ministers did give and take testimony at the hearings, they could not have participated in giving verdicts or pronouncing sentences.
>
> (Edmund Morgan, "Bewitched," *New York Review of Books* (9 January 1997))

Apparently, at some later date, a number of records, journals, diaries, etc. were systematically purged of references to the Salem trials. Presumably, this was due to embarrassment about the event.

8 There seems to have been a multitude of causes, all of which came together like a perfect storm to blow the trials in the direction they went. We are left like the proverbial blind men and the elephant to sort through the possibilities. The various explanations that have been given are too numerous to recount here, but there are some major theories worth paying attention to:

1. That the true cause was a clash of factions within Puritan society itself. In 1867, Charles Upham created a detailed map of the Salem area at the time and noticed that the accusers came from one part of town and the accused from another. Updating Upham, Paul Boyer and Stephen Nissenbaum proffered a very influential theory of economic factionalism in *Salem Possessed: The Social Origins of Witchcraft* (1974) that the conflict arose from rivalries between older farming families in Salem Village (where most of the accusers lived) and emerging, 'capitalist' merchant families who lived in Salem Town (where a harbor and most of the accused were located).

2. That the trials were an expression of patriarchal dominance and/or misogyny. Carol Karlsen's *The Devil in the Shape of a Woman* (1986) provides a patriarchal theory of the trials. Although the role gender plays in this affair is undeniable, it is difficult to pin down exactly what it is and how it affected events. Karlsen noted that the women most likely to be accused of witchcraft were women who were 'out of place': poor or homeless women, women who were childless, or women whose control of property went beyond the usual expectation.

3. That the frenzy had its roots in fear and trauma from the ongoing Indian wars and political frustration with the inability to stop them. In *In the Devil's Snare* (2002), Mary Beth Norton noticed that many of the key players in the witchcraft trials were individuals who had experienced trauma in the frontier Indian wars (King Philip's War, 1675–1678, and King William's War, 1688–1697). Norton created a masterly narrative, linking the almost PTSD-like symptoms of some of the accusers with the general fear of Indian atrocities (and, of course, the Puritans connected the 'dark' pagan Indians and their Catholic French allies with the Devil). Since the wars were going poorly for the Puritans, the witch trials also provided a convenient way for officials to demonstrate that they were doing *something* to combat Satan, according to Norton.

4. That the trials reflected a breakdown in legal institutions. "The Salem Village witchcraft phenomenon is a classic example of what happens when formal law fails, for various reasons, to help resolve disputes, and the burden falls on customary norms. Such norms had, for a generation, sufficed to regulate behavior in the Massachusetts Bay colony, but in the 1660s the capacity of the Congregational churches to resolve disputes failed; there were too many residents who were either not Puritans or not willing to submit to church discipline. We cannot fully understand what happened in Salem Village without appreciating the breakdown in the effectiveness of the law." Kermit Hall, *The Magic Mirror: Law in American History* (1989), pp. 35–36. This view embraces another take on the external pressures (recounted in Norton's narrative) and internecine conflicts (that Upham noticed), which were able to ignite into a larger conflagration due to the lack of institutional political and religious authority to quell them.

See generally John Demos, *The Enemy Within: A Short History of Witch-Hunting* (2008) (chap. 8). There are a number of good narratives and analyses of the Salem witch trials. Recommended in addition to those already mentioned are Stacy Schiff, *The Witches: Salem, 1692* (2015), John Demos, *Entertaining Satan: Witchcraft and the Culture of Early New England* (1982), and Peter Charles Hoffer, *The Salem Witchcraft Trials: A Legal History* (1997).

9 The later reaction of various Salem judges tells us only a little. Chief Justice William Stoughton was adamant in his support of the trials, never wavering throughout his life. Others initially supported them and later came to regret it. Both reactions mirrored the general public view. Reverend John Hale, the knowledgeable clergyman who initiated the witchcraft examinations, wrote a treatise entitled *A Modest Inquiry into the Nature of Witchcraft*, admitting mistakes in the Salem proceedings. Prominent citizens Cotton Mather and his father, Increase Mather, continued to support the trials (if somewhat less enthusiastically). But it should be noted that the Mathers were one of the most educated families in the English-speaking world, well-versed in the science of the day. Cotton Mather exemplifies how someone could hold both very religious and very scientific views at one and the same time. For example, in 1721, when it was objected that inoculations against small pox were blasphemous challenges to God's will, Mather defended the practice as being consistent with faith. All we know is that the Salem witch trials were one of the last instances of the so-called 'witch craze' that plagued Europe from the beginning of modernity (roughly, the 15th century) until the Enlightenment. The later reactions to the Salem trials may simply be evidence that the mind-set (or paradigm or episteme or whatever notion you wish to apply here) that accepted witchcraft as an acceptable explanation was in the process of disintegration. What we lack here as historians is a causal explanation of the change (if indeed such a change took place in the 18th century).

10 Nicholas Hytner, introduction to the Penguin edition of the screenplay, quoted in Edmund Morgan, "Bewitched," *New York Review of Books* (9 January 1997). The opinion most people today have of the Puritans (if any) has most likely been filtered through Nathaniel Hawthorne's *The Scarlet Letter* (1850) to be congealed in Arthur Miller's *The Crucible*. Despite the separation of a hundred years, these two authors present compatible views of the Puritans as prurient hypocrites. By the time Miller was writing, the stereotypical Puritan was thought to be someone horrified at the idea of sex, which was the physical manifestation of the 'original sin' that Christian doctrine says condemned mankind to depravity. The adjective itself became a synonym for a 'prude' and a 'killjoy.' On this, see Rochelle Gurstein, "'Puritanism' as Epithet: Common Standards and the Fate of Reticence," 101/102 *Salmagundi* (Winter-Spring, 1994), pp. 95–116. It took three centuries and many historical and

fictional iterations to create this caricature of Puritanism. The actual Puritans were not dour and joyless. Nor did they have an especially unhealthy attitude toward sex. See Edmund Morgan, "The Puritans and Sex," 15(4) *New England Quarterly* (1942), pp. 591–607.
11 *The Crucible*, p. 55. I base my analysis of the play on the Dramatists Play Service Inc.'s version of Arthur Miller, *The Crucible* (1980 [1952]). Miller revised the play later, including for the 1996 film version, but the revisions do not undermine any analysis here.
12 Building on *Powell v. Alabama*, 287 U.S. 45 (1932) (right to adequate legal counsel in death penalty cases), discussed in the Epilogue.
13 Worth pointing out here is the concern for the burden of proof and the presumption of innocence, which was not yet established as a fixed principle. The Puritan leader Increase Mather proclaimed in connection with the Salem trials: "It were better that Ten Suspected Witches should escape, than that one Innocent Person should be Condemned." *Cases of Conscience Concerning Evil Spirits Personating Men, Witchcrafts, infallible Proofs of Guilt in such as are accused with that Crime* (1692), p. 66. It is said that William Blackstone adapted this statement for his preeminent *Commentaries on the Law of England* (1765–1769) (Book IV, Chap. 27) as "[i]t is better that ten guilty persons escape than that one innocent suffer," now known as 'Blackstone's ratio.'
14 Spectral evidence was based on the belief that, if someone made a covenant with the Devil, the Devil could appear elsewhere in the form of that person. Most of the purported Salem victims testified that they had been tormented by specters in the form of someone they accused. If one accepted this piece of folk wisdom, then it would be evidence that the accused was in league with Satan. Yet, it was disputed among the learned whether the Devil could take the shape of persons with whom he had not covenanted. In his 1627 treatise on detecting witchcraft, *A Guide to Grand Jury-Men*, Richard Bernard wrote that the Devil could assume the appearance of "a common ordinary person, man or woman vnregenerate [sic] (though no Witch)" (*Guide to Grand-Jury Men*, Chap. XVII(v)). Thus, spectral evidence was not supposed to be definitive proof in itself although, by inference, the Devil could not appear in the form of a regenerate, innocent person. See Norton, *In the Devil's Snare*, p. 33. In a letter to John Foster dated 17 August 1692, Cotton Mather stated: "I do still think that when there is no further evidence against a person but only this, that a specter in their shape does afflict a neighbor, that evidence is not enough to convict them of witchcraft" (*Salem Witch Trials Documentary Archive*). Wendel Craker has argued that no defendants at Salem were convicted on spectral evidence alone ("Spectral Evidence, Non-Spectral Acts of Witchcraft, and Confession at Salem in 1692," 40 *Hist. J.* 331 (1997)). Nevertheless, when the General Court set up the new court system in the fall, Governor Phips (whose own wife had been accused) ordered that the Superior Court could no longer entertain spectral evidence, and no convictions were then forthcoming. See John Murrin, "Coming to Terms with the Salem Witch Trials," 110 *Proceedings of the American Antiquarian Society* 309 (2003), p. 343. This provides a useful illustration of what counts as evidence and how it counts within different legal paradigms.
15 The plea bargain system has been widely written about. For a critical perspective, see Carissa Byrne Hessick, *Punishment Without Trial: Why Plea Bargaining Is a Bad Deal* (2021); Donald A. Dripps, "Guilt, Innocence, and Due Process of Plea Bargaining," 57(4) *William & Mary Law Review* (2015–2016); William Stuntz, *The Collapse of American Criminal Justice* (2011); John H. Langbein, "Torture and Plea Bargaining," 46(1) *The University of Chicago Law Review* (Autumn, 1978). See also *Missouri v. Galin E. Frye*, 566 U.S. 134 (2012) (on attorney duties with respect to plea bargaining).

16 The play reproduces the transcript of countless lawsuits in which the credibility of a 'flawed' witness is attacked:

> DANFORTH. ... Do you not know that God damns all liars? Or is it now that you lie?
> MARY. No, sir – I am with God now.
> DANFORTH. You are with God now.
> MARY. Aye, sir.
> DANFORTH. I will tell you this – you are either lying now, or you were lying in the court, and in either case you have committed perjury and you will go to jail for it. You cannot lightly say you lied, Mary. Do you know that?
>
> (*The Crucible*, p. 60)

Interestingly, Miller says that he deviated from the historical record in this scene in order to make Judge Danforth more open-minded to contrary evidence than was apparent at the historical trial (Arthur Miller, "Introduction to *Collected Plays*," *The Collected Essays of Arthur Miller* (2017), p. 133).

17 For an interesting assessment of witness testimony in the context of the McCarthy hearings, see Herbert L Packer, *Ex-Communist Witnesses: Four Studies in Fact Finding* (1962).

18 Witness the exchange in the play between Martha Corey and Judge Hathorne:

> MARTHA. I am innocent to a witch. I know not what a witch is.
> HATHORNE. How do you know then that you are not a witch?
>
> (*The Crucible*, p. 49)

19 As the conventional view of Aristotle's *Poetics* has it, this is because the 'hero' may not be 'blameless' and must 'fall' from a 'height' if the play is to evoke the appropriate emotions of fear and/or pity in the audience (Aristotle, *Poetics*, 1452b30–1453a30). The reading of Aristotle's *Poetics* that emphasizes this has been widespread for centuries, but it is increasingly under question that Aristotle's views were as straightforward or as accurate a depiction of ancient tragedy as they have been made out to be. For example, see Page duBois, "Toppling the Hero: Polyphony in the Tragic City," 35(1) *New Literary History*, Rethinking Tragedy (Winter, 2004), pp. 63–81; Jean-Pierre Vernant and Pierre Vidal-Naquet, *Myth and Tragedy in Ancient Greece* (1988).

20 Arthur Miller, "Tragedy and the Common Man," *New York Times* (27 February 1949).

21 Terry Otten, *The Temptation of Innocence in the Plays of Arthur Miller* (2002), pp. 66–67.

22 The late Heidegger scholar Hubert Dreyfus dubbed this 'ontological tragedy' in his lectures at UC Berkeley on Aeschylus.

23 Jean-Pierre Vernant and Pierre Vidal-Naquet, *Tragedy and Myth in Ancient Greece* (1986 [1975]), p. 45, cited in Bernard Williams, *Shame and Necessity* (1993), p. 19. I agree with Williams that a better understanding of the tragic is achieved if one deletes the word 'supernatural.' Vernant and Vidal-Naquet view tragedy as the intersection of *ethos* and *daimon* (invoking Heraclitus' statement '*ethos anthropoi daimon*') with all the ambiguities those terms imply regarding human character and the non-human world. I cannot resist adding that the translation of Heraclitus' statement as 'a man's character is his destiny' may be the most misleading and unnuanced interpretation possible.

24 Terry Otten, *The Temptation of Innocence in the Plays of Arthur Miller* (2002), p. 75 (citations omitted).

25 Otten, p. 74. See also Terry Otten, "Historical Drama and the Dimensions of Tragedy: *A Man for All Seasons* and *The Crucible*," 6(1) *American Drama* (1996).

26 Ironically, in his later reflections on the play, Miller said that, if he had it to do again, he would not mitigate the evil in some of the characters as much as he did (Miller, "Introduction" to *Collected Plays*, pp. 133–34).
27 In a revision of the play, later discarded, Miller added a scene that muddies Abigail's character and may be read as confirming that she is genuinely mad.
28 Compare this to Thomas More swearing an oath that Richard Rich is lying in *A Man for All Seasons* – its credibility strengthened because his reluctance to take an oath is what brought him to trial in the first place.
29 If President Bill Clinton lied about sexual relations with Monica Lewinsky (as he almost certainly did, leading to his impeachment), many of his supporters argued that it was a 'natural' lie to tell about something that was no one else's business. One is also reminded of the 1995 murder trial of O.J. Simpson when, on the witness stand, Mark Fuhrman, the police officer in charge of the initial investigation, invoked his Fifth Amendment right against self-incrimination as to possible misconduct he engaged in (e.g., that he 'framed a guilty man'). Simpson's defense attorneys had the presence of mind to ask him whether he had falsified any police reports or planted evidence in his investigation of Simpson to which he responded by invoking his Fifth Amendment privilege not to answer. This punctured the truth of any other evidence to which Fuhrman may have testified and may have been sufficient for some jurors to find 'reasonable doubt' as to whether Simpson committed the murders.
30 The 1996 film version (but not the play) ends with the condemned (about to be hanged) reciting in unison the Lord's Prayer, which those in thrall to the Devil supposedly could not utter correctly. The scene echoes history. Just before Salem's former minister George Burroughs was executed for witchcraft, he recited the prayer perfectly, causing such unrest among the onlookers that Cotton Mather himself had to calm them down (Hoffer, p. 118; Schiff, p. 300).
31 *The Crucible*, p. 85.
32 Vividly illustrated, for example, in Edgar Allan Poe's tale of revenge, "Hop-Frog" (1849).
33 A procedure known as *peine forte et dure*. Giles Corey was the only victim of that particular form of torture in US history (Leonard Levy, *Origins of the Fifth Amendment* (1986), p. 362).
34 Hoffer, *The Salem Witchcraft Trials*, p. 126.
35 Stephen Marino, "Arthur Miller's 'Weight of Truth' in *The Crucible*," 38(4) *Modern Drama* (Winter, 1995), p. 489. Note that Marino uses a different version of the play than cited here.
36 Albert Camus, *The Myth of Sisyphus and Other Essays* (1955 [1942]), p. 91, echoing Nietzsche's 'yes' to the idea of eternal recurrence at the end of *Die Fröhliche Wissenschaft* [341] in Friedrich Nietzsche, *Werke* II (1981 [1882]), pp. 202–203.

References

Bernard, R. (1621). *A guide to grand jury-Men*.
Bigsby, C. (Ed.) (1990). *Arthur Miller and company*.
Bigsby, C. (2005). *Arthur Miller: A critical study*.
Blackstone, W. (1765–1769). Commentaries on the law of England.
Boyer, P., & Nissenbaum, S. (1974). *Salem possessed: The social origins of witchcraft*.
Camus, A. (1955 [1942]). *The myth of Sisyphus and other essays*.

Craker, W. (1997). Spectral evidence, non-spectral acts of witchcraft, and confession at Salem in 1692. 40(2) *Historical Journal* 331.
Demos, J. (1982). *Entertaining Satan: Witchcraft and the culture of early New England.*
Demos, J. (2008). *The enemy within: A short history of witch-hunting.*
Dripps, D. A. (2015–2016). Guilt, innocence, and due process of plea bargaining. 57(4) *William and Mary Law Review* 1343.
duBois, P. Toppling the hero: Polyphony in the tragic city. 35(1) *New Literary History*, Rethinking Tragedy (Winter, 2004).
Gurstein, R. (Winter–Spring, 1994). 'Puritanism' as epithet: Common standards and the fate of reticence. *101/102 Salmagundi* 95.
Hall, K. (1989). *The magic mirror: Law in American history.*
Hessick, C. B. (2021). *Punishment without trial: Why plea bargaining is a bad deal.*
Hoffer, P. C. (1997). *The Salem witchcraft trials: A legal history.*
Karlsen, C. (1986). *The devil in the shape of a woman.*
Langbein, J. H. (Autumn, 1978). Torture and plea bargaining. 46(1) *University of Chicago Law Review* 3.
Levy, L. (1986). *Origins of the fifth amendment.*
Marino, S. (Winter, 1995). Arthur Miller's 'weight of truth' in *The Crucible*. 38(4) *Modern Drama* 488.
Martin, R. A. (1987). Arthur Miller's *The Crucible*: Background and sources. In D. Parker (Ed.), *Essays in modern American drama.*
Mather. Increase. *Cases of Conscience Concerning Evil Spirits Personating Men, Witchcrafts, infallible Proofs of Guilt in such as are accused with that Crime* (1692).
McGill, Jr., W. J. (June, 1981). The crucible of history: Arthur Miller's John Proctor. 54(2) *New England Quarterly* 258.
Miller, A. (27 February 1949). Tragedy and the common man. *New York Times.*
Miller, A. (14 October 1996). Why I wrote 'The Crucible': An artist's answer to politics. *New Yorker.*
Miller, A. (2017). Introduction to *Collected Plays*. In *Collected Essays of Arthur Miller.*
Miller, A. (1980 [1952]). The crucible. *(Dramatists Play Service Inc.).*
Miller, P. (1954 [1939]). *New England Mind: from Colony to Province, 2.*
Morgan, E. (1942). The puritans and sex. 15(4) *New England Quarterly* 591.
Morgan, E. (9 January 1997). Bewitched. *New York Review of Books.*
Murrin, J. (2003). Coming to terms with the Salem witch trials. 110 *Proceedings of the American Antiquarian Society* 309.
Norton, M. B. (2002). *In the devil's snare.*
Otten, T. (1996). Historical drama and the dimensions of tragedy: *A Man for All Seasons* and *The Crucible*. 6(1) *American Drama* 42.
Otten, T. (2002). *The temptation of innocence in the plays of Arthur Miller.*
Packer, H. L. (1962). *Ex-communist witnesses: Four studies in fact finding.*
Salem Witch trials documentary archive. Retrieved from https://salem.lib.virginia.edu/home.html.
Schiff, S. (2015). *Witches: Salem, 1692.*
Stuntz, W. (2011). *The collapse of American criminal justice.*
Vernant, J.-P., & Vidal-Naquet, P. (1988). *Myth and tragedy in ancient Greece.*

Chapter 6

The Great Monkey Trial (1925)
Historical 'Memory' and the 'Politics of Eternity'

In 2002, Congressman Mike Pence (later, the Vice President of the United States) gave a speech on the floor of the US House of Representatives in which he shared with the American people his most cherished beliefs, one of which was that Charles Darwin's theory of evolution was not merely wrong, it exercised a pernicious influence on American morals and values. Pence explained, "In 1925, in the famous Scopes Monkey Trial, this theory made its way through litigation into the classrooms of America, and we have seen the consequences over the last 77 years."[1] It takes an extremely charitable reading to conclude that this statement is not outright mendacious. Nevertheless, it indicates the importance the case of *Tennessee* v. *Scopes* (1925)[2] has in the imagination of many.

History and memory

Over the past 30 years or so, historians and other scholars have worked with a distinction between 'history' and 'memory.' 'Memory' studies focus on the social or collective consciousness of historical events, which is often quite different from the analysis of actual historians.[3] In many ways, the term is as gossamer as what some historians used to call *mentalité*[4] or *Zeitgeist*.[5] Nevertheless, it is a useful term, which allows us to differentiate between the rigorous analysis in which historians actually engage and the sort of historical consciousness that loosely binds a society or group together with a collectively 'agreed-upon' story. These stories may be as dangerous as they are satisfying, but we must acknowledge the phenomenon. The respected Civil War historian David Blight put it this way:

> If history is shared and secular, memory is often treated as a sacred set of absolute meanings and stories, possessed as the heritage or identity of a community. Memory is often owned, history interpreted. Memory is passed down through generations; history is revised. Memory often coalesces in objects, sites, and monuments; history seeks to understand contexts in all their complexity.[6]

DOI: 10.4324/9781003302971-9

Moreover, the historical 'memory' we carry around in our heads is almost always embedded in a larger historical narrative with unspoken parameters and suppositions.

The historian Timothy Snyder has helpfully reconceived and explained two paradigmatic narratives to which Westerners today tend to resort (usually subconsciously) when they think and talk about 'memory': what Snyder calls the 'politics of inevitability' and 'the politics of eternity.' The 'politics of inevitability' includes the view that history 'progresses' – not necessarily in a straight line but ineluctably – toward some (hopefully) good goal. There are different versions of this, as mentioned in Chapter 2, including 'Whig' history and the so-called 'end of history' thesis (once propounded, for example, by Francis Fukuyama).[7] This general view of history is reflected in a motto often attributed to Martin Luther King, Jr.: "Let us realize the arc of the moral universe is long, but it bends toward justice." Thus, there are 'heroes' and 'villains' of history, depending on whether they hasten or hinder its 'march.'[8]

The 'politics of eternity' arises as a view of history when, for some reason, the 'politics of inevitability' collapses as an explanatory paradigm for people. What replaces it is a "cyclical story of victimhood. Time is no longer a line into the future, but a circle that endlessly returns the same threats from the past."[9] Those who work within the 'politics of eternity' tend to see themselves as 'victims' of some unfair encroachment by 'outsiders' or 'potential victims' of some 'outsider' threatening what they possess.[10] In Snyder's conception, the 'politics of eternity' abandons 'factuality' and concentrates on 'eternal moments,' portraying them as "moments of righteousness, discarding the time in between."[11] The historical 'process' does not matter, since the outside threat is perpetual. The focus is on symbolic moments that inspire resistance to a foe. For example, Benito Mussolini evoked the glory of the Roman Empire to inspire his Blackshirts as though the intervening millennia were irrelevant.[12] 'Eternal moments' may even be defeats. Many Serbs still see the Battle of Kosovo (Blackbird Field) in 1389 as defining their national character.

My argument in this chapter is that the play *Inherit the Wind* by Jerome Lawrence and Robert E. Lee and especially Stanley Kramer's 1960 film version of the play have usurped the cultural 'memory' of the Scopes trial in ways we may not realize without reflection – as indicated in Mike Pence's 2002 speech. Moreover, contemporary interpretations of *Inherit the Wind* (and, with it, the Scopes trial itself) are now almost entirely encased within one of these paradigms: the 'politics of inevitability' or the 'politics of eternity.' How does this work, and why does it matter? First, we need to examine what actually happened in that trial.

The stakes of the Scopes trial

Certainly, the Scopes 'monkey trial' lacked no component of spectacle. The case received widespread publicity and was followed intently all over the

United States – not only in the printed press but as the first courtroom trial ever to be broadcast via radio. The issue at stake – or so it was framed by the mass media – was nothing less than the truth of science versus the truth of revealed religion.[13] The very future of mankind (if the hype were to be believed) would be determined once and for all by a small-town judge in the backwater of Dayton, Tennessee, the issue to be argued by two titans of the American political stage whose names would forever be linked to that trial.

William Jennings Bryan, one of the most prominent political figures of his day, stood for the side of religion. Three times the (losing) candidate of the Democratic Party for president of the United States,[14] Bryan had a reputation as a brilliant speaker. His 1896 "cross of gold" speech[15] is counted among the greatest pieces of oratory in American history. Bryan, known popularly as 'the Great Commoner,' was an indefatigable friend of labor, an anti-imperialist, a proponent of both women's suffrage and the prohibition of alcohol, and a devout Christian with 'fundamentalist' leanings.[16]

On the side of science was Clarence Darrow, one of the most famous and effective lawyers of the twentieth century. Darrow was known as an agnostic in religion and a populist/progressive in politics. By the time of the Scopes trial, Darrow had represented defendants in some of the most notorious cases in US history. For example, in 1924, just before the Scopes trial, Darrow had represented the defendants in the infamous Loeb and Leopold case. Influenced by the writings of Friedrich Nietzsche, these two teenage boys had murdered 14-year-old Bobby Franks simply for the thrill of it. Through sheer tactical and oratorical brilliance, Darrow saved Richard Loeb and Nathan Leopold from the death penalty.[17] Although Darrow and Bryan had once been allies in the cause of labor, they were personal and ideological enemies by 1925.

The storm in the Scopes trial swirled around brief passages in George W. Hunter's 1914 high school textbook *A Civic Biology*[18] (approved and required by the State of Tennessee). One passage mentioned the evolution of *homo sapiens* from "races of men who were much lower in their mental organization" and "littler better than one of the lower animals" (*A Civic Biology* (1914), pp. 195–196). It also mentioned the so-called five races or varieties of man, each different "in instincts, social customs, and, to an extent, in structure" (Caucasians being the "highest sort"), and the 'science' of eugenics, which would help eliminate the "parasitism" on society of people born with genetic diseases or representatives of "a low and degenerate race."[19] Needless to say, the textbook linked the theory of evolution to a number of doctrines most people find repellent today. Indeed, opponents of evolution – including William Jennings Bryan – blamed Charles Darwin for the rise of the eugenics movement in Europe and the United States (many doctrines of which the Nazis would later implement in Germany after 1933).[20]

Bryan linked the rise of what is now called 'Social Darwinism'[21] not only with state policies of forced sterilization[22] but with rampant, predatory capitalism that kept the working man down – the notion (accepted explicitly by a number of prominent American industrialists such as Andrew Carnegie and John D. Rockefeller) that those who rise in the capitalist system deserve their position in society because they proved themselves the 'fittest for survival.' Thus, for Bryan, not only did the theory of evolution undermine Christian biblical faith, it threatened (he believed) the progressive social agenda he had worked for all his life by justifying unfettered capitalist exploitation of the workers.

The Butler Act and the origin of a lawsuit

The Scopes trial was an attempt by the newly-formed American Civil Liberties Union to challenge the constitutionality of the so-called Butler Act.[23] The Butler Act was the brainchild of John Butler, a representative to the Tennessee state legislature from a rural district near the Kentucky border. The story goes that Butler heard a preacher recount the tale of a young woman who went off to college, where she studied the theory of evolution; and, when she returned home, she was no longer a Christian. Fearful that such an evil doctrine might spread to high schools closer to home, Butler sat down on his 49th birthday and drafted a bill to ban the teaching of evolution in state schools.[24] The relevant text of the statute (1925 Tenn. House Bill 185) reads as follows:

Section 1. *Be it enacted by the General Assembly of the State of Tennessee*, That it shall be unlawful for any teacher in any of the Universities, Normals and all other public schools of the State which are supported in whole or in part by the public school funds of the State, to teach any theory that denies the story of the Divine Creation of man as taught in the Bible, and to teach instead that man has descended from a lower order of animals.

Section 2. *Be it further enacted*, That any teacher found guilty of the violation of this Act, shall be guilty of a misdemeanor and upon conviction, shall be fined not less than One Hundred $ (100.00) Dollars nor more than Five Hundred ($ 500.00) Dollars for each offense.

The statute went into effect on 13 March 1925.[25]

It cannot be said that Butler's bill was a model of statutory clarity. Must the theory taught explicitly deny the biblical story of creation? Or must it both deny the biblical creation story *and* teach that man descended from a lower order of animals? May the theory of evolution be taught as long as there is no mention of the Bible or man? To which Bible does the act refer – Catholic, Protestant, Jewish? Hebrew Torah, Greek Septuagint, Latin Vulgate, King James translation?[26] All of these issues became relevant in the Scopes trial.

Legal strategies and doctrines

The 'great monkey trial' might have led to a trailblazing legal decision, but it never got the chance. The trial began on 10 July 1925, during one of the hottest summers Dayton residents could remember, with John T. Raulston presiding as judge.[27] Raulston made no secret of his Christian faith and quoted Scripture handily during the trial. Once a jury was selected,[28] defense counsel moved to quash the indictment[29] by challenging the constitutionality of the Butler Act on various grounds including vagueness (that the statute did not make clear and thereby give a citizen reasonable notice of what behavior was being criminalized), violating a provision in the Tennessee Constitution to cherish science and education, and infringing the right to free speech and religion under the Constitutions of Tennessee and the United States. Under the doctrine of judicial review as it has developed in the United States, if a state law violates its own state constitution or the Constitution of the United States or if a federal law violates the Constitution of the United States, courts are obliged to strike down the law as invalid. If the defense could show that the Butler Act violated either constitution, then it would be overturned, and the basis for the indictment would be void.

The defense argument that the Butler Act violated the "cherish science" provision of the Tennessee Constitution never stood much of a chance, and it was unlikely that any free speech or religion argument under the Tennessee Constitution would be successful (Tennessee courts would have a great deal of latitude in their interpretation). The Tennessee Supreme Court ultimately ruled that such a provision was nonjusticiable. Therefore, the best shot at invalidating the Butler Act was to appeal to the US Supreme Court on the ground it violated the speech and religion provisions of the 1st Amendment[30] to the US Constitution. Yet, here, the arguments were at the cutting-edge of legal reasoning.

In the case of *Lochner v. New York*, 198 U.S. 45 (1905), the United States Supreme Court began utilizing an interpretive doctrine we now call "substantive due process" to strike down statutes. In the US system of federal government, 'sovereign' state governments have virtually unlimited 'police power' to regulate for the general health, safety, and welfare of their people unless such power is limited by a state's own constitution or the US federal Constitution. The federal Constitution only allows Congress to legislate in limited, specified areas; but, in these areas, the US Constitution and federal laws passed by Congress pursuant to the Constitution trump state laws. The doctrine of "substantive due process" (which sounds like an oxymoron[31]) derives from an interpretation of the 14th Amendment to the US Constitution, which prohibits a state from depriving "any person of life, liberty, or property, without due process of law." In *Lochner*, the US Supreme Court struck down a New York law limiting the number of hours bakers could work because the bakers' freedom of contract was protected by the 'liberty' clause of the 14th Amendment. Unless New York had a very good reason for exercising its 'police power,' said the Court, it could not deprive the bakers of their 'liberty' interest. In this case, the Court found that New York's reasons for the law were merely a pretext to protect large baker unions against competition from small bakeries with non-union employees. Therefore, the law was an invalid use of police power.[32]

Later, "substantive due process" was used to strike down other state laws. For example, in *Meyer v. Nebraska*, 262 U.S. 390 (1923), a Nebraska law, passed in the wake of World War I, forbidding all schools from teaching German was overturned because it interfered with parents' 'fundamental right' to control the upbringing of their children and the liberty interest of teachers to teach. However, because the law prohibited both private and public teachers from teaching German, the case was not directly on point for the Scopes situation, which only involved public school teachers.[33]

In another case, *Gitlow v. New York*, 268 U.S. 652 (1925), which was decided by the US Supreme Court just a month before the Scopes trial began, the Court announced the so-called 'incorporation doctrine,' which held that the Bill of Rights to the US Constitution (or, at least, some of them) could be applied to the states through the 14th Amendment.[34] The Bill of Rights is explicitly limited to the federal government[35] alone and, hence, acts only as a restriction on the power of the federal government. However, in this case, the Court held that the free speech rights guaranteed by the 1st Amendment were 'incorporated' through the 'liberty' clause of the 14th Amendment to apply to the states as well. By extension, the 1st Amendment's prohibition on the establishment of religion would also seem to apply. However, there is a 'state action' component to this principle, that is, only the state is prevented from violating an individual's right to free speech and religion (individuals – for example, private employers – may still do so). Here, obviously, the 'state action' component was fulfilled since the state legislature of Tennessee had passed the Butler Act to apply to public schools.

The defense strategy in the Scopes case was to argue for an extension of the substantive due process and incorporation principles to invalidate the Butler Act. The argument, in essence, was that Scopes could have violated the Butler Act only if teaching the theory of evolution *necessarily* requires a denial of the biblical story of creation. However, there are many ways to interpret the biblical story of creation that are compatible with a theory of evolution. If the Butler Act precluded all of those ways, then the Tennessee legislature was establishing one particular form of religion as 'official' as opposed to other forms. This would violate the 1st Amendment's prohibition on the governmental establishment of religion, which applies to the states through the 14th Amendment.

Judge Raulston ultimately rejected all the constitutional objections to the Butler Act, which was not unusual for a trial judge to do. For Raulston, the dispute was essentially a contractual one: the employer-employee relationship between the school and the teacher. The state has a right to establish the curriculum of the schools and the right as a master to dictate how the servant (the teacher) is to perform. If a teacher feels compelled by conscience to teach evolution, then he or she may find employment elsewhere.[36]

How a trial becomes a circus

The prosecution called only four witnesses, focusing less on the guilt of the defendant than showing that the textbook in question violated the law (even though the textbook was approved and required by the state!). Two students from Scopes' class were called to testify that Scopes had taught from the textbook[37] – particular emphasis was placed on a passage that stated that man was classified as a mammal. The prosecution also called the high school superintendent, Walter White, to testify that Scopes had taught from *A Civic Biology* and Frank Robinson, who owned the drugstore, to testify that he sold the textbook *A Civic Biology*,[38] that it was required by the state, and that Scopes had admitted teaching from it. With that, the prosecution rested, its case completed in the course of an afternoon.

Under Tennessee criminal procedure rules, if a defendant wished to testify on his own behalf, he had to do so at the beginning of the defense's case-in-chief. Darrow declined to put Scopes on the stand. Rather, he conceded, "Your honor, every single word that was said against this defendant, everything was true."[39] The tactic was not to prove the defendant's innocence but to attack the statute's validity and the prosecution's construction of it through expert testimony. When the defense tried to call witnesses on the scientific basis of evolution, the prosecution argued that the science of evolution was irrelevant to the interpretation of the statute upon whose validity the judge had already ruled. ACLU defense counsel Arthur Hays retorted that, since the defense intended to challenge the constitutionality of the statute on appeal, it was crucial for the defense to present evidence that it was beyond the state's police power. The rest of the Scopes trial turned on this point of law.

Judge Raulston allowed the testimony of one expert on evolution outside the presence of the jury.[40] The next day, the prosecution moved that such evidence be excluded as irrelevant. Teaching that man descended from a lower order of animals, they argued, simply *was* the offending act, whether or not theology might be reconcilable with it on some basis – even a 16-year-old boy could understand that. The defense insisted that virtually every aspect of the statute required explication, and no 16-year-old would be able to determine its meaning without special study. What, for example, does it mean for something to be a "lower order of animal" as opposed to merely a different genus?[41]

After considerable oratorical fireworks,[42] Judge Raulston (apparently, with some reluctance) held that the legislative intent of the Butler Act was clear and unambiguous and could be comprehended by the 'ordinary, non-expert mind.' The defense objected so vigorously that the prosecution accused them of disrespecting the court. Judge Raulston took no offense (at that point) but agreed to allow the defense to build the case for appeal as to their construction of the statute through affidavits by their expert witnesses. Darrow then asked for the rest of the day to prepare and submit the affidavits. Judge Raulston balked – why should it take so much time? Darrow peevishly objected:

Mr. Darrow – I do not understand why every request of the state and every suggestion of the prosecution would meet with an endless loss of time; and a bare suggestion of anything that is perfectly competent on our part, should be immediately overruled.
The Court – I hope you do not mean to reflect upon the court?
Mr. Darrow – Well, your honor has the right to hope.
The Court – I have the right to do something else, perhaps.[43]

Judge Raulston agreed to exclude scientific testimony. This occurred on Friday, 17 July.

On Monday, 20 July, Judge Raulston cited Darrow for contempt. Darrow offered his apology to the judge. Judge Raulston forgave him in the spirit of "the Man that I believe came into the world to save man from sin."[44] Due to the excessive heat in the courtroom, the judge adjourned to resume proceedings on the lawn. Arthur Hays then raised another point in the defense strategy. It was one thing, he argued, for the defense to show that the theory of evolution might be true, but the statute also required that the theory deny the biblical story of creation. The court had taken judicial notice of the King James version of the Bible, but what if other versions of the Bible contradicted the King James version? Hays wanted to create a record on this issue and – shockingly – called William Jennings Bryan as an expert witness on the Bible. Over the forceful objections of his fellow prosecutors, Bryan agreed to testify. What followed was the most famous direct examination in the history of American law – the exchange for which the trial is remembered.

Before a crowd of journalists and locals that afternoon, Darrow peppered Bryan with questions designed to demonstrate the foolishness of a literal reading of the Bible in light of modern science. This was well-trodden territory – many sceptics had raised these questions before. Indeed, Darrow and Bryan had debated ideas on biblical literalism in the *Chicago Tribune* newspaper as early as 1923.[45] How did Noah gather animals from all the different continents? From where did Cain get his wife? How could Joshua command the sun to stand still if the earth revolves around the sun? Bryan was in a rhetorically difficult position. Every concession he made to science (concessions he could hardly refuse) made his own case look weaker. Indeed, his strongest theological position made him appear stubborn and stupid: he had faith that the Bible was the Word of God and the truth – even if he, as a mere mortal, did not understand it.[46] Bryan was counting on being able to present countervailing evidence. He was confident that he would be able to show the flaws in the theory of evolution.

It was not to be. Bryan endured two grueling hours on the witness stand. The prosecution repeatedly objected to the defense line of questioning, but Bryan himself batted the objections away. The confrontation between the Great Commoner and Darrow grew more and more heated as Darrow exposed

Bryan's ignorance of science until Judge Raulston abruptly adjourned for the day. When proceedings resumed inside the courthouse the next morning, Judge Raulston immediately ruled that Bryan's testimony from the day before was to be stricken from the record. Darrow threw in the towel. Allowed no witnesses, the defense had no choice now, said Darrow, but to call in the jury and instruct them to find Scopes guilty. Yet, Darrow could deliver one final blow to Bryan. According to the court's procedural rules, if the defense waived its closing argument by asking for a guilty verdict, the prosecution could not provide one, either. Bryan was now definitively precluded from defending his reputation in the courtroom (sorely challenged by Darrow the day before) and delivering the elaborate attack on the theory of evolution he had been preparing, which he desperately wanted to be heard by the radio audience.

Yet, that is not the end of the bizarre twists in the case. The penalty to be imposed by the statute was a minimum fine of $100. While charging the jury, Judge Raulston stated that, if the jury wanted to impose a fine greater than $100, "then you must impose a fine not to exceed $500 in any event. But if you are content with a $100 fine, then you may simply find the defendant guilty and leave the punishment to the court."[47] After a brief deliberation, the jury found Scopes guilty. When asked whether they fixed the fine, the foreman stated that the jury would leave that to the court. Judge Raulston fined Scopes $100. Scopes stated that the fine was unjust, and the defense intended to challenge it.

The 'trial of the century' was over, and the appellate process began, taking the case all the way to the Tennessee Supreme Court (154 Tenn. 105, 289 S.W. 363 (1927)), which upheld the validity of the Butler Act against every objection, both state and federal. Nevertheless, the Court overturned Scope's conviction. The Constitution of Tennessee required any fine in excess of $50 to be assessed by a jury. In this case, the Court observed, the fine was not assessed by the jury but by the judge. Because the judge exceeded his jurisdiction, the Tennessee Supreme Court overturned the conviction – literally, on a 'technicality.' It is, perhaps, not unreasonable to suppose a certain cynicism in the Tennessee Supreme Court's ruling since the transcript could easily be read to indicate that the jury did assess the fine. Still, the ruling had the effect of upholding Tennessee law while precluding any danger that it might be declared invalid by the United States Supreme Court. The Scopes trial had now run its course through the legal system, but its impact on American culture and society had only begun. Indeed, it took on a second life in the form of fiction.

The prism and parallel of fiction

For all the evil Senator Joseph McCarthy did in the 1950s in the name of what we now call 'McCarthyism,' his anti-Communist antics at least inspired a number of popular protest plays (all based on trials in different historical eras) including Arthur Miller's *The Crucible* (1953), Robert Bolt's *A Man for All Seasons* (orig. ver. 1954), and Jerome Lawrence and Robert E. Lee's *Inherit the Wind* (1955).[48] Like the other two plays, *Inherit the Wind* draws heavily on actual trial transcripts[49] and historical records for its content, but (like Miller and Bolt) Lawrence and Lee very deliberately created a fictionalized version of the Scopes trial. Some of the changes are wholly superficial. The characters are given different names – William Jennings Bryan becomes Matthew Harrison Brady; Clarence Darrow becomes Henry Drummond; John Scopes becomes Bertram Cates – but they are clearly based on their real-life counterparts. Other deviations from the historical record are more significant.[50]

The plotline for all three plays may be (and has been) interpreted within the paradigm critique of 'the tyranny of the majority':[51] vindicating the right of the individual to dissent from majority opinion. In the case of *Inherit the Wind*, it is the right of Bertram Cates (John Scopes) to teach the theory of evolution in defiance of the religious prejudices of the townspeople of Hillsboro (Dayton). While the play/film illustrates the conflict inherent in a trial through the legal jousting of the various advocates, the actual legal issues[52] assume only a marginal role. They are merely the 'MacGuffin' on which to hang the drama.

Authorial intent in *Inherit the Wind*

When critics object to the play or film, they often point to the caricature of William Jennings Bryan presented in the form of Matthew Harrison Brady.[53] Like Bryan, Brady is supposed to be a man in decline, the shadow of a once admired and admirable statesman – now vain, gluttonous, and pompous, a populist demagogue but still capable of kindness and empathy. As portrayed by Fredric March in the film version, his bluster barely conceals the awareness of his own fragility. He is a man who needs adulation, a man to be pitied who nevertheless wreaks harm in his foolish self-righteousness. And it is undeniable to anyone who has read the transcripts that William Jennings Bryan sometimes acted like a fool during the Scopes trial. The only objection can be that Bryan was not so foolish as Brady. Perhaps. Brady still comes off infinitely more sympathetically than the alcoholic bully, Joe McCarthy.

By contrast (and in contrast to Clarence Darrow), Henry Drummond's advocacy does not take as strident an anti-religious stance as Brady's does a religious one – unless, of course, your definition of 'religious' encompasses nothing but a literal interpretation of the Bible. Instead, Drummond argues as more of an accommodationist: "The Bible is a book. A good book. But it's not the only book" (*Inherit the Wind*, p. 98). He forcefully and repeatedly argues that the trial is about "the right to think" (*Inherit the Wind*, pp. 72, 94). His is the classic libertarian position taken by John Stuart Mill in *On Liberty* (1859).[54] In a telling exchange during his examination of Brady, Drummond says, "Suppose Mr. Cates had enough influence and lung power to railroad through the State Legislature a law that only Darwin should be taught in the schools!" (*Inherit the*

Wind, p. 100). This, he implies, would be just as unacceptable as the law banning the teaching of evolution. At the very end of the play, Drummond picks up a copy of Darwin's book and a copy of the Bible. The stage directions (followed more or less in the 1960 film) read: "*he looks from one volume to the other, balancing them thoughtfully, as if his hands were scales. He half-smiles, half-shrugs. Then Drummond slaps the two books together and jams them in his brief case, side by side*" (*Inherit the Wind*, p. 129).

The message Lawrence and Lee wanted to convey was compromise and tolerance of individual conscience since there is no monopoly on truth. But, of course, there is no drama if there are no stakes for the individual involved. There must be a threat – and a real one – to the ostensible protagonist, Bertram Cates.[55] Lawrence and Lee embody this threat in the townspeople and do not shrink from making them hostile, prejudiced, and ignorant. They even introduce a preening, hellfire preacher[56] to articulate the townspeople's worst impulses – a preacher who, while extreme, is not unrecognizable from real life.[57] On the other hand, to balance the 'religious' threat, there is an equally sinister 'secular' threat in the form of the nihilistic newspaperman E.K. Hornbeck, whose real life counterpart was H.L. Mencken, the famous journalist who reported on the Scopes trial for the *Baltimore Sun*.[58] When Matthew Harrison Brady dies at the end of *Inherit the Wind*, Hornbeck cruelly remarks that it was due to a "busted belly" (in reference to Brady's gluttony). Clarence Darrow actually made that remark about Bryan's death. Yet, in the play, Drummond bridles against Hornbeck's cynicism and defends Brady: "I tell you Brady had the same right as Cates: the right to be wrong!" (*Inherit the Wind*, p. 127).

What Lawrence and Lee intended to be a plea for freedom of thought and speech eventually became entangled in a different conflict in American culture: the clash between religion and science. In Stanley Kramer's 1960 film version[59] of *Inherit the Wind*, free speech concerns (though still there) take a back seat to religious concerns – particularly, in the way the general public assessed it. So popular did the play and film become that they "all but replaced the actual trial in the nation's memory."[60] Indeed, the film's components proved to be supple enough to permit different 'readings' in changing contemporary circumstances – though almost always embedded in one of two broad interpretations of history (the 'politics of inevitability' or the 'politics of eternity'), neither of which has much to do with the intentions of the authors of *Inherit the Wind* but much to do with the intellectual climate in which they wrote the play and in which the film was made.

The 'politics of inevitability'

When Lawrence and Lee wrote *Inherit the Wind* some 30 years after the Scopes trial, it was very much within the paradigm of the 'politics of inevitability.' The Neo-Darwinian synthesis of the theory of evolution was firmly ensconced in scientific circles; any credibility the eugenics movement possessed had been quashed

124 Moderns

by association with the Nazis; and the respectability of 'Social Darwinism' had been thoroughly discredited thanks, among other things, to the ideological foundations of Franklin Delano Roosevelt's New Deal. The doctrine of evolution had been defanged of much to which William Jennings Bryan objected (which also made it easier for mainstream Christian churches to accommodate it). The Darwinism discussed in *Inherit the Wind* conspicuously lacks precisely those uncomfortable elements, which were present at the actual trial.[61]

The authors of the play could reasonably expect that their audience would recognize the otherwise milquetoast character of Bert Cates as a hero because he stood for a 'truth' that was now generally and easily accepted – even though the doctrine of evolution was still taboo in many public schools. There also seemed to be a lazy but congenial connection between the 'politics of inevitability' and the idea of an evolution that 'progresses' (see below). Moreover, the Cold War arms race and the Soviet launch of the first man-made satellite Sputnik in 1957 (just before the film was made) panicked US lawmakers to beef up science education in public schools and inclined audiences in a pro-science direction.

As a result, in the context of the late 1950s and early 1960s, it became attractive to see the Scopes trial (especially as interpreted through the play/film) as a little morality play that demonstrated how 'freedom of thought' generates 'progress.' The Scopes trial exposed the danger superstition posed to the advance of science – just as the trial of Galileo had.[62] As Drummond proclaims at the beginning of the trial, "All I want is to prevent the clock-stoppers from dumping a load of medieval nonsense into the United States Constitution" (*Inherit the Wind*, p. 417) – which, presumably, would hinder the march of history forward by pulling it backwards. Lawrence and Lee could use the Scopes trial as an effective metaphor to condemn McCarthyism precisely because there was a general consensus about the value of science in educated circles. Science was the engine of progress in history, and the train was back on track after the Scopes trial had diverted it. The message was that McCarthyites represented a suppression of 'freedom of thought' and, therefore, 'progress' just like the Butler Act did in the 1920s. If we can get the obstacles to thought out of the way, we can hasten progress and reap its benefits more thoroughly as a society.

The 'politics of eternity'

Yet, the very smugness of *Inherit the Wind*'s consensus view on Darwin also provided a platform for fundamentalist Christians to invoke a view of history that resembles the 'politics of eternity.' In 1963, the prominent American historian Richard Hofstadter could observe:

> Today the evolution controversy seems as remote as the Homeric era to intellectuals in the East, and it is not uncommon to take a condescending view of both sides. In other parts of the country and in other circles,

the controversy is still alive. A few years ago, when the Scopes trial was dramatized in *Inherit the Wind*, the play seems on Broadway more like a quaint period piece than a stirring call for freedom of thought. But when the road company took the play to a small town in Montana, a member of the audience rose and shouted "Amen!" at one of the speeches of the character representing Bryan.[63]

Remember that the Scopes trial ended in a legal 'victory' for 'religion.' However much the 'atheists' crowed that the trial made fundamentalism look preposterous, evolution had been kept out of the classroom in Tennessee and would remain excluded there and elsewhere for decades. However, some thirty years after the premiere of *Inherit the Wind*, reactions to the Scopes trial made it look like a cultural defeat to the fundamentalists.

In *Epperson v. Arkansas*, 393 U.S. 97 (1968), the US Supreme Court was at last able to rule on a statute almost identical to the Butler Act, holding that it was unconstitutional.[64] Yet, the Court did not agree on the grounds. Some justices believed the statute was too vague to be constitutional; others that it constituted an establishment of religion; some that it infringed on the teacher's free speech – all arguments raised during the Scopes trial. The *Epperson* ruling finally allowed the teaching of evolution in all public schools. Because they could no longer ban the teaching of evolution, some states tried a different tactic and passed legislation requiring schools to teach so-called "creation science" alongside evolution in order to 'balance things out.' The major test case on this issue came in *McLean v. Arkansas Board of Education*, 529 F. Supp. 1255 (E.D. Ark. 1982).[65] District Judge William Overton held that, since the sole purpose of the statute was to introduce a religious, biblical version of the creation story into the curriculum, it violated the Establishment Clause of the US Constitution by advancing particular religious beliefs (id., p. 1264).[66] Moreover, Judge Overton ruled that so-called 'creation science' simply did not meet the criteria of a 'science,' which required, *inter alia*, an explanation referencing natural laws that was falsifiable.[67] The biblical story of creation by definition "depends upon a supernatural intervention which is not guided by natural law" (id., p. 1267).

Creationists commenced litigation to challenge the outcome of the *McLean* case in next-door Louisiana. The result was the same as in Arkansas, but the parties appealed the case all the way to the US Supreme Court, which held, in *Edwards v. Aguillard*, 482 U.S. 578 (1987), that such 'creation science' statutes were an unconstitutional infringement of the Establishment Clause, just as Judge Overton had ruled.[68] This was literally the realization of the scenario anticipated by Henry Drummond: evolution was sanctioned to be taught in schools, but creationism was outlawed. For proponents of evolution, this sequence of events more or less confirmed the vision of history embedded in the 'politics of inevitability.' As fundamentalists saw it, the roles of Bertram Cates and Matthew Harrison Brady were reversed. It was Christianity that was being oppressed by 'atheistic,' secular society rather than the other way around – a reversal advocated for and achieved by, in no small part, the film version of *Inherit the Wind*.

Proponents of fundamentalism saw the film's deviations from the actual trial as deliberate distortions to undermine creationism in particular and religion in general.[69] Whereas, for example, Scopes volunteered to act as defendant (and, perhaps, never even taught the offending doctrine), the film shows authorities arresting Cates in the classroom in front of his students. In the film, Cates' students are depicted as supporting him – they are the wave of the future. In one scene, Bertram Cates is threatened with lynching, and a rock is thrown through the window of his jail cell – to demonstrate the mob mentality of the 'Christian' townspeople. Scopes, however, never spent a day in jail for the alleged misdemeanor. If Bert Cates was a 'hero,' fundamentalists thought, it was only because the film had thrown mud against Christians. The film's shameless indoctrination, they believed, resulted in an unfair 'emotional victory' for the 'secularists' over the 'Christians,' which became an 'eternal moment' of Christian victimhood. The 1960 film and the 1925 trial merged as the symbolic original sin against revealed truth by the Darwinists in the United States.

Mike Pence speaks for eternity

Congressman Mike Pence's 2002 statement on evolution (quoted earlier) is a good example of how the 1925 trial has become an ahistorical 'eternal moment' for fundamentalist Christians. Pence's statement reads as if it were based on notes he made five minutes before he gave the speech. He misunderstands fundamental concepts in the theory of evolution and reverses the basic facts of the Scopes trial. Clearly, the statement was not the result of intensive and original research on his part. Yet, as an apparently off-the-cuff disquisition, its mishmash of facts, mistakes, and misunderstandings is revealing. Apparently mixing up his emotional response to *Inherit the Wind* with the actual trial, Pence seems to have forgotten that the trial resulted in the banishment of the theory of evolution from many public schools and 'remembers' it as mandating that evolution be taught for the last "77 years in the classrooms of America as fact."[70] The 'fact' of evolution that Pence claims has been taught since 1925 is this:

> we can all see in our mind's eye that grade school classroom that we all grew up in with the linear depiction of evolution just above the chalkboard. There is the monkey crawling on the grass. There is the Neanderthal dragging his knuckles and then there is Mel Gibson standing in all of his glory.

Pence appears to argue that, because paleontologists have found evidence of 'non-linear' evolution, the entire evolutionary edifice on which Mel Gibson stands as pinnacle must fall. If so, Pence clearly misunderstands the nature of the scientific enterprise.

The 'linear depiction of evolution' to which Pence refers seems to be the so-called 'March of Progress' illustration[71] commissioned by Time-Life Books in 1965 for a tome called *Early Man*,[72] showing a series of ape-like figures ascending from a squat, gibbon-like creature to an erect *homo sapiens*. The artist notoriously but unintentionally gave the impression that man evolved in a straight line from beast to intelligent human being.[73] However, Pence is late to the party in taking exception to this view of evolution, which is contradicted in the very text of *Early Man* itself.[74] The illustration is now often parodied and regarded as scientifically distorted if not outright false. Even though the 'March of Progress' illustration is widely disseminated and a popular way of depicting the theory of evolution, both Darwin and the Neo-Darwinian synthesis reject any 'progressive' or 'linear' view of evolution in the sense that life inexorably becomes more complex and 'higher.'

To be fair, though, Hunter's *Civic Biology* on which the Scopes trial turned did accept it. Linnean in its origins, this notion of 'linear evolution' was still one of several Lamarckian speculations on evolution at the time Hunter was writing,[75] but it was not consistent with the point of *The Origin of Species*. Once Mendel's genetic principles were accepted as one of the microbiological mechanisms behind evolution, a Lamarckian/Linnean typology of 'higher' and 'lower' species no longer had any plausibility except as a convenient (but necessarily misleading) way to talk about speciation at a particular point in time. The concept of 'linear evolution,' already dubious in 1925, was obsolete by 1955 when *Inherit the Wind* was first performed.

Thus, Pence may have a justifiable complaint if public school teachers still teach children 'linear evolution' because, then, they would not really be teaching the theory of evolution as it is now (and has long been) understood. Such a mistake would be as egregious as if teachers still taught the Dunning School view of post-Civil War Reconstruction[76] or Galen's theory of humors[77] as viable. However, this was not Pence's complaint.

A common creationist trope, which Pence employs here, is that evolution is 'only' a theory and, thus, not an established fact. This is mere hair-splitting. If all that is meant is that a particular theory might at some point be falsified, then no scientific theory is ever an established fact. Theories become accepted as 'true' when their principles support a sufficient number of testable and verifiable predictions to be generally accepted by reasonable people. What is a 'good' theory at one point can become a 'better' theory later – or, perhaps, be completely discarded in favor of a more comprehensive explanation. By definition, details in every scientific theory from the theory of gravity to the theory of evolution to the germ theory of disease change over time as more experiments are done and more information is gathered.

Ptolemy's geocentric theory of the universe was testable and provided verifiable predictions but was discarded later for a different theory that provided predictions just as accurate (and, eventually, more accurate). Copernicus' heliocentric theory was made a better theory by Kepler's observations that the planets orbit the sun in ellipses (which undermined one of the basic reasons Copernicus proffered it in the first place – the beauty and perfection of simple circles).[78] Einstein's theory of relativity radically altered and improved Newton's theory of gravity. The theory of evolution has the same claim to 'facticity' as any of them. What 'creation science' and its sister hypothesis of 'intelligent design' lack is a testable hypothesis that has been verified.

Pence conflates the historical process of scientific investigation into a confused amalgam of a concept. Consistent with the 'politics of eternity,' 'truth' (for Pence) is eternal and unchanging, and historical processes are irrelevant. Echoing Plato's theory of forms, he thinks any 'truth claim' that might change over time is not a 'truth.' Given this skepticism, Pence advocates new legislation to require public schools to teach creationism (or its 'intelligent design' iteration) on the grounds that, because empirical science does not provide 'truth claims' as 'eternal' as 'truth' through divine revelation, students should be provided with the religious 'alternative' as well. This is why Pence is indifferent to the actual historical differences between the facts of the 1925 trial and its depiction in *Inherit the Wind*. Such differences do not matter if the 'truth' of revelation is unchanging. The irony is almost too satisfying that his position harmonizes with Henry Drummond's in *Inherit the Wind*. The irony is doubled in Pence's valedictory salute and concession to the emotional satisfaction of the other paradigm, the 'politics of inevitability': "I have no fear of science, I believe that the more we study the science, the more the truth of faith will become apparent."[79] That this should be a subject for legislation has both philosophical and historical implications. Clearly, the interpretation of law and what law is for may be affected by the conception of history one accepts. This shall be explored from a different angle in the Epilogue.

Notes

1 148(93) *Congressional Record* (July 11 2002), Daily Edition, 107th Congress (2001–2002) – 2nd Session.
2 For a good one-volume examination of the trial, see Edward J. Larson, *Summer for the Gods: The Scopes Trial and America's Continuing Debate over Science and Religion* (1998).
3 A classic example is the 'history' behind the reconceptualization of the American Civil War by white Southerners as a conflict over 'states' rights' rather than slavery. This is a story that became essential to 'Southern' identity as opposed to 'Northern' identity. See the masterly study by David Blight, *Race and Reunion: The Civil War in American Memory* (2002).
4 An examination of worldviews, usually associated with such *Annales* school historians as Marc Bloch and Fernand Braudel.
5 'Spirit of the times' analysis, often popularized by followers of Hegel and Herder. An excellent example of this type of history might be Allan Janik and Stephen Toulmin, *Wittgenstein's Vienna* (1973) or Johan Huizinga's classic *Autumntide of the Middle Ages* (1919).
6 David W. Blight, "Historians and 'Memory'," 2(3) *Common-Place* (April, 2002).

7 Francis Fukuyama, *The End of History and the Last Man* (1992), which, to summarize it crudely, builds on the ideas of Alexandre Kojève (who, in turn, leans on Hegel) to show that the end of the Cold War represents the triumph of liberal, democratic values worldwide. Fukuyama has modified his views since then.
8 Ironically, the 'politics of inevitability' undermines historical responsibility since the thesis is that eventually everything will work out. This may be comforting for those who suffer 'temporary' setbacks in a just cause, but it can also 'justify' atrocities in the moment in order to achieve some future utopia – as happened with Stalinism.
9 Timothy Snyder, *The Road to Unfreedom* (2018), p. 8. It is important to emphasize that Snyder is not arguing that these are inescapable categories of thought. To the contrary, both are opposed to and cloud a real understanding of history.
10 The classic example is the Nazi claim that all defeats and setbacks experienced by Aryans were caused by the eternal outsider, the Jew. See Timothy Snyder, *Black Earth: The Holocaust as History and Warning* (2015). This conception is consonant with Nazi theorist Carl Schmitt's notion that the political is essentially an existential distinction between friend and enemy. See Schmitt, *The Concept of the Political* (2007 [1932]), which in turn evokes the ever shifting re-definition of the 'enemy' in George Orwell's *1984*.
11 Snyder, *Road to Unfreedom*, p. 166.
12 It is where we get the term 'fascism,' derived from the Latin term *fasces*, a bundle of rods wrapping an axe that symbolized the power of ancient Roman magistrates. Ironically, the Nazis invoked as one of their 'eternal moments' the Battle of Teutoburg Forest (9 C.E.) in which the German tribes wiped out three Roman legions.
13 For a more detailed discussion of the religious and scientific background of this case, see the Appendix 3 below.
14 1896, 1900, and 1908.
15 This was the speech that won Bryan his first nomination as presidential candidate. Bryan, a champion of the working man, railed against proponents of the gold standard. Even Americans who have no clue about the great controversy over silver-based versus gold-backed currency recognize Bryan's famous words, "You shall not press down upon the brow of labor this crown of thorns; you shall not crucify mankind upon a cross of gold." In the (disputed) allegorical reading of L. Frank Baum's *The Wizard of Oz* (1900), Bryan is thought to be the model for the cowardly lion. See, for example, Henry M. Littlefield, "The Wizard of Oz: Parable on Populism," 16 *American Quarterly* 47 (Spring, 1964); Hugh Rockoff, "The 'Wizard of Oz' as Monetary Allegory," 98 *Journal of Political Economy* 739 (1990); Ranjit Dighe, *The Historian's Wizard of Oz: Reading L. Frank Baum's Classic as a Political and Monetary Allegory* (2002).
16 'Fundamentalism' is the name given to a Christian movement that came to prominence during the early part of the 20th century, its principles loosely captured in a series of essays published by the Bible Institute of Los Angeles between 1910 and 1915 called *The Fundamentals*. 'Fundamentalism' held that there were five doctrines that were essential or 'fundamental' to the Christian faith, including a belief in the inerrancy of the Bible as the inspired Word of God. Fundamentalism stood in contrast to more mainstream Christian churches that accepted 'modernism' and 'higher criticism' in their interpretation of Christianity. 'Higher criticism,' for example, used the tools of historical criticism to understand ancient texts, taking into consideration the historical contexts in which ancient texts were written and developing critical apparatuses on the basis of variations in existing manuscripts. 'Modernism' in Christianity is associated with such movements as 'Liberal Christianity,' which tends to interpret the Bible in metaphorical rather than literal terms, and the 'Social Gospel' movement, which sought to operationalize the Lord's Prayer in Matthew 6:10 by working for social justice on earth.

17 The Loeb and Leopold case was also touted by many as the 'trial of the century.' It served as the inspiration for such films as *Compulsion*, starring Orson Welles, and Alfred Hitchcock's *Rope*.
18 The 'civic' in the title refers to the intent to provide practical applications of biology to society in general. The Tennessee Textbook Commission dropped Hunter's text shortly after Scopes' indictment. The textbook was later revised and its controversial section on evolution deleted (Larson, *Summer for the Gods*, p. 231). For a comprehensive discussion, see Adam Shapiro, *Trying Biology: The Scopes Trial, Textbooks, and the Antievolution Movement in American Schools* (2013).
19 *A Civic Biology*, p. 196. The textbook includes a section with the following remarks:

> If such people were lower animals, we would probably kill them off to prevent them from spreading. Humanity will not allow this, but we do have the remedy of separating the sexes in asylums or other places and in various ways preventing intermarriage and the possibilities of perpetuating such a low and degenerate race. Remedies of this sort have been tried successfully in Europe and are now meeting with some success in this country.
>
> (Id., p. 263)

It is worth pointing out that Clarence Darrow was not an advocate for eugenics. He believed environment was much more determinative of human character and behavior than genetics – *vide* his defense of Loeb and Leopold.
20 See Edwin Black, *War Against the Weak: Eugenics and America's Campaign to Create a Master Race* (2012).
21 On this topic, see James Allen Rogers, "Darwin and Social Darwinism," 22 *Journal of the History of Ideas* 265 (1972); see generally, though now dated, Richard Hofstadter, *Social Darwinism in American Thought 1860–1915* (1944). On the complex interactions between Darwinism and Lamarckianism in political and economic thinking in the years following Darwin's death, see Piers J. Hale, *Political Descent: Malthus, Mutualism, and the Politics of Evolution in Victorian England* (2014).
22 Culminating in the repugnant statement of Justice Oliver Wendell Holmes in *Buck v. Bell*, 274 U.S. 200, 207 (1927) (upholding the constitutionality of a state compulsory sterilization law) that "three generations of imbeciles are enough." See Adam Cohen, *Imbeciles: The Supreme Court, American Eugenics, and the Sterilization of Carrie Buck* (2016).
23 The story is generally known. The ACLU placed an advertisement in newspapers across Tennessee, offering to provide legal and financial support to a teacher who would volunteer to test the validity of the Butler Act. This ad caught the attention of George W. Rappleyea, a resident of Dayton. Rappleyea opposed the Butler Act because he thought the theory of evolution could be reconciled with Christianity. However, when he read the ACLU's offer, Rappleyea also saw an opportunity to help the local economy. He envisioned a lawsuit that would put Dayton on the map, and he hurried down to the drugstore, where a now infamous meeting took place with some of the prominent personages of the town. Rappleyea contacted the ACLU, which accepted an arrangement to challenge the Butler Act in Dayton. Local prosecutors and brothers Herbert E. and Sue K. Hicks (named for his mother, who died giving birth to him and, supposedly, the inspiration for Johnny Cash's song "A Boy Named Sue") agreed to prosecute the case if a local teacher who taught evolution after the passage of the Butler Act could be found. The ACLU offered to pay their expenses, but they declined. District attorney Tom Stewart also joined the prosecution team. The conspirators next enlisted a 24-year-old teacher, John Scopes, into their cause. Scopes taught physics, math, and football at the Rhea County Central High School in Dayton and had been filling in for the biology teacher. In his later memoirs, Scopes said he did

not recall whether he actually taught evolution, but he assigned the students to read from Hunter's *Civic Biology* to prepare for their final exam – and that textbook certainly discussed evolution. He agreed to stand as defendant. An arrest warrant was arranged by the local justice of the peace, and Scopes went off to play a game of tennis. The publicity garnered the attention of William Jennings Bryan, who had been preaching antievolutionism on the Chautauqua circuit. Even though he had not practiced law in decades, Bryan volunteered to assist the prosecution without compensation. The Hicks brothers accepted. In response, Clarence Darrow volunteered to assist the defense along with a consulting attorney, Dudley Field Malone. John Neal, whom the ACLU had selected to defend Scopes, accepted their offer without consulting ACLU headquarters. Thus, in one fell swoop, the ACLU lost control of the legal parameters by which the case would be decided. It was now the great antagonists – Darrow and Bryan – who would set the agenda in the circus atmosphere that surrounded the court.

24 See Shapiro, *Trying Biology*, at 89.
25 The Governor of Tennessee Austin Peay signed the bill into law, stating: "I can find nothing of consequence in the books now being taught in our schools with which the bill will interfere in the slightest manner" (quoted in Shapiro, *Trying Biology*, p. 7). The 1914 edition of Hunter's *Civic Biology* was still the required textbook in virtually all of Tennessee. The governor might technically be correct about this, as Hunter's *Civic Biology* does not *explicitly* say man evolved from lower animals but from a more 'primitive' man. Still, the book does categorize man as a mammal among the other animals.
26 Or, for that matter, which story of the divine creation of man in Genesis is authoritative – the one in Genesis 1:27 or the one in Genesis 2:7? Ultimately, the court took judicial notice of the King James version as an authoritative text.
27 Raulston indulged in the practice of addressing the attorneys in the case by military titles. Darrow and Malone became 'colonels,' Stewart a 'general' (for attorney-general). See Larson, *Summer for the Gods*, p. 149.
28 The transcript of the *voir dire* (jury selection) process provides some of the trial's most entertaining passages. The play/film *Inherit the Wind* gives a sense of it.
29 There was some initial squabbling over the use of an opening prayer at the beginning of each day's session. The defense (supported by a petition from Jewish, Unitarian and Congregationalist clergymen) argued that any denominational prayer might prejudice the jury since religious issues would inevitably be raised during the course of the trial. The objection was overruled.
30 "Congress shall make no law respecting an establishment of religion, or prohibiting the free exercise thereof; or abridging the freedom of speech, or of the press; or the right of the people peaceably to assemble, and to petition the government for a redress of grievances" (First Amendment, US Constitution).
31 That is, on its face, 'due process' is merely a procedural concept – the government may only deprive you of certain rights if it follows certain procedural steps laid out in law. In 'substantive due process,' the legislature violates the 'due process' required to pass legislation if it invades certain 'substantive' areas of the law (life, liberty, and property) without sufficient justification.
32 Oliver Wendell Holmes dissented in the case, saying: "The Fourteenth Amendment does not enact Mr. Herbert Spencer's Social Statics" (*Lochner*, p. 197).
33 Because it prohibited speech in its entirety. If public school teachers only were prohibited to teach German, then free speech rights might not necessarily be violated (according to doctrine at that time) because private school teachers could still teach German – one could simply choose to go to a private school to teach or learn it.
34 Although the doctrine was first articulated in *Chicago, Burlington & Quincy Railroad Co. v. City of Chicago*, 166 U.S. 226 (1897) (holding that the takings clause of the 5th Amendment applied to the states).

35 I.e., "Congress shall make no law ..."
36 *The World's Most Famous Court Trial: Tennessee Evolution Case: A Complete Stenographic Report of the Famous Court Test of the Tennessee Anti-Evolution Act* (1925), p. 102.
37 After the end of the appeals process in 1927, a reporter at the trial, William Kinsey Hutchinson, wrote an article in which he claimed that Scopes admitted he had not taught evolution and that the students had been coached about what to say by the lawyers – implying that the whole enterprise was a fraud. See L. Sprague de Camp, *The Great Monkey Trial* (1968), p. 435. In his memoirs of the trial, *Center of the Storm*, Scopes himself seems to lend some credence to this – though attributing the students' testimony to faulty memory.
38 Darrow jokingly cautioned Robinson against self-incrimination. Robinson replied that the crime was to *teach* the textbook, not to sell it.
39 *The World's Most Famous Court Trial*, p. 133.
40 One of the many ironies of the Scopes case was that the members of the jury – townspeople who had clamored to get onto the jury so they could have a front-row seat to the proceedings – were, for all practical purposes, excluded from the rest of the trial.
41 *The World's Most Famous Court Trial*, p. 155.
42 During the afternoon session of 16 July, Bryan finally rose and mounted an eloquent attack on the theory of evolution: "the Christian believes that man came from above, but the evolutionist believes he must have come from below" (*The World's Most Famous Court Trial*, p. 174). Bryan mocked the notion that man might have descended from the monkey – and "[n]ot even from American monkeys, but from old world monkeys." A ploy frequently used by Bryan at the trial should be noted – he addressed the audience in the court as much as (or more than) the judge. Excoriating Hunter's *Civic Biology*, he boomed: "There is the book they were teaching your children that man was a mammal and so indistinguishable among the mammals that they leave him there with thirty-four hundred and ninety-nine other mammals ... including elephants?" (id. at 175). The reference to elephants is a joke, a Democrat's satirical jab at the symbol of the Republican Party. No expert testimony was necessary, Bryan concluded: "The one beauty about the Word of God is that it does not take an expert to understand it" (id., p. 181).
43 Id., p. 207.
44 Id., p. 226.
45 Larson, *Summer for the Gods*, pp. 72–73.
46 Darrow succeeded in flustering Bryan to the point of this exchange:

> Q – When was that Flood?
> A – I would not attempt to fix the date. The date is fixed, as suggested this morning.
> Q – About 4004 B.C.?
> A – That has been the estimate of a man that is accepted today. I would not say it is accurate.
> Q – That estimate is printed in the Bible?
> A – Everybody knows, at least, I think most of the people know, that was the estimate given.
> Q – But what do you think that the Bible, itself says? Don't you know how it was arrived at?
> A –I never made a calculation.
> Q – A calculation from what?
> A – I could not say.
> Q – From the generations of man?
> A – I would not want to say that.
> Q – What do you think?
> A – I do not think about things I don't think about.

> Q – Do you think about things you do think about?
> A – Well, sometimes.
>
> (*The World's Most Famous Court Trial*, p. 287)

Ironically, many fundamentalists later criticized Bryan for conceding at one point that, when the Book of Genesis refers to 'days' with respect to the Creation, this might mean indeterminate periods. Interestingly, *Inherit the Wind*'s version of this exchange is cited by the dissent in *Lloyd Corporation v. Whiffen*, 849 P.2d 446, 475 n.9 (1993).

47 *The World's Most Famous Court Trial*, pp. 310–311.
48 Lawrence and Lee, "Notes from the Authors" in program for *Inherit the Wind* (1985); Jonathan Mandell, "Inherit the Controversy," *Newsday*, 17 March 1996, cited in Gad Guterman, "Field Tripping: The Power of *Inherit the Wind*," 60(4) *Theatre Journal* (December, 2008), p. 567.
49 The authors claim, "Only a handful of phrases have been taken from the actual transcript of the famous Scopes Trial." Jerome Lawrence and Robert E. Lee, Preface to *Inherit the Wind* (2003 [1951]), unpag. However, this is disingenuous. Certainly, the broad structure of the play, subplots, etc. differs from the events in Dayton and the film differs slightly from the play, but much of the dialogue in the courtroom scenes may be traced to the trial transcript (even if altered a bit).
50 For example, the play/film works on the premise that the defense is sincerely working to acquit Bert Cates. In the film version, Cates even threatens to change his plea to 'guilty' if Drummond does not do as he asks. The whole point of the actual trial, however, was to achieve a guilty verdict, so that the attorneys could appeal it and, perhaps, have the Butler Act declared unconstitutional.
51 See the discussion in the chapter on Plato's *Apology*.
52 The distinguished constitutional law scholar Gerald Gunther was so appalled by the play's representation of the legal issues that he stormed out of a performance "in disgust" (Larson, *Summer for the Gods*, p. 242; Guterman, "Field Tripping," p. 570).
53 Sue Hicks, one of the prosecutors, apparently called the film version of Bryan a "travesty" (Larson, *Summer for the Gods*, p. 243).
54 Mill asserts that, "if any opinion is compelled to silence, that opinion may, for aught we can certainly know, be true. To deny this is to assume our own infallibility." (*On Liberty*, p. 95) See the chapter on Plato's *Apology*.
55 As real as the narcissistic Henry VIII or the witch hunters of Salem.
56 Whose daughter provides the fictionalized, schmaltzy 'romantic interest' in the play/film as Cates' sweetheart.
57 The type satirized by Sinclair Lewis in *Elmer Gantry* (1927), a fictional portrait widely criticized by evangelicals at the time. One recognizes the type in real life in such mountebanks and frauds as Jimmy Swaggart and Jim Bakker.
58 Mencken was a notorious atheist and proponent of eugenics and once labelled 'fundamentalists' as *homo boobiens*. Mencken also first called the event the 'Monkey Trial.' Early in the play/film, Hornbeck appears, munching on an apple – like the fruit of knowledge in the Garden of Eden.
59 Throughout his career, Kramer was known for making 'message' films with strong political viewpoints, including *On the Beach* (1959), *Judgment at Nuremberg* (1961), and *Guess Who's Coming to Dinner?* (1967).
60 Larson, *Summer for the Gods*, p. 241 (referring to the play, however). The remark still applies since the film magnified the influence of the play.
61 Notable, too, by their absence are references to Bryan/Brady's 'leftist' leanings. This, of course, simplified a reading of the play's anti-McCarthy sentiments and placed Brady's fundamentalism in a camp more familiar to the culture of the 1950s. By 1955, fundamentalist Christianity had become firmly yoked to a conception of laissez-faire

capitalism that was utterly alien to the Social Gospel movement and 19th-century Christian socialism, both of which contributed to Bryan's passionate support for labor. See Kevin M. Kruse. *One Nation Under God: How Corporate America Invented Christian America* (2015).

62 By coincidence, Bertolt Brecht wrote the third version of his *Life of Galileo* in 1955 although it contained a very different warning about potential dangers in the 'progress' of science. Dudley Malone in one of the most passionate colloquies in the Scopes trial invoked Copernicus and Galileo in his defense of freedom of speech and thought. According to various reports of the trial, the spectators had greeted Bryan's speech castigating evolution with enthusiasm, but the courtroom exploded with cheers and applause at the end of Malone's. Even Bryan is reported to have told Malone that it was the greatest speech he had ever heard (Donald McRae, *The Old Devil Clarence Darrow: The World's Greatest Trial Lawyer* (2009), p. 202). According to H.L. Mencken, Darrow at one point feared Malone might persuade some of the jurors (resulting in a hung jury) or, perhaps, even the judge to their side when an acquittal would have defeated their purpose (H.L. Mencken, *Heathen Days* (1943), pp. 236–237).

63 Richard Hofstadter, *Anti-Intellectualism in American Life* (1963), p. 129.

64 The *Epperson* case followed other 'defeats' for the fundamentalists in the US Supreme Court: *Engel v. Vitale* (1962) (holding that recitation of a prayer written by a school violated the 1st and 14th Amendments) and *Abington School District v. Schempp* (1963) (holding that public-school-sponsored Bible reading and religious activities are also prohibited). It is still a common rhetorical trope for fundamentalist Christians to claim that the United States began its decline as a superpower when prayer was banished from the schools. Among white Southerners especially, however, the first major attack was reckoned as *Brown v. Board of Education* (1954), which overturned segregation by race, which some fundamentalists believed had been ordained by God. See Daniel Williams, *God's Own Party: The Making of the Christian Right* (2010), pp. 44–46, and *Bob Jones University v. United States*, 461 U.S. 574 (1983) (overturning tax-exempt status of racially segregated school). As segregation became gradually less accepted as a policy, Southern fundamentalists also began to abandon it as an important religious principle.

65 The plaintiffs here were religious leaders who opposed the teaching of 'creation science' in the schools because it promoted a *particular* religious view.

66 The court applied a test on Establishment Clause questions developed in *Lemon v Kurtzman*, 403 U.S. 602 (1971) (which required a statute 1) to have a secular legislative purpose, 2) neither advance nor inhibit religion, and 3) not result in an 'excessive government entanglement' with religion).

67 Echoing a definition of science propounded by such figures as Karl Popper in *The Logic of Scientific Discovery* (1959) on the tentative nature of scientific induction. Some argue that this precludes religious explanations by definition; others that it shows that science and religion are "non-overlapping magisteria" (Stephen Jay Gould, *Rocks of Ages: Science and Religion in the Fullness of Life* (1999)). Yet, the very inductive nature of science leaves open to religion the so-called 'God of the gaps' explanation: that where science has not yet explained a phenomenon, religion may claim 'God did it.'

68 Almost 20 years again after *Edwards*, 'creation science' in the guise of 'intelligent design' was also rejected as violating the Constitution in the case of *Kitzmiller v. Dover Area School District*, 400 F. Supp. 2d 707 (M.D. Pa. 2005). For a useful one-volume overview of the controversy, see Eugenie C. Scott, *Evolution v. Creationism: An Introduction* (2005).

69 See, for example, Phillip Johnson, *Defeating Darwinism by Opening Minds* (1997), p. 25:

> *Inherit the Wind* is a masterpiece of propaganda, promoting a stereotype of the public debate about creation and evolution that gives all the virtues and intelligence

to the Darwinists. The play did not create the stereotype, but it presented it in the form of a powerful story that sticks in the minds of journalists, scientists and intellectuals generally.

See Larson, *Summer for the Gods*, p. 232–233 (on the impact of the trial on 'fundamentalism' as a movement); Kevin M. Kruse. *One Nation Under God: How Corporate America Invented Christian America* (2015)(on the politicization of Christian fundamentalism); Daniel Williams, *God's Own Party: The Making of the Christian Right* (2010) (taking the history beyond the 1980s).
70 148(93) *Congressional Record* (July 11 2002); Daily Edition, 107th Congress (2001–2002) – 2nd Session. Here, Pence repeats briefly many of the common tropes used by 'creationists' to 'refute' Darwin's theory of evolution.
71 Also called 'The Road to Homo Sapiens.'
72 F. Clark Howell and the editors of *Life*, *Early Man* (1976 [1965]), pp. 41–45.
73 Kevin Blake, "On the Origins of 'The March of Progress,'" *Washington University ProSPER* (17 December 2018). It also encourages creationists to misunderstand Darwin's theory as demonstrated by the often-asked question: 'If man evolved from monkeys, why are there still monkeys?,' which misses the entire point of the theory.
74 For example, *Early Man* discusses the 'missing link' fraud surrounding the Piltdown Man, which attempted "to reconcile Darwin's theory of the descent of man with the doctrine of a 'chain of being' leading back to Creation" (*Early Man*, p. 24).
75 Building on the theory of the ancient 'great chain of being,' the notion that all creatures (including angels) may be located on a ladder of 'higher' and 'lower.' Comp. Arthur O. Lovejoy, *The Great Chain of Being: A Study in the History of an Idea* (1936). See also Appendix 3.
76 Named for William Archibald Dunning, who around the turn of the 19th century advocated a racist interpretation of the post-Civil War era, popularly depicted in the silent film *Birth of a Nation*.
77 Ancient Greek physician who synthesized the most prominent theory of medicine for many centuries based on the balance of the four 'humors' or 'fluids' of the body.
78 See Thomas Kuhn, *The Copernican Revolution* (1957), pp. 171–181.
79 148(93) *Congressional Record* (July 11 2002), Daily Edition, 107th Congress (2001–2002) – 2nd Session.

References

Blake, K. (17 December 2018). On the origins of 'the march of progress'. *Washington University ProSPER*.
Blight, D. (April, 2002). Historians and 'memory'. 2(3) *A Common-Place: The Journal of Early American Life*.
Blight, D. (2002). *Race and reunion: The Civil War in American memory*.
Cohen, A. (2016). *Imbeciles: The Supreme Court, American eugenics, and the sterilization of Carrie Buck*.
de Camp, L. (1968). *The great monkey trial*.
Dighe, R. (2002). *The historian's* Wizard of Oz: *Reading L. Frank Baum's classic as a political and monetary allegory*.
Fukuyama, F. (1992). *The end of history and the last man*.
Gould, S. J. (1999). *Rocks of ages: Science and religion in the fullness of life*.
Guterman, G. (December, 2008). Field tripping: The power of *Inherit the Wind*. 60(4) *Theatre Journal* 563.
Hale, P. J. (2014). *Political descent: Malthus, mutualism, and the politics of evolution in Victorian England*.

Hofstadter, R. (1944). *Social Darwinism in American thought* 1860–1915.
Hofstadter, R. (1963). *Anti-intellectualism in American life*.
Howell, F. C. and the editors of *Life*. (1976 [1965]). *Early man*.
Huizinga, J. (2020 [1919]). *Autumntide of the Middle Ages*.
Janik, A., & Toulmin, S. (1973). *Wittgenstein's Vienna*.
Johnson, P. (1997). *Defeating Darwinism by opening minds*.
Kruse, K. M. (2015). *One nation under God: How corporate America invented Christian America*.
Kuhn, T. (1957). *The Copernican revolution*.
Larson, E. J. (1998). *Summer for the gods: The Scopes trial and America's continuing debate over science and religion*.
Lawrence, J., & Lee, R. E. (2003 [1951]). *Inherit the wind*.
Littlefield, H. M. (Spring, 1964). The Wizard of Oz: Parable on populism. 16(1) *American Quarterly* 47.
Lovejoy, A. O. (1936). *The great chain of being: A study in the history of an idea*.
McRae, D. (2009). *The old devil Clarence Darrow: The world's greatest trial lawyer*.
Mencken, H. L. (1943). *Heathen days*.
Popper, K. (1959). *The logic of scientific discovery*.
Rockoff, H. (1990). The 'Wizard of Oz' as monetary allegory. 98 *Journal of Political Economy* 739.
Rogers, J. A. (1972). Darwin and Social Darwinism. 22 *Journal of the History of Ideas* 265.
Schmitt, C. (2007 [1932]). *The concept of the political*.
Scott, E. C. (2005). *Evolution v. creationism: An introduction*.
Shapiro, A. (2013). *Trying biology: The Scopes trial: Textbooks and the antievolution movement in American schools*.
Snyder, T. (2015). *Black earth: The holocaust as history and warning*.
Snyder, T. (2018). *The road to unfreedom*.
Williams, D. (2010). *God's own party: The making of the Christian Right*.
World's most famous court trial: Tennessee evolution case: A complete stenographic report of the famous court test of the Tennessee anti-evolution act (1925).

Epilogue
The Vicissitudes of a Fictional Character: Time, Atticus Finch, and Constitutional Evil

To Kill a Mockingbird (1960) – Harper Lee's beloved novel of a brother and sister, Jem and Scout, and their lawyer father Atticus Finch – is a canonical work in the 'law and literature' movement. Apparently, the first thing Harper Lee submitted for publication was a manuscript we now know as the novel *Go Set a Watchman* (2015),[1] which is set in the 1950s and narrated by an adult Jean Louise Finch (Scout). The book deals with important issues of law and race raised by the turbulent reaction in the American South to the US Supreme Court's ruling in *Brown v. Board of Education*, 347 U.S. 483 (1954), which overturned *de jure* racial segregation in public schools throughout the United States. It is said that Lee's editor did not like the novel but saw potential in the writer – particularly, in the flashbacks to the heroine's childhood, set about 20 years earlier in the Alabama of the 1930s. So, as Harper Lee put it, she dutifully went back to her desk and did what she was told – and wrote the book we know today as *To Kill a Mockingbird*, placing its dramatic climax in Atticus' defense of a black man accused of raping a white woman.

Historical context and literary theory: The trials of the Scottsboro Boys

It has become accepted as a commonplace that Harper Lee's inspiration for Tom Robinson's trial came – at least, obliquely – from the trials of the nine 'Scottsboro Boys,'[2] who were accused of raping two white women[3] on a freight train near Scottsboro, Alabama in 1931. These trials became a worldwide sensation and were at the height of their infamy between 1932 and 1935, precisely the years in which *To Kill a Mockingbird* was set. Harper Lee seems to have deliberately evoked the spirit of the Scottsboro Boys cases but without as many of their procedural flaws.

For one thing, whereas, in their first trial, the Scottsboro Boys had woefully incompetent legal representation (an alcoholic Tennessee real estate lawyer and a senile Alabama practitioner), Tom Robinson has more than adequate counsel in the form of Atticus Finch. Moreover, Tom is a single individual and an adult (as opposed to a 'pack' of juvenile delinquents)[4] and, thus, has a better chance

DOI: 10.4324/9781003302971-10

of eliciting the sympathy of a jury. Like some of the Scottsboro Boys, Tom is crippled.[5] He is reputed to be a hard worker and a good family man – not (as the white community of Alabama characterized the Scottsboro Boys) scruffy, uneducated vagrants, some of whom were thought to be violent and 'physically intimidating.'[6] Tom has only one accuser, Mayella Ewell, whom most Maycomb residents would classify as 'white trash' as many Northerners (and some Southerners) called the alleged victims in the Scottsboro case. Paralleling the threats of lynching made against the Scottsboro Boys at their first trial,[7] an attempt is made to lynch Tom Robinson. There are also similarities between Judge Taylor and Judge Horton (who presided over the first retrial of Haywood Patterson)[8] in that the judge is aware of the biases against black defendants and will not tolerate their most blatant manifestations, though without challenging customary procedures outright. An important difference, however, may be noted in the 'factual' circumstances of Tom Robinson's situation: in the Scottsboro cases, there was medical evidence to indicate that no rape had been committed. In Tom Robinson's case, there was no medical evidence at all. Lee has trimmed down the particulars to create a more pristine lab setting in which to examine the relationships between race, gender, and class.[9]

Atticus' challenge is to convince an all-white (male) jury that they should believe a 'good Negro man' over a 'bad white girl' who, Atticus insinuates, was not only willing to engage in miscegenation but may have incest in her past as well.[10] Yet, Atticus 'knows' that, even if the jury 'knew' Tom was innocent, they would still convict him. The real strategy is to create a record for appeal and win in appellate or federal court as happened with the Scottsboro Boys (at least, for a time).[11] By simplifying the legal niceties and courtroom complications, Harper Lee shows how insidious a flaw racism is in Southern culture and society. Race, in effect, trumps class and gender.[12] Viewed from this standpoint, the implication of the narrative is that, even if every other factor had been favorable to the Scottsboro boys, they still would have been convicted because of their race.

But what are we to make of Atticus' strategy? Is it sincere or cynical? Obviously, the answer depends on how we read his character. But how might we determine this? Do we rely on narrative signals alone? Or should the historical context in which the book was written provide us with clues – for instance, the example of the Scottsboro Boys trials? Indeed, to what extent should historical context ever affect our understanding of a work of art? To what extent should the time and place in which it was created affect its interpretation? Should later events play a role? For example, to what extent, if any, should the Holocaust affect our interpretation of Shakespeare's *Merchant of Venice*? Or would that simply impose anachronistic values that would cloud our aesthetic judgment of the work? Is it even possible to interpret an artwork except through our own circumstances?

Traditional literary criticism, for instance, includes an author's biography and historical milieu as a matter of course in the interpretation of a text. Thus,

Herman Melville's experience as a seaman and relationship to a famous judge, Lemuel Shaw, would be highly relevant to any interpretation of *Billy Budd*[13] just as the McCarthy hearings might be for the three modern plays discussed in this book. By contrast, New Criticism, which includes the poet T.S. Eliot as a leading proponent, argues against historical context even if it is the source of the author's inspiration. A work of art should be considered on its own terms for its inherent aesthetic appeal. We should not waste our time wondering whether Shakespeare agreed with Macbeth's conclusion that life is "a tale told by an idiot, full of sound and fury, signifying nothing."[14] The pronouncement is only relevant in the context of the play and the actions of its characters.[15] Reader-response criticism, however, focuses on the reception of a work of art or a text. This theory acknowledges that the 'meaning' of a text, for example, may change in changing circumstances. A text contains "an autonomous space of meaning which is no longer animated by the intention of its author."[16] Thus, we both can and should allow our knowledge about the Holocaust to influence our understanding of *The Merchant of Venice*.

Each of these critical schools assumes in its own way a particular approach to history (its relevance or irrelevance) and how historical context should affect our understanding of an artwork. Each approach also affords different implications for how to understand *To Kill a Mockingbird* and the character of Atticus Finch. From our perspective, however, we should also note that the approach to history we choose (which is intertwined with the literary approach we choose) often brings with it a tacit understanding of how law 'ought' to be interpreted.

Constitutional faith and constitutional evil[17]

Put in the simplest terms possible, a central issue here is whether one's interpretation of 'law' is oriented toward the future (an 'aspirational' interpretation not unlike Robert Cover's notion of a 'redemptive' *nomos*) or toward the past (for example, an 'originalist' interpretation[18]). In the 'aspirational' model, the proper interpretation of law is one that is consistent with the goals the society purports to attempt to achieve in the future – e.g., a "more perfect Union" as the preamble to the US Constitution exhorts. The doctrine of "living constitutionalism"[19] (the notion that the meaning of the values and principles set forth in the US Constitution may change over time) is consistent with this 'aspirational' model. Indeed, the very genius of the English common law system, it has been claimed, is its flexibility, its ability to change the law in accordance with new values and perspectives that develop over time.[20] Thus, an 'aspirational' model might interpret general principles of law differently in different eras as our understanding of those principles develops. For example, people have argued that the extent to which 'equal protection of the laws' applied to blacks, women, children, the disabled, etc., has changed and should change as people's perceptions of who counts as a 'person' entitled to that protection has changed. To this extent, the 'aspirational' model has resonances with Cicero's apothegm that what right reason dictates *is* law.

In the 'originalist' model, the proper interpretation of law is one fixed in the past, ostensibly when the law was promulgated. In 2013, US Supreme Court Justice Antonin Scalia (who claimed to be an 'originalist') provocatively asserted before an audience of law students that the Constitution "is not a living document. It's dead, dead, dead."[21] What he meant by this is not entirely clear, but at the very least it seems that subsequent circumstances and contexts are not supposed to affect the interpretation of a law. Scalia's view was influenced by Jeremy Bentham's 'legal positivist' approach to the law. Both the aspirational and the originalist orientations allow for a multitude of different conceptions of law and interpretation and different conceptions of the narrative to which they belong.[22]

How this framing of the issue makes a difference in the interpretation of law may be illustrated by the positions taken in the 19th century by William Lloyd Garrison (a fervent abolitionist opposed to slavery) and Frederick Douglass (an escaped slave).[23] Garrison argued that the institution of slavery in the United States was so evil that the US Constitution was "a covenant with death, and an agreement with hell."[24] The Constitution's initial compromise with slavery made it irredeemable since the very structure of the Constitution prevented an abolition of slavery in the United States.[25] Garrison looked backwards in time at the way the Constitution had 'always' been read as condoning slavery. Thus, he accepted that the 'proper' interpretation of the Constitution – one that is 'faithful' to the Constitution – must be one that accepted the institution of slavery as it had existed up to that point. For Garrison, since that meant accepting an 'evil' institution, the Constitution itself embodied evil and should be resisted. Of course, for someone like John C. Calhoun (Vice President of the United States and apologist for slavery), a 'faithful' interpretation of the Constitution was one that saw slavery as a positive good, not as an evil. Therefore, there was no moral quandary in remaining 'faithful' to an interpretation of the Constitution that preserved (or expanded) slavery.[26]

By contrast, Frederick Douglass eventually rejected Garrison's position and argued audaciously that the Constitution was actually 'anti-slavery' – among other things, by noting the (deliberate) absence of the words 'slavery,' 'slave' or 'white' in the text of the Constitution and drawing implications from the otherwise inclusive language in the document.[27] Douglass rejected an 'originalist' interpretation of the Constitution[28] and looked forward in time to a society in which the Constitution was read the way it 'should' be – as 'aspiring' to eliminate the institution of slavery. But where does this 'should' come from? Abraham Lincoln maintained that the 'silver frame' of the Constitution should be interpreted in the light of the 'golden apple' of the Declaration of Independence, which held that all men are created equal. But did he mean that the goals were set in 1776 and had been misinterpreted up to that point? Or did he mean that, while the Declaration set forth abstract values to be attained, what those values actually mean changes over time as mankind develops its moral senses? This, for example, is what Justices Brennan and Marshall argued in the 1970s and '80s from the perspective of 'living constitutionalism' when they opposed the death penalty under any circumstances as "cruel and unusual punishment" (8th Amendment) based on "the evolving standards of decency that mark the progress of a maturing society," (*Gregg v. Georgia*, 428 U.S. 153, 173 (1976), citing *Trop v. Dulles*, 356 U. S. 100, 101 (1958)).[29]

Atticus Finch as 'liberal hero'[30]

Harper Lee's success with *To Kill a Mockingbird* led to the fortune (or misfortune) of an even more successful film version, released in 1962. If Atticus Finch is the moral center of the book, Gregory Peck's superb performance in the role as defender of the innocent and protector of the downtrodden cemented the character as an icon in American consciousness (and around the world). Atticus is not just *a* hero; he is *the* hero, named by the American Film Institute as the greatest hero in the history of American cinema!

Yet, it is unwise to conflate film and book. The Atticus we see in the movie is not exactly the same as the Atticus in the book. The movie came out just after the Freedom Riders[31] in the South were making the news. These were exciting times in the history of civil rights, and people were called on to take sides. Gregory Peck himself was well-known for his support of civil rights and other liberal causes – enough so that President Richard Nixon later put the actor on his so-called 'enemies list.' In the context of the times, it seemed natural to believe that (as portrayed by Peck) Atticus, too, was at heart a liberal who supported racial equality and civil rights, that he would be the kind of white Southerner who would have defended and supported the Freedom Riders.[32]

This interpretation of Atticus has been read into one of the most memorable scenes in the book and movie: the mad dog scene.[33] On this reading, the mad dog symbolizes Southern white racism (inverting signs one could see posted throughout the South: 'no dogs or colored allowed'). This is the kind of racism you could find among the working poor and 'white trash' in Maycomb – the Cunninghams and the Ewells, in other words. Calpurnia (the most significant black character in the story) is the first to recognize the dog as 'mad,' and she is the one to warn all the neighbors, including the white ones. Heck Tate, the sheriff, represents Southern elected officials who were unable to deal with white racism even though they were obliged to under the law – hence, the nobility of someone like Atticus who steps up to deal with the problem.[34] The metaphor has been interpreted optimistically – Atticus may lose with Tom Robinson, but eventually education and enlightenment (for which Atticus stands) will prevail in the South, and the rule of law will, at some point, be restored (implying that this will be good for civil rights). The film version virtually trumpets this heroic view of Atticus, and it has inspired many.[35]

Yet, Harper Lee did not create the character of Atticus as an unadulterated 'liberal hero.' The 'aspirational' reading of *To Kill a Mockingbird* that people take from the film, while supported by this interpretation of the 'mad dog' scene, is almost entirely a projection of values from outside the book derived (one reasonably speculates) from a 'progressive' conception of history and the notion of a "Constitution that can do no wrong"[36] – that is, a presumption that the principles and values of the Constitution cannot include 'evil' or 'moral wrong' – to which (it is presumed) racial discrimination belongs.

Atticus Finch as antihero?

If we pay close attention, however, the portrayal of Atticus is more nuanced – especially in the novel. For example, Atticus is shown to be spectacularly wrong about a number of things. When Jem asks Atticus about the Ku Klux Klan, Atticus replies that the KKK was just a 'political organization' that had gone away forever and, apparently, never done any harm – at least, around their parts. When Jem points out that they had threatened the sole Jew in town, Sam Levy, Atticus scoffs. Levy had shamed them by pointing out that he had sold them the sheets they were wearing (subtly – and, hopefully, unconsciously – evoking a Jewish stereotype). Granted, the heyday of the Klan was in the 1920s, and it declined as an organization in the 1930s. Yet, Atticus is or, at least, can be read to seem quite gullible about the Klan's power.[37] Indeed, Atticus makes these remarks in the context of dismissing the idea that a lynch mob might gather in Maycomb to kill Tom Robinson – about which he is very mistaken, placing his own life, the life of Tom Robinson, and even the lives of his children in grave jeopardy.[38] Atticus' naïve optimism also turns out to be dangerously mistaken at another crucial moment in the novel. When Bob Ewell spits in Atticus' face in the town square, Atticus believes that is the end of it – Ewell has blown off his steam.[39]

Moreover, the idea that Atticus has an 'aspirational' faith in a constitutional principle of racial equality is dashed in the novel as well. If we compare the most inspirational passages of the book and the film, we can see the difference. For example, in his closing argument to the jury in the film, Atticus says:

> Now, gentlemen, in this country our courts are the great levelers. In our courts, all men are created equal. I'm no idealist to believe firmly in the integrity of our courts and of our jury system. That's no ideal to me. That is a living, working reality!

This speech is a condensation of the one in the book. It cannot exactly be said to be an unfaithful rendition, but its phrasing allows an interpretation consistent with 'white liberal aspirations' to a society without racial divide. When Atticus invokes Thomas Jefferson's 'all men are created equal,' he adds the words 'in our courts,' and he phrases it this way in order to persuade the white, male jurors to apply the law the way they 'ought' to and disregard racial prejudices when they deliberate the evidence. Many of us choose (and the speech in the film allows us) to believe that an unstated premise in Atticus' mind is that the law (the Constitution) requires racial equality. The truly 'faithful' interpretation of the law is one that recognizes that racial equality must be realized as a principle.

While the concept of 'equality' is present in Atticus' speech in the book, it is couched in much more ambiguous and less 'aspirational' terms. Atticus goes to some lengths to explain away Jefferson's phrasing in the Declaration when he says: "We know all men are not created equal in the sense some people would have us believe."[40] Rather, equality means 'equality before the law' as implemented in the court system — and not necessarily anywhere else. The Atticus in both film and book dismisses contemptuously the notion that "*all* Negroes lie, that *all* Negroes are basically immoral beings, that *all* Negro men are not to be trusted around our women." However, the Atticus of the book is careful to qualify this with the statement that "some Negroes lie, some Negroes are immoral, some Negro men are not to be trusted around women — black or white" (*To Kill a Mockingbird*, p. 208). He is making a rhetorical point to allow for reasonable doubt: although prejudice may encourage jurors to assume that some traits are universal, logically they are not. Therefore, the jurors need not abandon their 'general' views about the 'inferiority of Negroes' in order to find Tom Robinson innocent.

By the late 1960s, the film's portrait of Atticus as 'white liberal hero' came to be seen by some as patronizing and condescending — particularly with the rise of the Black Power Movement. It was objected that the film depicted blacks as passive and incapable of agency. In 1999, law professor Steven Lubet, an expert in trial advocacy, pointed out a few things to think about in terms of Atticus' defense of Tom Robinson.[41] He asked: what if Mayella was telling the truth? After all, Tom's deformed arm doesn't necessarily prove anything — he could have beaten her with the back of his hand. Viewing it objectively, we have to admit that the defense Atticus uses is, in effect, the same defense any sleazy lawyer would use in a rape case — i.e., the victim wanted it.[42] After all, Atticus insinuates that she was so starved for sex/affection that she would resort to a black man. However politely it was done, this is about as cruel as you can be to a witness in the context of the 1930s. Our sympathies disappear if Mayella was lying. But what if she wasn't? The film makes a choice about which interpretation to illustrate (indeed, it almost has to), but in the book one could read her testimony in a different way[43]: that, while she is on the stand, she comes to realize just how despised she is by the town. We ordinarily read her emotional reaction upon cross-examination as evidence she is lying, but we could also understand it as the confusion and dismay she feels at this humiliation.

Atticus' back-up defense is another sleazy criminal lawyer trick — my client did not do this crime, but somebody in this courtroom did, implying that it was Mayella's incestuous father who beat her! This is a classic ploy to create reasonable doubt, familiar to any fan of Erle Stanley Gardner's Perry Mason stories.[44] Yet, as Lubet pointed out, once you start pulling on the threads, you start to see that Tom Robinson's testimony might not be as credible or Mayella's as implausible as they are usually made out to be. For example, is it plausible that Mayella would plan something like this for a 'slap year' in which she saved up seven nickels and then send her siblings off without knowing whether Tom would come by that day?[45] Is it plausible that the Ewells would possess two chiffarobes?[46] Or are they just flaws in Harper Lee's craftsmanship? These are interpretive questions the text allows us to ask, and we might be able to be construct answers. In the larger context of the book's reception, however, most of us are loathe to believe that Harper Lee meant for us to think Tom Robinson was guilty![47]

Malcolm Gladwell, following up on Lubet's article, provides another perspective on Atticus' performance.[48] Atticus, Gladwell asserts, was not the great civil rights advocate we want him to be. Rather, he is a racial accommodationist. Gladwell compares Atticus to Big Jim Folsom, who was governor of Alabama in the 1950s and a 'moderate' on racial issues – in the sense that he viewed and treated blacks as citizens 'like any other citizen' but did not challenge the Jim Crow laws or segregationist views of his fellow whites. The view was that 'people are people' and there is good and bad in all of them. People can only change society by changing people's hearts. This was a pretty common attitude among whites (and even some blacks) in the 1950s and '60s, but it is deemed to be on the losing side of history now. Still, this is precisely what Atticus tries to do with the jury, to change their hearts – and he succeeds to a tangible if, ultimately, futile extent (the jury deliberates for two hours).[49]

The indeterminacy of context: *Go Set a Watchman*

This more negative view of Atticus received unexpected support from Harper Lee herself with the publication of *Go Set a Watchman* in 2015. Whereas the climax of *To Kill a Mockingbird* comes with Scout watching her father defend Tom Robinson from the courthouse balcony, the emotional climax of *Go Set a Watchman*, the event that triggers everything that happens afterwards, is a grown-up Jean Louise watching her father from that same balcony as he presides over a White Citizens' Council meeting. White Citizens' Councils were white supremacist organizations that sprang up in the South right after *Brown* to oppose racial integration. They were open and legal, did not explicitly advocate violence, and have been accurately said to pursue the KKK's agenda through the Rotary Club's rhetoric.[50]

Jean Louise's suspicions about her father are triggered by a pamphlet she finds in his house called 'The Black Plague.' Eventually, it is revealed that Atticus is not a proponent of racial equality at all. He thinks blacks are decidedly inferior to whites, and he is all for segregation. As he puts it bluntly to Jean

Louise: "Do you want Negroes by the carload in our schools and churches and theaters? Do you want them in our world?" (*Go Set a Watchman*, p. 245). The answer he expects is clearly 'no.'

The other telling example in *Go Set a Watchman* involves Calpurnia. The loyal housekeeper of the Finch household is retired. In the novel's most moving moment, Jean Louise visits her and finds her to be cold and distant. Only then does Jean Louise realize that, all the while Calpurnia was looking after her and Jem, she had her own children – whom she neglected for the sake of earning a living.[51] It turns out that her grandson Frank has run afoul of the law – he killed a drunk white man while speeding in his car. Atticus has volunteered to defend him free of charge, but it is clear that it is only to prevent the NAACP from getting involved. And the problem with the NAACP, Atticus says, is that they might bring "colored" lawyers in and demand "Negroes on the juries" – and, maybe even worse, use "every legal trick in their books" (*Go Set a Watchman*, p. 149) to force the judge into an error, so they can get into federal court, which might not only enforce but expand the civil rights of blacks, as happened not only in the *Brown* case but the Scottsboro Boys cases.

Just as John C. Calhoun saw no moral quandary in the institution of slavery, the Atticus of *Go Set a Watchman* sees no moral quandary in the doctrine of 'separate but equal' established by *Plessy v. Ferguson*, 163 U.S. 537 (1896). Atticus' view of constitutional law is consistent with *Plessy*'s view of the 14th Amendment (that 'equal protection of the laws' does not require race mixing) and a certain reading of the 10th Amendment (which, according to some, establishes 'state's rights' and implies 'state sovereignty').[52] In Atticus' eyes (and even in Jean Louise's), the sin of *Brown v. Board of Education* was in imposing 'outside' values on what was supposed to be determined by state law authorities, forcing integration of the races where the local sentiments (of whites) opposed it. For this Atticus, as long as individuals regardless of race are afforded adequate legal protections, then 'separation' of the races is no problem. In fact, because the Atticus of *Go Set a Watchman* believes "our Negro population is backward" (p. 242), it is a positive good and 'faithful' to the Constitution.[53] This certainly conflicts with the sentiments of most Americans today, but it may be enough to indicate that *Brown*'s reasoning might seem 'aspirational' and, therefore, illegitimate to those whose theory of constitutional interpretation is oriented toward the past.

The Jean Louise in *Go Set a Watchman* is also "furious" at the *Brown* decision because (in her view) it tried to implement the 14th Amendment while ignoring the 10th Amendment, which in her mind "meant the most, somehow" (p. 239). While Jean Louise's understanding of the Constitution seems naïve and muddled to us now, it was not an unusual position among many conservatives at the time. Local mores and customs were felt to be more important than the abstract values enshrined in the 14th Amendment (especially if they could be interpreted another way). Yet, while agreeing with Atticus on many fundamental issues, she pleads for a future-oriented, 'aspirational' interpretation of the Constitution: "You deny them [blacks] hope. Any man in this world, Atticus, any man who has a head and arms and legs, was born with hope in his heart" (p. 251). For Jean Louise, the problem was not just that blacks were 'backward' but that they were being *held* back. They had a right to improve their lives just like any white person. The 'meddling' of the NAACP was the price the South had to pay for ignoring and suppressing the aspirations of its non-white citizenry. Therefore, the constitutional trump card was hope that racial equality could be achieved; this prospect of a better nation ultimately justified *Brown*'s interpretation of the 14th Amendment.

What are we to make of the differences between Atticus the liberal hero in the film version of *To Kill a Mockingbird* and the racist Atticus of *Go Set a Watchman*? Is the Atticus of *Watchman* the same as in the Atticus of *Mockingbird*, only older and crustier? Should we reconsider everything we thought about Atticus in light of new information? A New Critic would have no problem resolving this. These are two separate works of fiction. Just because most of the protagonists have the same names does not necessarily mean that they are the same characters. Is James Bond played by Sean Connery the same as the James Bond played by Roger Moore or Daniel Craig? The different Atticuses must be viewed and interpreted on the premises and within the confines of their own works. Thus, if we want to retain the Atticus of *Mockingbird* as the pristine liberal hero of the movie, we can.

But we can also use the elements we find in *Go Set a Watchman* and the critiques of Lumet and Gladwell to craft a nuanced character, a more realistic Atticus who is both heroic and flawed in a complex, disturbing, and very human way. It is perfectly historically plausible that a Southern white man in the 1930s (or 1950s) would be comfortable with a 'separate but equal' interpretation of the Constitution – one that 'acknowledges' inherent differences between the races but insists on the impartial application of the law to all people even if social mores permit discrimination in other ways. In other words, the character of Atticus Harper Lee intended to create might well be the perfect Southern gentleman who would lament the boorish racism of less refined folk and defend and protect a black man from injustice but never dream of socializing with him as an equal. If such an Atticus is a hero, it is not because he is a champion of equality and civil rights but because he is a champion of the rule of law as an alternative to violence.[54]

Notes

1 On the controversy surrounding its publication, see Ed Pilkington, "Go Set a Watchman: Mystery of Harper Lee Manuscript Discovery Deepens," *The Guardian* (2 July 2015). For general analysis, see Helle Porsdam, "Literary Representation and Social Justice in an Age of Civil Rights: Harper Lee's *To Kill a Mockingbird*," in K. Dolin (ed.), *Law and Literature* (2018), pp. 255–272.
2 Clarence Norris (19), Charlie Weems (20), Hayward Patterson (18), Ozie Powell (16), Willie Roberson (17), Eugene Williams (13), Olen Montgomery (17), Andy Wright

(19), and his brother Roy Wright (12 or 13). The nine boys were subjected to a series of trials, characterized by some as a "legal lynching" (Hollace Ransdall, Report on the Scottsboro, Ala. Case for the American Civil Liberties Union (27 May 1931)). Their case twice went to the US Supreme Court, which overturned their convictions – the first time for inadequate legal counsel, *Powell v. Alabama*, 287 U.S. 45 (1932), the second time for bias in jury selection, *Norris v. Alabama*, 294 U.S. 587 (1935). In 1937, the charges against Willie Roberson, Olen Montgomery, Eugene Williams, and Roy Wright were dropped. The others were convicted. For more comprehensive accounts of the Scottsboro Boys trials, see also Dan T. Carter, *Scottsboro: A Tragedy of the American South* (1969) and Gerald Horne, *Powell vs. Alabama: The Scottsboro Boys and American Justice* (1997).

3 Victoria Price and Ruby Bates. In a later trial, Ruby Bates recanted her testimony and asserted that no rapes had taken place.

4 Such a characterization arouses a mob mentality in the general community not unlike that surrounding the miscarriage of justice in the so-called Central Park Five case in which five black and Latino teenagers were wrongfully convicted of assaulting and raping a white female jogger in 1989. They were later exonerated in 2002. See Sarah Burns, *The Central Park Five: The Untold Story Behind One of New York City's Most Infamous Crimes* (2012).

5 Olen Montgomery was almost blind. Ozie Powell was later assessed as having a very low IQ, and Willie Roberson suffered from a crippling case of syphilis and gonorrhoea.

6 Though the prosecution does point out Tom Robinson's size and physique, implying that he is (despite his handicap) 'intimidating.'

7 The governor called out the National Guard to protect them.

8 Although Patterson was convicted by the jury, Judge Horton overturned the verdict because "the law declares that a defendant should not be convicted without corroboration where the testimony of the prosecutrix bears on its face indications of improbability or unreliability and particularly when it is contradicted by other evidence" (J. Michael Martinez, *The Greatest Criminal Cases: Changing the Court of American Law* (2014), p. 55). See Matthew C. Heise, "The Scottsboro Boys Trials and Judge Horton's *Ex Parte* Meeting: History's Verdict," 7(2) *The Dartmouth Law Journal* 208 (2009).

9 For a different comparison of *To Kill a Mockingbird* and the Scottsboro Boys case, see James A. Miller, *Remembering Scottsboro: The Legacy of an Infamous Trial* (2009), pp. 220–234.

10 Recalling defense attorney Sam Leibowitz's futile attempt to impeach Victoria Price's testimony in Haywood Patterson's second trial by implying she was promiscuous and/or a prostitute.

11 None of the Scottsboro Boys' trials ended in acquittal, but some of the convictions were overturned on appeal. An intriguing unanswered question raised by Harper Lee's two novels is whether Atticus would have appealed exclusively in the state court system, where the Scottsboro Boys lost (except for one minor victory), or in federal court, where they won. The text is ambiguous but seems to contemplate only the state system. See below on this issue in *Go Set a Watchman*.

12 Race relations dominate the movie, and class and gender issues are only hinted at. Yet, the important *Bildung* aspect of the novel is the way Scout has to learn to negotiate the pitfalls of class, gender, and race. She is constantly being pressured to stop being a tomboy and put on a dress, act like a lady. This is the focus of her entire relationship with Aunt Alexandra, who does not appear in the movie. At the same time, she is learning the delicate social mores that govern class relations – the Cunningham boy pouring syrup on his meal, for example. In addition, Maycomb's class hierarchy is clearer in the book: there is the white middle class at the top (to which Atticus, the judge, Miss Maudie belong); there are the white working poor

(to which the Cunninghams belong), and there is 'white trash' (to which the Ewells belong). But 'white trash' need somebody below them: by default, black people. It is an old sociological truism that so-called 'white trash' elements of society are the most virulent racists because race and race alone distinguishes them from their poor black neighbors.

13 On this, see Robert Cover, *Justice Accused: Antislavery and the Judicial Process* (1975), esp. "Of Creon and Captain Vere."
14 *Macbeth,* Act V, scene v, lines 26–28.
15 This sort of divide may be found among judges/legal scholars who advocate 'textualist' approaches and those who rely on some form of context to interpret law. It is common among disciplines that rely on hermeneutics. Compare the traditional approaches to the history of ideas discussed, for example, in Quentin Skinner, "Meaning and Understanding in the History of Ideas," 8(1) *History and Theory* (1969), pp. 3–53.
16 Paul Ricoeur, *Hermeneutics and the Human Sciences* (1981), p. 174. See Stanley Fish, *Is There a Text in This Class?* (1980).
17 'Constitutional evil' is a term employed by Mark Graber especially in his book *Dred Scott and the Problem of Constitutional Evil* (2006). The book is a meditation on the notorious case of *Dred Scott v. Sandford,* 60 U.S. 393 (1857) in which the US Supreme Court tried to resolve the inflammatory issue of slavery by holding that no black person could be a citizen of the United States and that the Missouri Compromise of 1820 (limiting the spread of the institution of slavery) was unconstitutional.
18 A theory of constitutional interpretation that the binding legal authority of the words of the Constitution are limited to 1) the original intention of the Framers of the Constitution with respect to those words or 2) the original public meaning of those words at the time the Constitution was drafted and ratified, depending on the theory of 'originalism' to which one subscribes. This applies *a fortiori* to the Constitution's amendments as well. For an overview of 'originalism' as an interpretive theory, see, for example, Lawrence B. Solum, "What is Originalism? The Evolution of Contemporary Originalist Theory," Georgetown University Law Center, http://scholarship.law.georgetown.edu/facpub/1353http://dx.doi.org/10.2139/ssrn.1825543 (2011); Daniel A. Farber, "The Originalism Debate: A Guide for the Perplexed," 49 *Ohio St. L.J.* 1085 (1989); Jack Rakove, *Original Meanings: Politics and Ideas in the Making of the Constitution* (1997).
19 The term itself was used at least as early as the 1830s and the doctrine it refers to was articulated by Chief Justice of the Supreme Court John Marshall in *McCulloch v. Maryland,* 17 U.S. (4 Wheat.) 316, 415 (1819). It is frequently associated with Supreme Court Justice William J. Brennan, Jr., "The Constitution of the United States: Contemporary Ratification," Text and Teaching Symposium, Georgetown University, Washington, D.C. (12 October 1985). See Lawrence B. Solum, "Originalism Versus Living Constitutionalism: The Conceptual Structure of the Great Debate," 113(6) *Northwestern University Law Review* 1243 (April, 2019).
20 One of dozens of sources to express this sentiment puts it this way:

> Inherent in the common law is a dynamic principle which allows it to grow and to tailor itself to meet changing needs within the doctrine of *stare decisis,* which, if correctly understood, was not static and did not forever prevent the courts from reversing themselves or from applying principles of common law to new situations as the need arose. If this were not so, a court must succumb to a rule that a judge should let others 'long dead and unaware of the problems of the age in which he lives, do his thinking for him.
>
> (*Bielski v. Schulze,* 16 Wis. 2d 1, 11 (1962))

'Living constitutionalism' is often equated with "common law constitutionalism." See, for example, Lawrence B. Solum, "Legal Theory Lexicon: Living Constitutionalism," *Legal Theory Blog* (25 November 2018).

21 "Constitution a 'dead, dead, dead' document, Scalia tells SMU audience," *Dallas Morning News* (28 January 2013). For a critical assessment of Scalia's originalism, see Rick Hasen, *The Justice of Contradictions: Antonin Scalia and the Politics of Disruption* (2018).

22 As an aside, it should be noted that the two modes of reasoning cannot be so easily distinguished simply by their orientation toward future or past. After all, the goals of the 'aspirational' model must in one way or another have been settled upon in the past – either explicitly or as a mode of reasoning accepted in the past that assumes its values may change in the future. And if that is the case, then can't it be said that this is merely another form of 'originalist' jurisprudence – one that provides a method for realizing the past's aspirations for the future? In this sense, it is not a contradiction to speak of "living originalism" (see Jack M. Balkin, *Living Originalism* (2011)) even though 'originalism' was once thought to be the antonym of 'living constitutionalism.'

23 Manumission from his 'master' was later purchased by two wealthy British women so that fugitive slave laws could not be used against him when he returned to the US from a tour through the British Isles.

24 Quoted by Graber, *Constitutional Evil*, pp. 226–227 from a resolution introduced by Garrison to the Massachusetts Anti-Slavery Society in 1843.

25 Paul Finkelman, "Frederick Douglass's Constitution: From Garrisonian Abolitionist to Lincoln Republican," 81(1) *Missouri Law Review* 1 (Winter, 2016), p. 8 ("had there been no civil war and slavery continued, to this day, in 2016, the fifteen slave states that existed in 1860 could block a constitutional amendment to end slavery"). The 13th Amendment to the Constitution abolishing slavery was only feasible because the Southern states had ostensibly withdrawn from the Union, triggering the American Civil War, and had no vote on the amendment.

26 For a discussion of this moral quandary, see Jeffrey M. Schmitt, "Slavery and the History of Congress's Enumerated Powers" *Arkansas Law Review* (forthcoming), available at SSRN: https://ssrn.com/abstract=3912752 (arguing that 'originalism' in constitutional interpretation is so tied to the institution of slavery that it is morally compromised and, therefore, 'living constitutionalism' is to be preferred).

27 Douglass explained that

> it has been said that Negroes are not included within the benefits sought under this declaration. This is said by the slaveholders in America ... but it is not said by the Constitution itself. Its language is "we the people"; not we the white people, not even we the citizens, not we the privileged class, not we the high, not we the low, but we the people; ... if Negroes are people, they are included in the benefits for which the Constitution of America was ordained and established.
> (Frederick Douglass, "The Constitution of the United States: Is It Pro-Slavery or Anti-slavery?" (1860) (speech before the Scottish Anti-Slavery Society, Glasgow, Scotland, 26 March 1860))

28 As Douglass put it:

> [W]here would be the advantage of a written Constitution, if, instead of seeking its meaning in its words, we had to seek them in the secret intentions of individuals who may have had something to do with writing the paper? What will the people of America a hundred years hence care about the intentions of the scriveners who wrote the Constitution?
> (Id.)

29 One cannot help noticing a certain 'Whiggishness' to the justices' conception of history.
30 The term 'liberal' is used in the modern American context here in which 'freedom' is linked to notions of 'equality' and 'social justice' – more Franklin Delano Roosevelt than John Stuart Mill.
31 Mixed race groups that boarded interstate buses to challenge racial segregation in the South.
32 On the history of the civil rights movement, see, for example, Richard Kluger, *Simple Justice: The History of* Brown v. Board of Education (1975) and Taylor Branch's three-volume biography of Martin Luther King, Jr., esp. *Parting the Waters: America in the King Years 1954–63* (1988).
33 As interpreted by Joseph Crespino, "The Strange Career of Atticus Finch," 6(2) *Southern Cultures* (Summer, 2000), pp. 9–30.
34 It is also significant for the *Bildungsroman* aspects of the book in that Scout and especially Jem begin to look at their father differently, realizing for the first time that he is more than just a wise and kind but essentially useless member of the community: Atticus meets the overarching requirement for masculinity in the South – proficiency with a gun. That he both mastered it and rejected it is telling.
35 Including the author of this book. I want to emphasize this since Atticus will be examined in less flattering terms in the following.
36 Gerard N. Magliocca, "The Constitution Can Do No Wrong," 3 *University of Illinois Law Review* 3 (2012), pp. 723–735, available at SSRN: https://ssrn.com/abstract =1779505 or http://dx.doi.org/10.2139/ssrn.1779505.
37 Perhaps, Harper Lee intends us to see Atticus' remarks as naïve. She knows, after all, what happens after the 1930s. For example, she knows about farcical trials like those of the Scottsboro Boys; she knows about Emmet Till, a 14-year-old boy savagely beaten to death allegedly for whistling at a white woman.
38 In the book, the actual danger was mitigated somewhat since it turns out that Mr. Underwood, the newspaper editor and intractable racist, was keeping an eye on the incident with a loaded shotgun.
39 Atticus says, "We don't have anything to fear from Bob Ewell, he got it all out of his system that morning" (*To Kill a Mockingbird*, p. 222). The spitting scene is powerfully refashioned in the film to illustrate Atticus' consistent Christian pacifism in the book. Atticus' different reactions in the book and film to Tom Robinson's death also illustrate something. Tom was 'shot while escaping', a euphemism in the South that meant he was gunned down in cold blood by white guards. Yet, in the film, Atticus innocently believes that that this account is true ("they shot to wound him"). In the book, there is no pretense of trying to wound Tom – it was 17 shots to kill, but Atticus immediately puts himself in the shoes of the guards who killed him ("What was one Negro, more or less, among two hundred of 'em?," p. 239). Indeed, one can even sense in the book that Atticus blames Tom for lacking faith in the legal strategy Atticus was pursuing. It is left to the reader who is more familiar with the ways of the South to determine whether or not Tom actually tried to escape or was simply executed to save the State the trouble of an appeal.
40 In the book, the full context of Atticus' remark reads:

> One more thing, gentlemen, before I quit. Thomas Jefferson once said that all men are created equal, a phrase that the Yankees and the distaff side of the Executive branch in Washington are fond of hurling at us. There is a tendency in this year of grace, 1935, for certain people to use this phrase out of context, to satisfy all conditions. The most ridiculous example I can think of is that the people who run public education promote the stupid and idle along with the

industrious—because all men are created equal, educators will gravely tell you, the children left behind suffer terrible feelings of inferiority. We know all men are not created equal in the sense some people would have us believe—some people are smarter than others, some people have more opportunity because they're born with it, some men make more money than others, some ladies make better cakes than others—some people are born gifted beyond the normal scope of most men.
(*To Kill a Mockingbird*, p. 209)

Only then does he argue for the courts as the 'great leveler.'

41 Steven Lubet, "Reconstructing Atticus Finch," 97(6) *Michigan Law Review* (1999), pp. 1339–1362.
42 In *Go Set a Watchman*, the narrator Jean Louise relates that Atticus won an acquittal for a 'colored boy' on the charge of the rape of a white girl – the only time that had ever happened in Maycomb. Atticus won by proving the woman consented. "Consent was easier to prove than under normal conditions – the defendant had only one arm." *Go Set a Watchman*, p. 109. Now, besides the obvious parallels to Tom Robinson, think for a minute what this says implicitly about the concept of 'rape' at this time. It is not rape if the girl could have fought her way out of it. Thus, in the original manuscript, Atticus used the 'she asked for it' defense, and it worked.
43 After all, the narrator (Scout) might not have the best or the most reliable comprehension here. Jem vouches to the Reverend Sykes that she does not understand when the term 'rutting' is uttered in Bob Ewell's testimony. Still, the inconsistency of the narrator's voice (sometimes naïve, sometimes sophisticated) has been considered a consistent aesthetic flaw in the novel.
44 Popular in the 1930s and given new life on radio and television in the 1940s and 1950s, though Perry Mason was never meant to be considered a 'sleazy' lawyer.
45 See Lubet, "Reconstructing Atticus Finch," p. 1347.
46 Though it may be one chiffarobe, which is a 'true' detail that slips into both Tom's and Mayella's stories, albeit in different ways. A possible scenario that seems never to be discussed is that Tom and Mayella were engaged or about to engage in consensual intercourse but were interrupted by the return of Bob Ewell. This would provide both Tom and Mayella a motivation to lie. Moreover, if Mayella is telling the truth, then there is a reason to bring charges against Tom. However, if Tom's story is true, what is the motivation of the Ewells to make the incident public? Might Mayella be lying to cover up being caught by her father while she was with Tom Robinson? If they were caught *in flagrante*, so to speak, the Ewells might not want it publicized. But it is also plausible that Mayella would make up the rape charge to mollify her father after he caught her alone with a black man.
47 The book's ultimate decision seems to be: "Atticus had used every tool available to free men to save Tom Robinson, but in the secret courts of men's hearts Atticus had no case. Tom was a dead man the minute Mayella Ewell opened her mouth and screamed" (*To Kill a Mockingbird*, p. 245). This is Scout's conclusion after reading the racist Mr. Underwood's bitter newspaper editorial, likening Tom's death to the slaughter of a songbird.
48 Malcolm Gladwell, "The Courthouse Ring: Atticus Finch and the Limits of Southern Liberalism," *New Yorker* (10 August 2009).
49 For Gladwell (and many others), Atticus' real moral test comes at the end: when his own family has been threatened, when he agrees to become complicit in an obstruction of justice and endorse the lie that Bob Ewell fell on his knife – all, as Gladwell puts it, "in the name of saving their beloved neighbor the burden of angel-food cake." In the end, Gladwell says, Atticus supports a discriminatory law – one law for genteel whites, one for white trash, one for blacks. He is really no different from the jury that convicted Tom Robinson.

50 Charles M. Payne, *I've Got the Light of Freedom: The Organizing Tradition and the Mississippi Freedom Struggle* (2007), p. 34.
51 This contrasts with *To Kill a Mockingbird* in which Scout as a girl recognizes that Calpurnia has a life separate from hers. The premise of the critically-acclaimed television series *I'll Fly Away* (1991–1993) was a retelling of *To Kill a Mockingbird* from Calpurnia's point of view but set during the heyday of the Civil Rights Movement.
52 Based on the still-controversial theory of states' rights accepted by many Southerners, which accommodated the now-discredited doctrines of nullification and secession. For an overview, see Sanford Levinson (ed.), *Nullification and Secession in Modern Constitutional Thought* (2016).
53 Atticus explains this to Jean Louise: "It might benefit you to go back and have a look at what some of our founding fathers really believed, instead of relying so much on what people these days tell you they believed" (id., p. 244).
54 To illustrate the complexity of assessing even 'heroic' American characters on race, consider President John Quincy Adams (famed for his abolitionist sentiments), who after his presidency argued the infamous Amistad case in favor of slave mutineers before the US Supreme Court. This same man wrote an essay on Shakespeare's *Othello* in which he condemned the lascivious character of Desdemona:

> The blood must circulate briskly in the veins of a young woman, so fascinated, and so coming to the tale of a rude, unbleached African soldier. The great moral lesson of the tragedy of *Othello* is, that black and white blood cannot be intermingled in marriage without a gross outrage on the law of Nature.
> (J.Q. Adams, "Misconceptions of Shakespeare, Upon the Stage," in James Hackett, *Notes and Comments upon Certain Plays and Actors of Shakespeare* (1864), p. 224)

See James Shapiro, *Shakespeare in a Divided America* (2020).

References

Balkin, J. M. (2011). *Living originalism*.
Branch, T. (1988). *Parting the waters: America in the King years 1954–63*.
Brennan, Jr., W. J. (12 October 1985). The Constitution of the United States: Contemporary ratification. *Text and Teaching Symposium*, Georgetown University, Washington, D.C.
Burns, S. (2012). *The Central Park five: The untold story behind one of New York City's most infamous crimes*.
Carter, D. T. (1969). *Scottsboro: A tragedy of the American South*.
Cover, R. (1975). *Justice accused: Antislavery and the judicial process*.
Crespino, J. (Summer, 2000). The strange career of Atticus Finch. 6(2) *Southern Cultures* 9.
Douglass, F. (1860). *The Constitution of the United States: Is it pro-slavery or anti-slavery?*
Farber, D. A. (1989). The originalism debate: A guide for the perplexed. 49 *Ohio St. Law Journal* 1085.
Finkelman, P. (Winter, 2016). Frederick Douglass's constitution: From Garrisonian abolitionist to Lincoln Republican. 81(1) *Missouri Law Review* 1.
Fish, S. (1980). *Is there a text in this class?*
Gladwell, M. (10 August 2009). The courthouse ring: Atticus Finch and the limits of southern liberalism. *New Yorker*.
Graber, M. (2006). *Dred Scott and the problem of constitutional evil*.
Hasen, R. (2018). *The justice of contradictions: Antonin Scalia and the politics of disruption*.

Horne, G. (1997). *Powell v. Alabama: The Scottsboro boys and American justice.*
Heise, M. C. (2009). The Scottsboro boys trials and Judge Horton's *ex parte* meeting: History's verdict. 7(2) *Dartmouth Law Journal* 208.
Kluger, R. (1975). *Simple justice: The history of* Brown v. Board of Education.
Lee, H. (2015). *Go set a watchman.*
Lee, H. (1988 [1960]). *To kill a mockingbird.*
Lubet, S. (1999). Reconstructing Atticus Finch. 97(6) *Michigan Law Review* 1339.
Magliocca, G. N. (2012). The Constitution can do no wrong. 3 *University of Illinois Law Review*, available at SSRN: https://ssrn.com/abstract=1779505 or http://dx.doi.org/10.2139/ssrn.1779505.
Martinez, J. M. (2014). *The greatest criminal cases: Changing the course of American law.*
Miller, J. A. (2009). *Remembering Scottsboro: The legacy of an infamous trial.*
Payne, C. M. (2007). *I've got the light of freedom: The organizing tradition and the Mississippi freedom struggle.*
Pilkington, E. (2 July 2015). Go set a watchman: Mystery of Harper Lee manuscript discovery deepens. *The Guardian.*
Porsdam, H. (2018). Literary representation and social justice in an age of civil rights: Harper Lee's To Kill a Mockingbird. In K. Dolin (Ed.), *Law and Literature.*
Rakove, J. (1997). *Original meanings: Politics and ideas in the making of the Constitution.*
Ransdall, H. (27 May 1931). *Report on the Scottsboro, Ala. case for the American Civil Liberties Union.*
Ricoeur, P. (1981). *Hermeneutics and the human sciences.*
Schmitt, J. M. (Forthcoming). Slavery and the history of Congress's enumerated powers. *Arkansas Law Review* [in press], available at SSRN. Retrieved from https://ssrn.com/abstract=3912752.
Shapiro, J. (2020). *Shakespeare in a divided America.*
Skinner, Q. (1969). Meaning and understanding in the history of ideas. 8(1) *History and Theory* 3.
Solum, L. B. (April, 2019). Originalism versus living constitutionalism: The conceptual structure of the great debate structure of the great debate. 113(6) *Northwestern University Law Review* 1243.
Solum, L. B. (2011). What is originalism? The evolution of contemporary originalist theory. Retrieved from http://scholarship.law.georgetown.edu/facpub/1353http. Georgetown University Law Center. https://doi.org/10.2139/ssrn.1825543.
Solum, L. B. (25 November 2018). Legal theory lexicon: Living constitutionalism. *Legal theory blog.*

Appendix 1 Summary of Historical Background and New Testament Source Differences

It may be helpful for those uninitiated in biblical studies to summarize a bit about the historical background and differences among the gospels in their accounts of Jesus' trials.

Historical background

Alexander the Great conquered an empire that stretched from Macedonia to Egypt to India. When he died, his empire broke up into five, then four, then three kingdoms: the Ptolemies (Egypt), the Seleucids (Mesopotamia), and the Antigonids (Macedonia and Greece). The area we call Israel or Palestine today was split roughly between the Ptolemies and the Seleucids and was divided into various administrative units – the largest of which were Judea, Samaria, and Galilee. The Maccabean Revolt (167–160 B.C.E.) was an attempt by Jews living in Judea to rebel against an aggressive Hellenizing effort by the Seleucid Empire. Around 63 B.C.E., Pompey the Great made Syria into a Roman province during the Third Mithridatic War, and he was invited to set up a puppet government in Jerusalem. In 40 B.C.E., Rome had Herod the Great declared "King of the Jews" to rule Judea. Around 6 C.E., Judea and Samaria were combined into a Roman district called Iudaea, which was a satellite of the province of Syria. Publius Sulpicius Quirinius was appointed governor, and he instituted a census of the region for tax purposes. Pontius Pilate was procurator (or prefect) of this district between 26 and 36 C.E.[1]

The trial of Jesus (assuming it took place) occurred in Jerusalem during the reign of the Roman emperor Tiberius. At the time, according to the Jewish historian Josephus (born around 37 C.E.), there were three basic philosophies predominant in the Jewish religion: the Pharisees (who held strictly to the laws set forth in the Torah as well as such rules as could be deduced from the Torah through an oral tradition), the Sadducees (who were responsible for the Temple in Jerusalem, usually descendants of the priestly class, who considered only the Torah authoritative), and the Essenes (a smaller, communal, almost monastic sect). Josephus also mentions the Zealots (a word that describes Jews who were particularly hostile to the rule of "foreigners"), a group that may have been founded in revolt against Quirinius' tax measures. We know Jesus was not a Sadducee, and we may deduce from the gospel accounts of his teachings that he was hostile to the Pharisees. According to the gospel accounts, the chief priests, Pharisees, and scribes all plot against Jesus. However, there is no agreement among the gospels as to what exactly Jesus did to merit their hatred. Whatever the reason – whether it was driving the moneychangers from the Temple, violating the Sabbath, or just generally rousing rebellion,[2] the stories all agree that Jesus was hauled before the authorities and, ultimately, crucified. Indeed, the *kerygma* (i.e., the central message of Jesus' ministry) of the gospel stories is that it was *necessary* for him to be crucified in order to save mankind – although there is not unanimous evidence that *Jesus* thought it was necessary (*vide* in Mark's account when Jesus asks for this cup to be taken from him). The four gospels do not agree on the details of this trial but generally describe it as having two phases – a Jewish trial and a Roman trial.

The Jewish trial

All four gospels relate that Jesus was taken to the Sanhedrin or, at least, brought before a prominent Jewish official after his arrest in Gethsemane.[3] There is no certainty about what the procedures of the Sanhedrin were at this time. However, according to the Mishnah (the oral tradition of Jewish law, which began to be written down in Jesus' time but was not really compiled in a comprehensive written form until around 200 C.E.), it was illegal to hold trials in capital cases at night, and the verdict also had to be reached in the daytime (Mishnah Sanhedrin 4.1).

Mark (chap. 14) and Matthew (chap. 26) say that the high priests sought testimony to put Jesus to death but found none. Many bore false witness, but their testimony did not agree. Some (in Mark) or two (in Matthew) testify that they heard Jesus say he would destroy the Temple made with hands and, in three days, build another not made with hands. However, in Mark, even they did not agree. To be convicted of a crime under Jewish law, two witnesses, testifying to the same thing, were required – or a confession. Hence, in Mark but not in Matthew, there were insufficient witnesses to convict Jesus of anything.[4] Nevertheless, in both accounts, the high priest asks Jesus to answer these charges, but he does not reply. He then asks Jesus, "Are you the Christ?"[5] In Matthew and Luke, when Jesus is asked this, he replies with a variation of "you say so" or "are you saying so."[6] In Mark alone, Jesus says, "I am."

Here, in the narrative, the high priest rends his garment[7] and announces that there is no need for witnesses now, because all present have heard Jesus' blasphemy. Blasphemy was defined as using the "name" of God disrespectfully (Mishnah 7.5) and was punishable by death by stoning. It might also be blasphemous to compare oneself to God. In Mark and Matthew, the chief priests, elders, and scribes say that Jesus deserves death (leaving open whether they actually do condemn him).

According to Mark, the trial was held and Jesus condemned at night. The next morning, the chief priests and the council held a consultation – possibly, implying that they recognized that Jesus' condemnation was not kosher, so to speak.[8] Thus, in Mark, it seems that Jesus was not condemned by the Sanhedrin, because the trial before it was illegal. In Matthew, the witnesses are sufficient to condemn Jesus. However, it is not clear at this point in the text that he *was* condemned. The next morning, the chief priest and elders take counsel on whether to have Jesus executed and then send him to Pilate. It is later affirmed indirectly in Judas' colloquy with the council that Jesus *was* condemned by them in a trial that might not have been legal (because it was held at night). In Luke (for yet another variation), there is no trial at night although he is taken to the high priest. According to Luke, Jesus is only brought before an assembly of elders, chief priests, and scribes when day comes, and he is asked whether he is the Christ and the Son of God. Jesus replies, 'you say I am,' and the council agrees that this is blasphemy.

The Gospel of John's account of these episodes (chapter 18) is very different. First of all, Jesus is not only arrested by a group of Jewish officers but a 'band of soldiers,' which indicates that Roman authorities were involved from the beginning. Moreover, they take Jesus first to Annas, Caiaphas' father-in-law. When the high priest questions Jesus about his teachings, it is a soldier who strikes Jesus for responding improperly. Peter follows along in every gospel, but only in John is there "another disciple known to the high priest" who is present in the court. Hence, only in John is there any indication of who might have related the story of what happened during Jesus' interrogation – but we do not know who it was. In John's account, Annas sends Jesus on to Caiaphas, who then sends him on to the *praetorium* (Pilate's palace). The Jews refuse to enter the *praetorium* – ostensibly, to avoid being defiled, and Pilate comes out to meet them (an extremely unlikely action on his part as a Roman official). When asked to judge Jesus, Pilate tells them to take him and judge him by their own laws. The Jews then claim that "it is not lawful for us to put any man to death." This is puzzling, as there seems to be plenty of evidence that Jews could and did exercise the death penalty in this era. However, there is evidence in the Jerusalem Talmud (J. Sanh. 1.18a; 7.24b) that the Sanhedrin lost the power of capital punishment forty years before the destruction of the Temple. But this is contradicted elsewhere in the Mishnah and the New Testament.[9]

Did Jesus commit blasphemy? This is an almost impossible question to answer adequately. Even if Jesus answered as affirmatively in all the gospels as he does in Mark, it would not be clear. Blasphemy is cursing the name of God or denying one of his attributes. See Mishnah Sanh. 7.5. To the extent we understand the Jewish doctrine of blasphemy at the time of Jesus, nothing Jesus says can be said to be blasphemy; but, of course, that would be consistent with one story the gospels want to relate – that Jesus was unjustly condemned! – yet inconsistent with other ostensive messages. However, the penalty for blasphemy was stoning and, if there is one thing the gospels all agree on, it is that Jesus was crucified – a Roman penalty, not a Jewish one – and that it had something to do with him being 'King of the Jews.'[10]

The Roman trial

All four gospels agree that Jesus was taken before Pontius Pilate, the Roman administrator of the area. Josephus indicates Pilate ruled the Jews somewhat heavy-handedly (*Antiquities of the Jews* 18). However, the gospel accounts portray a Roman administrator almost bending over backwards to give Jesus a fair shake but nevertheless condemning him. Interestingly, we find in Luke and John attempts by Pilate to get rid of the case on jurisdictional grounds. In John, the crowd does not explain the charge against Jesus except that he is "an evildoer." We can speculate that Pilate assumed this was a religious charge or, at least, some charge only relevant to Jewish law. So, he tells them to judge Jesus "by your own law" (κατὰ τὸν νόμον ὑμῶν). In Luke, once Pilate hears that Jesus is from Galilee, he immediately sends him to Herod (presumably, Herod Antipas[11]), who questions him and then sends him back to Pilate. Only Luke has this episode, and it is strange in a number of ways – at first, Herod is 'glad' to meet Jesus, but when questioning occurs and Jesus does not respond, Herod and his soldiers mock him. However, from that day, we are told, Herod and Pilate became good friends. We are not told why.

In every version, Pilate asks Jesus whether he is 'King of the Jews.'[12] In Mark, Pilate seems to know about the claim beforehand. Jesus always replies with a version of 'you say so.' In the Synoptic Gospels, Jesus is taciturn, barely responding to Pilate or the charges against him.[13] However, in John, they engage in a comparatively extended conversation about the nature of kingship, ending with Pilate's (in)famous words, 'what is truth?'

All four versions speak of the custom of releasing a prisoner in honor of the holiday (the only evidence we have of such a custom). Pilate asks the crowd whether they would release Jesus or Barabbas,[14] someone who was already in prison for insurrection (in Mark and Luke) or robbery (in John). Only Matthew gives us the story of Pilate's wife, who warns him away from this case.

In three versions (Matthew, Luke, and John), Pilate states that he finds no crime in Jesus. In Mark, Pilate understands that the chief priests are acting out of envy and asks the crowd what evil Jesus has done. They merely shout 'crucify him.' So, it is puzzling – to judge from the gospel accounts – what crime by Jesus Pilate finds to justify crucifixion. A common reading of the gospels is that, since Jesus replies ambiguously but not unequivocally negatively to the question 'are you King of the Jews,' Pilate condemns him under the Roman law of treason (the *lex maiestatis*)[15] for which crucifixion would be an appropriate punishment. The notion is that, if Jesus claims to be King of the Jews, he is claiming secular authority at odds with Roman authority. In short, if Jesus is claiming to be king of the Jews, that is insurrection. But it is interesting to note that it is after he asks whether Jesus is king of the Jews that Pilate says he find no crime in Jesus.[16] In Luke, at least, Pilate is then told that Jesus is perverting the nation, 'forbidding us to give tribute to Caesar' and that 'he stirs up the people.' This would be evidence of a dangerous, insurrectionary group, and Jesus' behavior in the temple (chasing out the moneylenders) may have been consistent with the crime of treason as described in Roman law by Ulpian. However, if the charge was insurrection, why didn't they try to arrest the other disciples? Certainly, at least one of them was armed when Jesus was arrested.[17] And what sense, then, does it make to condemn Jesus for insurrection, while releasing another prisoner already condemned for insurrection (in those accounts in which Barabbas is a terrorist)?

In the end, it is unclear from the gospels why Pilate would condemn Jesus, except that the narrative requires Jesus to be condemned to the Roman punishment of crucifixion and it makes sense in the story that he be condemned unjustly. All four gospel versions of the story seem to imply that Pilate, who is "just and upright, if timid and ineffectual,"[18] is reacting to the sentiments of the crowd, a move that seems to want to shift the narrative blame from the Romans to the Jews. Matthew does this in a way that had a horrific effect in later Western history when he has the crowd shout, "His blood be on us and on our children" (Matthew 27:25). The twist makes sense if the speculations are true that, by the time the gospels were written, it was in the interest of Christians to downplay the role of the Romans.[19] Perhaps, this is why Matthew has Pilate wash his hands of the innocent man's blood. The gospels "were intended and calculated to absolve the Roman governor of all responsibility for the crucifixion, though there was no escaping the initial premise that it was he who had ordered it to be carried out, and to place that responsibility squarely and solidly upon the shoulders of the Jews."[20] However, as to its historical plausibility, we have to wonder whether it is likely that a Roman administrator would bow to the wishes of a rowdy mob – perhaps, he would; perhaps, he wouldn't. It must be noted, however, that "timid and ineffectual" is not the view Josephus gives us of Pilate.[21]

Notes

1 The Roman historian Tacitus mentions Pilate as a procurator (*The Annals* 15.44), which was the term for certain provincial governors appointed by Caesar Augustus and later emperors. An inscription was discovered in 1961 referring to Pilate as "Prefect of Judaea." 'Prefect' was the earlier term for 'proconsul.' It is possible Tacitus mixed up the terms. Matthew calls him a "governor" (*hegemon*) (Matthew 27:2). If Pilate had the rank of 'prefect,' then he certainly had *imperium* or legal authority to sentence Jesus even without a trial since Jesus was not a Roman citizen. See generally A.N. Sherwin-White, *Roman Society and Roman Law in the New Testament* (1963), pp. 1–47, esp. p. 12.
2 See Alan Watson, *The Trial of Jesus* (1995), pp. 32–33.
3 Mark and Luke say he was taken to the chief priests. Matthew mentions the high priest Caiaphas by name.
4 If the chief priests were trying to rig the trial against Jesus in Mark, one wonders why they did not do a better job of coaching their witnesses.

160 Appendix I

5 In Mark (14:61), he asks, are you the Christ, "Son of the Blessed" (ὁ υἱὸς τοῦ εὐλογητοῦ); in Matthew (26:63), "the Christ, the Son of God" (ὁ υἱὸς τοῦ θεοῦ).
6 Luke omits the search for witnesses, but apparently his reply to this question is enough for them to bring him before Pilate and they need no more 'testimony' (μαρτυρίας) (Luke 22:71)
7 In Jewish tradition, priests were forbidden to rend their sacred garments, but if Jews heard someone blaspheme, they were expected to tear their garment. It is worth noting that Leviticus 21:10 forbids a priest from rending his vestments. This raises the question of whether the chief priest violates this law. If the trial was illegal (at night and in a private home), the chief priest might not have been wearing vestments. See Alan Watson, *The Trial of Jesus*, p. 39.
8 See Watson, *The Trial of Jesus*, p. 73.
9 See Morna Hooker, *A Commentary on The Gospel According to St. Mark* (1995), p. 354; Watson, *The Trial of Jesus*, pp. 100–112.
10 John makes the most of this. In John's version, the title 'Jesus of Nazareth, the King of the Jews' is written on the cross in Hebrew, Latin, and Greek (Ἑβραϊστί, Ῥωμαϊστί, Ἑλληνιστί, John 19:20). The chief priests object that it should say 'This man said, I am King of the Jews.' However, Pilate replies, 'What I have written I have written.'
11 Son of Herod the Great – in other words, not the Herod who was responsible for the 'Massacre of the Innocents' in Matthew. An inference here might be that this Herod was in Jerusalem for the Passover and not in Galilee. See Edith Z. Friedler, "The Trial of Jesus as a Conflict of Laws?," p. 417.
12 Or, perhaps, the 'King of the Judeans.'
13 According to Alan Watson, this refusal to answer alone would explain Pilate's sentence of flogging and crucifixion. Watson, *The Trial of Jesus*, p. 48.
14 Matthew does not mention him by name but calls him a 'notorious prisoner.'
15 Presumably, the relevant law here was a version of the treason law reformed by Augustus (but may have been Julius Caesar) called the *lex Julia de maiestate*, which reflected a combination (previously done by Sulla) of the laws of *perduellio* (an offense against the State and its officers for which the penalty was death; originally, the crime was aiding enemies) and *maiestas* (any act damaging the sovereignty of the State; later, it included slander against the *princeps* or his family). Unfortunately, we no longer have the original text, only excerpts in other documents. In the *Digest of Justinian*, for example, Ulpian describes the Julian law in this way:

> The crime of treason is that which is committed against the Roman people or against their safety. He is liable, by whose agency a plan is formed with malicious intent to kill hostages without the command of the emperor; or that men *armed with weapons or stones* should be, or should assemble, *within the city against the interests of the state*, or should occupy places or temples; or that there should be an assembly or gathering or that men should be called together for seditious purposes; or by whose agency a plan is formed with malicious intent to kill any magistrate of the Roman people, or anyone holding imperium or power; or that *anyone should bear arms against the state*; or who sends a messenger or letters to the enemies of the Roman people, or gives them a password, or does anything with malicious intent whereby the enemies of the Roman people may be helped with his counsel against the state; or who persuades or incites troops to make a sedition or tumult against the state.
>
> (*The Digests of Justinian*, Vol 4, 48.4. (ed. by Alan Watson) (1985) (emphasis added))

Tacitus notes about Tiberius (emperor during Jesus' trial) that: "he had revived the law of treason, the name of which indeed was known in ancient times, though other

matters came under its jurisdiction, such as the betrayal of an army, or seditious stirring up of the people, or, in short, any corrupt act by which a man had impaired 'the majesty of the people of Rome.' Deeds only were liable to accusation; words went unpunished. It was Augustus who first, under colour of this law, applied legal inquiry to libellous writings, provoked, as he had been, by the licentious freedom with which Cassius Severus had defamed men and women of distinction in his insulting satires."
Annals of Tacitus 1.72, trans. by Alfred Church and William Brodribb (1942 [1876]).

As a non-Roman, Jesus would not have the rights a Roman citizen would have under the law – as opposed to the apostle Paul, who was a Roman citizen. Consequently, Christian tradition has it that, when he was martyred, Paul was beheaded, while Peter (a non-Roman) was crucified upside-down.

16 In Luke, echoing the three denials of Peter, Pilate says three times he will scourge Jesus and release him, and the crowd shouts this down.
17 It is mentioned in all four gospels that, when Jesus was arrested at Gethsemane, there was a disciple (or disciples) armed with a sword who attacked a slave of the high priest. In three accounts, the slave's ear is cut off (Luke and John say it is his right ear). John says it was Peter who cut off the ear and the slave's name was Malchus.
18 Haim Cohn, *The Trial and Death of Jesus* (1972), p. 327.
19 As Haim Cohn puts it,

> if it could be made out that the Roman governor in Jerusalem had been satisfied of the legitimacy and harmlessness of Jesus' works and doctrines, there would be no sense or justice in persecuting Christians in Rome for adopting and following them.... all the 'fantasies' and 'historical carelessness' of the Gospel authors assume new qualities: in the given situation, they would have done the greatest disservice to their faith – indeed, they might have been persuaded that they would jeopardize its very survival – by reporting the truth that Jesus had been found guilty of the capital *crimen maiestatis* and duly tried and crucified in accordance with Roman law.
>
> (Haim Cohn, *The Trial and Death of Jesus*, p. xvi.)

20 Id., pp. 326–327.
21 See Josephus, *The Jewish War*, Book II and *Jewish Antiquities* XVIII, par. 55–62.

References

Cohn, H. (1972). *The trial and death of Jesus*.
Friedler, E. Z. (1997). The trial of Jesus as a conflict of laws? 32 *Irish Jurist* 398.
Hooker, M. (1995). *A commentary on the gospel according to St. Mark*.
Sherwin-White, A. N. (1963). *Roman society and Roman law in the New Testament*.
Tacitus. (1942 [1876]). *Annals of Tacitus*, trans. by A. Church and W. Brodribb.
Watson, A. (Ed.). (1985). *The digests of Justinian*.
Watson, A. (1995). *The trial of Jesus*.

Appendix 2 Procedural Issues in the Trial of Thomas More

Was the actual trial of Thomas More a mockery, a mere kangaroo court? This has been the traditional view over the centuries, and it is certainly the position of Robert Bolt's *A Man for All Seasons*. However, almost the only thing historians agree on about the procedural aspects of More's trial is that the king assumed More's conviction was a foregone conclusion. We know this because Henry VIII issued a circular letter publicly declaring the treasons of Thomas More and Bishop John Fisher on 25 June 1535. At that point, Fisher had already been executed, but More had not yet been tried.[1] One might reasonably conclude that this could unduly influence a court and a jury.

The surviving official records of the trial, found in the so-called "Bag of Secrets" (*Baga de Secretis*, a store of secret documents kept by the English government), give us only scanty information.[2] We know the date of the trial, 1 July, and that More pleaded not guilty. A commission of *oyer and terminer* (to hear and determine) was established to try More, which was not unusual. It consisted of a number of councillors – only a bare majority of whom were lawyers and included known enemies of More such as Anne Boleyn's father, uncle, and brother (which might be considered irregular). We also know that the 'petty jury' of twelve men, which acts as the trier of fact in the common law system, contained persons with personal grudges against More. According to the procedures of the time, More would not have been afforded an attorney to speak on his behalf (though, it is often pointed out by scholars, he could hardly have found a better advocate than himself).[3] Moreover, he would not have been apprised of the charges against him until the indictment was read aloud.[4]

J. Duncan M. Derrett published an influential interpretation (and what may now be called a consensus view) that treated More's trial not only as a serious legal process but, possibly, as having reached the correct legal outcome.[5] Crucial evidence of this is Derrett's interpretation of the 'articles'[6] in More's indictment as 'counts' (which may be summarized thus):

> The first was that in the Tower on 7 May 1535, before Cromwell and other commissioners, More had maliciously refused to give his opinion on

the king's supremacy, saying that 'I wyll not meddyll with any such matters, for I am fully determyned to serve God, and to thynk uppon his passion and my passage out of this worlde.' The second was that on 12 May More had written a letter to Fisher reporting his own silence and maliciously encouraging the bishop in his treason. Third, he had maliciously conspired with Fisher, both men comparing the Act of Supremacy to a two-edged sword. The fourth count accused More, in conversation with Richard Rich on 12 June, of maliciously depriving the king of his title, and supplied an account of their verbal exchanges essentially identical to that Rich had written down for Cromwell.[7]

The consensus view, following Derrett, holds that More brilliantly and successfully argued for the dismissal of the first three 'counts.' According to the Guildhall Report, More argued that the evidence was lacking for 'count' two because all the correspondence between himself and Bishop Fisher had been burned. Since he had sworn an oath that the content of such letters was not treasonable, the only evidence pointed toward his innocence.

To refute the first 'count,' More argued that the statute required the *mens rea* [mental state] of 'malice' on the part of the perpetrator. Since More neither said nor did anything, he could not act with 'malice,' and the law provided no penalty for silence. More also invoked the civil law maxim "*qui tacet, consentire videtur*" ("one who keeps silent seems to consent"), which implied that, absent any other evidence, silence must be interpreted as consent to the king's title. As for 'count' three, More also claims that his reference to "a two-edged sword" (whether it was in a (now destroyed) letter to Fisher or in his interrogation at Lambeth) was hypothetical and, therefore, could not be malicious.[8]

Derrett claims that the only evidence adduced at trial was on the fourth 'count.' Therefore, the court must have dismissed the other three charges – "otherwise the Attorney-general would not have dared to abandon, as he plainly did, three-quarters of the Crown's carefully-prepared case."[9] Moreover, William Roper indicates that More was convicted solely on the testimony of Richard Rich, which would also support Derrett's conclusion that only the fourth 'count' remained. If Derrett is correct about this, the trial should not be considered a complete sham – indeed, it indicates "an especially honourable, courageous exercise of judicial independence."[10]

Henry Kelly[11] recently called Derrett's 'revisionist' reading of the trial into question. Kelly argues that More was charged and tried on the whole indictment, not just the final 'count.' As Kelly notes, the Guildhall Report itself states that, when the petty jury was called after More's response to the indictment, it was to consider "capita accusationis" ("chapters of accusation," i.e., in the plural). Moreover, if it is true, says Kelly, that the entire case against More was based on Rich's testimony, then why doesn't the Guildhall Report say anything about it? Instead, the report states that, after More responded to the 'two-edge sword' accusation, the petty jury was called and the prisoner was found guilty. So, Rich plays no role at all in the Guildhall Report. This cannot mean, Kelly implies, that all the other sources are wrong about Rich's role in the trial. Rather, it means that we should read the entire account not as reporting various stages in the arraignment and trial but as a conflation of what happened during the entire procedure – that is, it reports the charges against More and the responses he gave to them later, a logical but not a chronological presentation of the information.[12]

Was Thomas More guilty?

Whatever one thinks about Thomas More's actions or inactions in a moral or religious context, we must still ask ourselves whether Thomas More was *legally* guilty. On what basis could we assess this? Any determination must take into account at least these three issues:

a) Was the statute's requirement of 'malice' a separate component of the crime?

The Act of Treasons specifically stated that the prohibited act had to be done 'maliciously.' There has been much debate about whether Parliament intended this term as mere redundancy or as a limitation on the definition of treason. There is evidence on both sides. One argument is that the term 'malice' merely meant an intent to do the act in question – to rule out unintentional acts.[13] If so, as long as More acted intentionally, he was guilty under the statute. However, 'malice' could also mean 'ill will,' that is, the act must be done with an intent to do evil or cause harm. As a good lawyer, of course, More seized upon the term as evidence of a supplemental requirement for conviction – an element that the prosecution had to prove in addition to any act on his part. As son-in-law Roper put it, "where there is no malice, there can be no offense."[14] Hence, More's legal defense was, in effect, 'even if I did it, I didn't mean any harm by it. Therefore, I cannot be guilty of a crime.' If one accepts this view, then the putting of hypothetical cases between More and Rich could not be 'malicious' since it did not affirm any particular opinion and could not have ill will. However, a jury need not accept More's interpretation of the hypothetical. As Derrett points out, the premise of the hypothetical itself can be interpreted as an implicit violation of the statute:[15]

> More's comment that other nations did not accept what had been done in the instance alluded to by Rich looks at first sight like a piece of gratuitous comment. In fact it is relevant. Had the other nations unanimously accepted that Henry VIII was Supreme Head of the Church of England, had they even agreed that their respective kings were supreme heads of

their national churches, there might be some ground for suggesting that the general consensus of Christians allowed this development, that some sort of substitute for a general council had spoken, and that what parliament had taken upon itself to do was retrospectively adopted or ratified. But in default of such evidence the Act was not binding upon the citizen whether in morals or law.[16]

And, if that were the case, then a jury *could* have reasonably concluded that More was depriving the King of his title Supreme Head of the Church. Thus, it would have been an overt act (not mere 'silence'). But was this act in and of itself 'malicious'? Or was other evidence of an intent to harm required?

b) More's silence

More's view of the proper interpretation of 'maliciously' also implies that mere silence cannot be 'malicious' because silence is not an act.[17] According to the Guildhall Report, the prosecution argued that More's silence on the issue of the King's supremacy "was a sure indication and a not obscure sign of evil thought."[18] It was in response to this that More invoked the presumption that silence implies consent. However, the issue is not so straightforward. First, it is questionable whether the presumption even applied in a criminal law context at the time.[19] Many have also viewed the argument as excessively technical especially since there is no reason to suppose that silence implies consent specifically to the king's title as Head of the Church. One interpretation of More's aim here is that this evidentiary presumption should be respected because it comported with the faithful subject's duty to consult his own conscience. This, however, implies that there was reasonable doubt about the legitimacy of the king's title.[20] One might also argue that, since the Treasons Act makes it a crime to "wish, will or desire" to deprive the king of a title, "[t]hat silence could be evidence of the wish or will is not impossible...."[21]

c) Did Richard Rich commit perjury?

According to the indictment, Rich claimed that, in the 'putting of cases' exchange, More had denied the king could be "Supreme Head on Earth of the English Church." In no source are we given Rich's testimony at trial. We are told in Roper's *Life* that More responded with these words: "In good faith, Master Rich, I am sorrier for your perjury than for my own peril."[22] Therefore, assuming Rich's testimony was consistent with the indictment, we must work out what More meant (assuming More was telling the truth – some have speculated that More did, indeed, let something slip in their conversation).[23] In Roper's account, More said that Parliament could not "make the king supreme head of the Church." However, in context, one may read this as saying that More was not depriving Henry of the title of

Supreme Head of the Church of England. Rather, he denied the proposition that Parliament could declare a king Supreme Head of the universal Catholic Church, which would not directly deprive the king of his title.[24] Another reading is that Rich told the truth but that More relied too much on the technicality of a 'putting of cases' – that is, the hypothetical nature of the discussion. In other words, More was too much the lawyer. He believed a hypothetical did not count as proof of 'malice' since it affirmed no positive fact. Again, as Derrett has pointed out, the jury may not have appreciated the fine distinction.

Either way, More tried to rebut Rich's testimony by attacking his character and swearing that Rich's testimony was not true. As Roper reports, More said: "'If I were a man, my lords, that did not regard an oath, I needed not, as it is well known, in this place, at this time, nor in this case, to stand here as an accused person."[25] It would be up to the trier of fact (the jury) to decide between the two witnesses. We learn from the Guildhall Report that the jury deliberated for fifteen minutes before rendering a verdict of 'guilty.'[26] Whether the jury deliberated well or merely caved to pressure is a question we must evaluate from the totality of the evidence by our best lights.

Notes

1 Henry Ansgar Kelly, "A Procedural Review of Thomas More's Trial," in Henry Kelley, Louis Karlin and Gerard Wegemer (eds.), *Thomas More's Trial By Jury* (2011), p. 1.
2 For everything else, we are dependent on a few sources of evidence – all of which have problems. 1) We have More's indictment, which was first published in Elsie Vaughan Hitchcock's *Harpsfield's Life of More* (1932). 2) We have an eyewitness account of the trial reconstructed by More scholar J. Duncan M. Derrett, based on a version published in August 1535 in a *Paris News Letter* and a Latin manuscript of this account found in the Guildhall (known now as the "Guildhall Report"). 3) We have the account by More's son-in-law, William Roper, *The Life of Sir Thomas More*, which was written around 1556 during the reign of Queen Mary. Roper himself was not present at the trial. 4) Reginald Pole, an English cardinal in exile, also wrote an account of the trial in a work called *Pro ecclesiasticae unitatis defensione*, which he claims was based upon eyewitness testimony. 5) There is also an account written by one of the commissioners, Sir John Spelman, in a private book of memoirs.
3 But violating the old adage: "A man who is his own lawyer has a fool for a client." In the play, More makes this comment: "The currents and eddies of right and wrong, which you find such plain sailing, I can't navigate. I'm no voyager. But in the thickets of the law, oh, there I'm a forester. I doubt if there's a man alive who could follow me there, thank God." Bolt, *A Man for All Seasons*, p. 26. But is this hubris on More's part?
4 J. Duncan M. Derrett, "The Trial of Sir Thomas More," 79(312) *The English Historical Review* (1964), p. 455. There is speculation that More was not condemned by bill of attainder this time only because Parliament was not in session at the time. See Karlin and Oakley, "A Guide to Thomas More's Trial for Modern Lawyers," in *Thomas More's Trial By Jury,* p. 73.
5 J. Duncan M. Derrett, "The Trial of Sir Thomas More," pp. 449–477.

6 'Articles' would be the term used for 'charges' in an ecclesiastical court at the time but not necessarily a common law court hearing a criminal action. See Kelly, "A Procedural Review of Thomas More's Trial," *Thomas More's Trial*, p. 7. However, the 'articles' might not be 'counts' but "a series of material facts alleged in support of the single charge of treason." Karlin and Oakley, "A Guide to Thomas More's Trial for Modern Lawyers," *Thomas More's Trial*, p. 79.
7 Peter Marshall, "The Last Years," p. 130.
8 After several interrogations, Cromwell at one point demanded point blank that More state his opinion as to whether the Act of Supremacy was lawful or not. When More (in effect) remained silent on the issue, Cromwell noted that the king could compel an answer. More's reply is worth quoting in full:

> If it so were that my conscience gave me against the statutes (wherein how my mind giveth me I make no declaration), then I nothing doing nor nothing saying against the statute, it were a very hard thing to compel me to say either precisely with it against my conscience to the loss of my soul, or precisely against it to the destruction of my body.
> (Letter to Margaret Roper, 3 June 1534, in *Selected Letters*, p. 251)

This was sufficiently like the answer Bishop John Fisher (who was also imprisoned for refusing to swear the oath) gave to a similar question that More was accused of colluding with the Bishop ("the Statute is like a two-edged sword" – answer one way, one's conscience is imperilled, answer the other way, one's life is). As a result, Cromwell ordered that all More's books and writing paper be confiscated. On this occasion, Richard Rich, who was Cromwell's Solicitor General, entered into the hypothetical 'putting of cases' upon which More was ultimately condemned.
9 Derrett, "The Trial of Thomas More," p. 456; see Marshall, "The Last Years," p. 130.
10 Karlin and Oakley, "A Guide to Thomas More's Trial for Modern Lawyers," p. 85.
11 Kelly, "A Procedural Review of Thomas More's Trial".
12 As Kelly says,

> more plausible is the conclusion that Guildhall portrayed More as subsuming the whole of the Rich charge, even though it made up a full third of the indictment in length, in the first article, where he was accused of impugning the act by refusing to given [sic] an answer about it. This would fit with Reginald Pole's informant's account as well (except that he also ignored the charge of colluding with Fisher).
> (Id., p. 36)

13 "Judicial Commentary on Thomas More's Trial," in Henry Kelley, Louis Karlin and Gerard Wegemer (eds.), *Thomas More's Trial By Jury* (2011), p. 114.
14 Roper, *The Life of Sir Thomas More*, p. 50. In his final interview with More, Cromwell demanded that More "confess it lawful that his Highness should be Supreme Head of the Church of England or else to utter plainly my malignity." Letter to Margaret Roper, dated 3 June 1535, in *Selected Letters*, p. 250. This, of course, allowed More to reply that he had no malignity, escaping the trap.
15 Derrett, "The Trial of Thomas More," p. 468.
16 J. Duncan M. Derrett, "The 'New' Document on Thomas More's Trial," *Moreana*, no. 3 (June 1964), p. 9. This is additional evidence that More held conciliarist views. Current popular opinion aside (including, perhaps, Bolt's interpretation), More never acknowledged the supremacy of the papacy as such but, rather, relied in all his argumentation on the superiority of the *consensus fidelium*, "Christendom's consensual unity, which was inspired by the Holy Spirit and made known in determinations of general

councils, [and which] was the dogmatic equivalent of the mystical body of Christ." Rockett, "Thomas More's Quarrel," pp. 205–206. See also Roper, *Life of Thomas More*, p. 53:

> this realm, being but one member and small part of the Church, might not make a particular law disagreeable with the general law of Christ's universal Catholic Church, no more than the city of London, being but one poor member in respect of the whole realm, might make a law against an act of Parliament to bind the whole realm.

17 Interestingly, in 2010, the Thomas More Law Center made a similar argument against President Obama's healthcare initiative (known popularly as 'Obamacare') that the so-called 'individual mandate' (which required people to purchase health insurance or pay a fine) was unconstitutional because precedent governing the application of the "necessary and proper" clause to the "interstate commerce clause" had regulated 'activities.' Not buying health insurance, it was argued, was 'inactivity,' not an 'activity.' See *Thomas More Law Center v. Obama*, 720 F. Supp.2d 882 (E.D. Mich. 2010). Ultimately, the 'individual mandate' was upheld as a tax, not as a commerce regulation.
18 In Reginald Pole's account of the trial, the judges even cried out "Malice! Malice!" at this point to underscore the point. Reginald Pole, *Pro ecclesiasticae unitatis defensione*, fols. 89v–90 (nos. 5–6) (1535–1536), cited in Kelly, "More's Trial by Jury," p. 26.
19 In the Guildhall Report, More refers to the maxim as a principle of "jus commune." Whether this civil law principle would be accepted as a general principle of common law applicable in all situations is highly disputed. Nor is "jus commune" to be confused with English "common law." Pope Boniface VIII endorsed it as a "rule of law" in 1298, but the next "rule of law" he endorses is "one who remains silent neither confesses nor denies." See Kelly, "Thomas More's Trial by Jury," pp. 22–26.
20 Karlin and Oakley, "A Guide to Thomas More's Trial for Modern Lawyers," pp. 77–78.
21 J. Duncan M. Derrett, "More's Silence and His Trial," *Moreana*, no. 87–88 (November, 1985), p. 27.
22 Roper, *Life of Sir Thomas More*, p. 50. This is also the occasion for one of the more memorable lines in Robert Bolt's play. In the play, Richard Rich appears to testify wearing a chain of office indicating that he has been appointed Attorney General for Wales. The character of More remarks, "Why, Richard, it profits a man nothing to give his soul for the whole world... But for Wales!" *A Man for All Seasons*, p. 100.
23 G.R. Elton, *Policy and Police: The Enforcement of the Reformation in the Age of Thomas Cromwell*, p. 415.
24 See Kelly, "A Procedural Review of Thomas More's Trial," p. 37.
25 Roper, *Life of Sir Thomas More*, p. 49.
26 Apparently, no direct coercion was applied to the jurors. However, it is said that, earlier, when a jury refused to convict three Carthusian priors, Cromwell browbeat them until they did. Might this have influenced the jury in More's trial?

References

Bolt, R. (2013 [1960]). *A man for all seasons*.
Derrett, J. (1964). The trial of Sir Thomas More. 79(312) *English Historical Review* 449.
Derrett, J. (June, 1964). The 'new' document on Thomas More's trial. 3 *Moreana* 5.
Derrett, J. (November, 1985). More's silence and his trial. 22(87–88) *Moreana* 25.
Elton, G. R. (1972). *Policy and police: The enforcement of the reformation in the age of Thomas Cromwell*.

Hitchcock, E. V. (1932). *Harpsfield's life of More*.
Kelley, H., Karlin, L., & Wegemer, G. (Eds.) (2011). *Thomas More's trial by jury*.
Marshall, P. (2011). The last years. In G. M. Logan (Ed.), *The Cambridge companion to Thomas More*.
More, T. (1961). *Selected letters*, E. Rogers (Ed.).
Rockett, G. W. (2012). Thomas More's Quarrel with Reform. 92 *Church History and Religious Culture* 201.
Roper, W. (2003 [1556]). *The life of Sir Thomas More*, G. Wegemer & S. Smith (Eds.).

Appendix 3 A Digression on Evolution and Religion

The connection of ideas such as 'eugenics' and the 'survival of the fittest' with Darwin is unfortunate if somewhat understandable, although untangling all the threads in the story is difficult. The theory of evolution did not spring full-blown from the mind of Charles Darwin in 1859.[1] It had been taken seriously as a scientific concept for at least a century before the publication of *On the Origin of Species*. However, until Gregor Mendel's work on the principles of genetic inheritance became well known, there was no good scientific theory on how evolution actually worked at the microbiological level. Thus, what gets called "Darwinism" in the late 19th and early 20th centuries is not always consistent with the scrupulous work Darwin did. Darwin also 'muddied the waters,' so to speak, by trying to explain his innovative and (for 19th-century minds) difficult theory in terms used by earlier evolutionists (with whom more people were familiar) and by making concessions to criticisms of some aspects of his work for which he did not yet have sufficient evidence.

Prior to the work of Darwin and Mendel, the paradigm for biology was the system epitomized in the 18th century by Carl Linneaus, who classified all creatures by kingdom, genus, species, etc. The Linnean system is still used today for many purposes. The principle behind the classification, however, was much older – one that presumed that all creatures with their individual characteristics were merely examples of "types" that were eternal, like Plato's eternal Forms. Just as, according to Plato's theory, individual chairs in the physical world were merely imperfect manifestations of the perfect form of a chair, individual organisms were merely imperfect examples of the perfect form of the species. Individual dogs might differ in a variety of characteristics, but they could never exhibit differences beyond the limits imposed by the 'eternal nature' of the species. In effect, it was the species that was 'really real.' This systematic biology comported well with the Biblical account in Genesis that God specially created all the various types or kinds of plants and animals. That all the varieties could be classified in such a systematic manner was counted as evidence of God's design in the universe and confirmation that the book of Nature and the book of Scripture were never in contradiction.[2]

However, just as Copernicus had challenged the Biblical conception of the solar system (manifested in the story of Joshua halting the course of the sun), natural scientists in the 17th and 18th centuries began questioning the story of the Deluge and Noah's ark. For one thing, the story did not seem to fit with the distribution of species across the face of the earth; and, for another, more and more fossils were being found of species that had vanished or appeared to be very, very different from anything still living – which would not be the case, it was thought, if species were eternal and unchanging.[3] A number of natural scientists including Charles Darwin's grandfather, Erasmus Darwin, began to think that the species we see today must somehow have evolved from the earlier specimens we see in fossilized remains.

In 1801, Jean-Baptiste Lamarck, for example, postulated a theory of evolution that was accepted by many scientists even after Mendel's discoveries.[4] Lamarck's theory was teleological in the sense that he believed that organisms evolved to become ever more complex and sophisticated, ascending the so-called chain of being. God, for Lamarck, resembled Newton's God, a deist God who started the machine of the world in motion and then left it to its own devices (perhaps, intervening occasionally to keep it on track). Organisms adapted to their environments and improved themselves over time. These changes explained the differences we see between living species and their fossilized relatives. Moreover, in Lamarck's theory, living organisms not only adapted to their environments but the characteristics acquired by such organisms during their lifetimes could be passed down to their offspring. The classic example was the evolution of the giraffe's neck – because giraffes spent their lives stretching their necks to reach leaves in tall trees, they passed down their gradually more and more elongated necks to their offspring.[5] Thanks to Mendel, among others, the theory that acquired characteristics can be inherited has been rejected,[6] but it was accepted by many far into the twentieth century – including in Stalin's Soviet Union and Mao Zedong's China, where Trofim Lysenko's rejection of Mendel led to agricultural catastrophe.[7]

Darwin's theory explains the elongation of the giraffe's neck by a different mechanism. Evolution, according to Darwin, occurs slowly over a long period of time through the inherited accumulation of incremental changes[8] in individual organisms. Because (the assumption is) living organisms must compete for scarce resources, those with incremental advantages for acquiring those resources tend to be able to reproduce more often. In the case of the giraffe, individuals with longer necks were able to acquire more food and had a statistically better chance of surviving to reproduce. Through such "natural selection," descendants with longer necks tended to reproduce more often and wound up dominating their environmental niche. A "species" is, thus, not an eternal Form that determines the characteristics of individual organisms. Rather, it is a linguistic designation of convenience for a general population of organisms with similar characteristics at a particular point in time, a statistical description of a population. Used in this fashion, the difference between one 'species' and another may be entirely arbitrary such as the distinction between breeds of dogs and wolves. Consequently, today, "species" are normally defined in terms of their ability to produce fertile offspring rather than their physical characteristics. But even this is not 'permanent.' As the process of evolution continues, there is no reason that, at some distant point in the future, descendants of individuals deemed to be in the same species today might vary so significantly that they are not able to reproduce or that descendants of individuals of different species today might be able to reproduce. There is no teleology in Darwin's theory; a "species" is never a fixed or immutable thing.

Unfortunately, many people in the 19th century did not quite grasp this revolutionary insight provided by Darwin. For them, the most shocking thing about *On the Origin of Species* was its implication that man might have been the result of the same process of natural selection as the other animals. To the 19th-century Western mind, it is one thing to acknowledge that animals might evolve over time – after all, that is exactly what happens when humans breed animals artificially for certain characteristics – but man was supposed to have been specially created in God's image. The notion that man might be no different from the animals was considered repugnant to many.

Darwin left no doubt about this proposition when he published *The Descent of Man* in 1871, which focused on sexual selection as one of the important factors in evolution. Unlike other evolutionists, such as co-discoverer Alfred Wallace, Darwin did not think that the development of humans could only be explained by supernatural intervention. The development of man, he theorized, could be explained through perfectly ordinary evolutionary mechanisms. Darwin himself did not ruminate on any religious or ethical ramifications his theory might involve. However, many who called themselves Darwinists (and many who did not) happily indulged in such speculations.

If one accepted the notion that human beings are animals and evolved through natural selection, then some thinkers also drew the conclusion that human beings could also be 'bred' for certain characteristics on the same principles as artificial selection. While Charles Darwin never advocated such a thing, his half-cousin Francis Galton became very interested in the heritability of human characteristics and coined the term 'eugenics' in 1883. The so-called 'eugenics movement,' which was dedicated to the biological improvement of the human race, flourished in the first half of the 20th century – resulting in legislation in many places, including anti-miscegenation laws and compulsory sterilization laws.[9] It was popular (though not universally so) among both progressive and conservative politicians as a way to improve the lives of ordinary people (by averting hereditary diseases, for example) or as a way of preventing the degradation of society with 'inferior' specimens (for example, by sterilizing so-called 'imbeciles'). Unfortunately, the movement was a hodgepodge of theories and assumptions, some deriving from Darwinian principles, some from Lamarckian principles, some deriving from completely separate traditions such as the racialist theories of Arthur de Gobineau (*An Essay on the Inequality of Human Races*, 1853–1855) and Madison Grant (*The Passing of the Great Race*, 1916) (both works purporting to show the superiority of the Aryan or Nordic race).[10] However, due to the widespread misunderstanding of Darwin's theory, many people, including William Jennings Bryan, tarred all of Darwin's thinking with the eugenics brush.

Biblical literalists objected to Darwin's theory on a variety of grounds. For one thing, it denied the special creation of man and man's dominion over the animals and that God created eternal 'kinds' of animals. Moreover, if Darwin's gradualist theory were true, the earth would have to be much, much older than anyone had ever speculated it could be – and certainly older than the approximately 6,000 years that, in 1650, Bishop James Ussher had determined by adding up the ages of the patriarchs in the Old Testament, concluding that God created the world in 4004 B.C. (on 23 October). More fundamentally, people objected that, if man were nothing but an animal, then there could be no basis for morality – it was literally a 'dog-eat-dog' world, confirming their worst fears about Tennyson's "Nature, red in tooth and claw."[11]

Notes

1 Many of the phrases we connect today with Darwin's theory of evolution did not originate with Darwin. The "struggle for existence," for example, could be found in works by Jeremy Bentham in 1790, Thomas Malthus in 1798, and G.W.F. Hegel in 1817. It is worth noting that Darwin and Alfred Wallace each developed the theory of evolution through natural selection independently after meditating on Malthus' *An Essay on the Principle of Population*, which theorized that, since food production increases arithmetically and population increases exponentially, population will always outstrip the food supply. "Survival of the fittest" was coined by Herbert Spencer as early as 1852. Darwin utilized these concepts as metaphors to explain his theory of evolution, but what he meant by the terms is not identical with what these or later authors meant by them.

> By using metaphorical concepts from Malthus and Spencer, Darwin made it more difficult to disassociate his new discovery in biology from older patterns of social thought. It was not what Darwin said that had little impact, but it was the manner in which he said it that led those, who were looking for scientific support for opinions already held, to infer that he meant what they already believed.
> (Rogers, "Darwin and Social Darwinism," p. 268)

2 The classic book on this is William Paley's *Natural Theology* (1802), which makes use of the famous watchmaker analogy for the design of the universe.

3 One can find in the writings of many natural scientists in the late 18th and early 19th centuries an almost panicked attempt to avoid a conclusion that the Almighty allowed species to become extinct. Over time, this position became more and more difficult to sustain. See generally Michael Ruse, *The Darwinian Revolution: Science Red in Tooth and Claw* (Chicago 1979) and Charles Coulston Gillispie, *Genesis and Geology: The Impact of Scientific Discoveries upon Religious Beliefs in the Decades before Darwin* (1951).

4 Until Mendel's genetic theory became well-known, there was no clear explanation of the biological mechanism behind evolution. As a result, Lamarckian explanations had more plausibility at the time than they do now. Therefore, one could be a

respectable scientist and still favor a Lamarckian theory over Darwin's or an amalgamation of Lamarck and Darwin, which explains why so many so-called Darwinians could hold theories of species and race that were not compatible with Darwin's own stated theories.

5   Lamarck's theory was richer and also a bit more confusing than this, but it was this aspect of it that was emphasized in the 19th and early 20th centuries. See, for example, Stephen Jay Gould, "Shades of Lamarck," *The Panda's Thumb* (1980).
6   Current research into epigenetics may nuance this a bit.
7   See generally David Joravsky, *The Lysenko Affair* (1970) and Jasper Becker, *Hungry Ghosts: Mao's Secret Famine* (1998).
8   At the time, Darwin had no explanation of where the incremental changes came from. Most biologists at the time, for example, thought that offspring displayed a 'blending' of the characteristics of their parents – a theory that was relatively easily exploded by observation but only definitively refuted by Mendel.
9   Eugenics laws in various forms were passed in 30 states in the United States and many European countries such as Sweden, Germany, and the United Kingdom.
10 It must be pointed out for the sake of clarity that any theory based on maintaining the 'purity' of a race or species cuts against Darwin's theory of natural selection. Darwin himself does not address this issue directly, but the strong implication of Darwin's theory is that it is diversity that ensures the survival of offspring, not 'purity.' The racialist theories of thinkers such as Gobineau or Grant derive from non-Darwinian sources. It is easy to misread Darwin, however, thanks to the confusion in the 19th century of such terms as 'species,' 'race' or 'variety' – particularly, after the abandonment of Linnaean principles, which were confused enough already. To take one obvious example: Darwin uses the term 'race' to mean something like a 'variety' – he speaks in the *Origin of Species*, for example, of 'races' of cabbages; whereas Gobineau, who wrote his most influential works (influential on Nazi ideology, for example) prior to 1859, speaks of racial characteristics as permanent, the human 'races' as different 'species' with different origins.
11 Alfred, Lord Tennyson, "In Memoriam A.H.H." (1849).

References

Becker, J. (1998). *Hungry ghosts: Mao's secret famine*.
Gillispie, C. (1951). *Genesis and geology: The impact of scientific discoveries upon religious beliefs in the decades before Darwin*.
Gould, S. J. (1980). Shades of Lamarck. *The panda's thumb*.
Joravsky, D. (1970). *The Lysenko affair*.
Rogers, J. A. (1972). Darwin and Social Darwinism. 22 *Journal of the History of Ideas* 265.
Ruse, M. (1979). *The Darwinian revolution: Science red in tooth and claw*.

Index

Aeschylus 32n52, 110n22
Agamben, Giorgio 73
Aristophanes 17, 18, 23, 24, 28n6
Aristotle 5, 12n20, 27n1, 28n14, 30n30, 30n32, 30n35, 34, 47n10, 78; cycle of regimes 39, 50n32–34; tragedy 101, 110n19
Athens: democracy 19–21; juries 21–23

Blasphemy 65, 66–67, 73n46, 156–157
Bolt, Robert 77–79, 84, 85, 88, 93n46, 94n56, 97 101, 102–103, 105, 167n16
Brecht, Bertolt 77, 88n1, 94n56, 134n62
Bryan, William Jennings 115–116, 120–121, 122–124, 129n15, 131n23, 132n42, 132n46, 134n61–62, 173
Burnyeat, Miles 25
Bush, George W. 3, 44, 54
Butler Act 116–117, 118, 119, 121, 124, 125, 130n23, 133n50

Calhoun, John D. 140, 145
Camus, Albert 84, 93n46, 100, 105, 106
Chicago 7 2–4
Cicero 1, 33–38, 41–46, 78, 140; career 36–37, 48n17; life 34–35, 47n7; republicanism 36, 39, 51n40
Cohn, Haim 67, 161n19
Collingwood, R.G. 8–9, 11n13–17, 20, 29n17, 97
Confessions 64, 65, 67, 85, 92n39, 99, 104, 156
Cover, Robert 56–57, 62, 65, 69n7, 72n34–35, 139, 148n13
Crespino, Joseph 150n33
Cromwell, Thomas 77, 80, 85, 86–87, 88–89, 93n44, 167n8, 167n8, 167n14, 168n26

Darwin, Charles 113, 115, 124, 127, 170–173

Darrow, Clarence 115, 119–121, 123, 130n19, 131n23, 131n27
Delcourt, Marie 77
Derrett, J. Duncan M. 162–64
Dikasterion 21, 29n25
Douglass, Frederick 92n40, 140, 149n27–28

Eco, Umberto 6
Elton, G.R. 90n20, 90n23, 93n43
Erasmus, Desidirius 78
Eugenics 115, 170–171

Finch, Atticus 17, 88, 94n58, 137–146

Garrison, William Lloyd 140
Gladwell, Malcolm 144, 146, 11n49
Gospel of John 58, 69n4, 72n42, 157–158

Harris, Robert 34, 35, 41–45, 47n6, 48n18, 48n20, 52n45
Henry VIII 77–79, 82, 91n25
Historical imagination 8–9, 10, 11n13
Hunter, George 115, 127, 130n18, 131n23, 131n25
Hytner, Nicholas 97, 108n10

Incorporation, doctrine of 118
Isonomia 21

Jewish trial of Jesus 64–65, 156–158
Josipovici, Gabriel 68, 73n32

Kelly, Henry 163–164, 167n12

Lamarck, Jean-Baptiste 171, 173n4, 174n5
'Law and humanities' 4–6, 56
'Law and literature' 4, 137
Lee, Harper 137–138, 144, 147n1
Liberalism 20–21, 51n42

Living constitutionalism 139, 141, 149n20, 149n22
Lubet, Steven 143–144

McCarthy, Joseph 10, 77, 96, 106n3, 110n17, 121, 122, 139
Machiavelli, Niccolò 34, 39–42, 52n39–40
MacLeish, Archibald 6
Mantel, Hilary 77, 90n20
'March of Progress' illustration 127, 135n73
Marino, Stephen 105
Melville, Herman 5, 139
'Memory' studies 113–114
Mendel, Gregor 127, 170, 171, 174n8
'Messianic secret' 60–61, 64
Miller, Arthur 4, 31n47, 96–97, 101–102, 103, 106n4, 107n7, 109n11, 110n16, 111n26–27
Miller, Perry 96
More, Thomas: 17, 31n47, 77; charges 80–81; life 78–79; trial 86–88,162–66

New Criticism 139, 146
Nomos 22, 23, 29n20, 29n23, 56, 62, 65, 72n35, 139

Oaths 26, 29n29, 31n47, 31n50, 81–82, 83–84, 87, 91n27, 91n41, 93n44, 111n28, 163
Originalism 5, 8, 139–140, 148n18, 149n21–22, 149n26

Pence, Mike 113, 126.128
Perjury 87, 93n42, 102, 165
Pilate, Pontius 65–68, 155, 157, 158–59, 159n1
Plato 6, 17, 23; relation to Socrates 17–19; theory of forms 128, 170; works 18–19, 27n1
Plea bargaining 99, 109n15
Polybius 34, 39, 47n4, 50n33–35
Pompey the Great 43–45, 155

Quirinius, Publius Sulpicius 69n3, 155, 156

Raulston, John T. 117–121
Rich, Richard 31n47, 87, 88, 111n28, 163, 164, 165–66
Right to counsel 93n47, 98, 109n12, 147n2
Roman trial of Jesus 65–68, 158–159
Rome: criminal law 48; republicanism 35–36

Salem witch trials: causes 96–97, 107n8
Scopes trial 119–121
Scottsboro Boys 137–138, 145, 146n2–3
Shakespeare, William 17, 21n11–12, 78, 138, 139, 152n34
Skinner, Quentin 8, 12n18, 29n19, 47n9, 51n40, 148n15
Snyder, Timothy 114, 129n9–11
Social Darwinism 115, 124, 130n21, 173n1
Socrates: acquaintances 19–20: charges 23, 27; *daimonion* 24–27, 31n43, 49; oracle of Delphi 24, 26, 31n40; problem of 17–19
'Son of God' 58, 61, 70n15, 71n29, 157, 160n5
'Son of man' 59, 61, 62, 63, 65, 66, 71n20
Sophocles 5, 7, 22, 29n23, 32n52, 81, 102
Spencer, Herbert 131, 173n1
Substantive due process 117–118, 131n31
Synoptic Gospels 58, 60, 64, 68n2

Tragedy 11n11, 26, 27, 101–102, 103, 105, 110n19–23
Treason 80–81, 83, 85, 87, 91n26, 92n38, 158–159, 160n15, 167n6

Verres, Gaius 37; trial 42–43

Watson, Alan 65, 72n36, 160n13
Whig history 33, 114, 150n29
White, James Boyd 4–5

Xenophon 17, 18, 20, 27n2–4, 30n32, 30n36, 30n38, 31n40

Printed in the United States
by Baker & Taylor Publisher Services